Understanding Early Years Education across the UK

The four nations of the UK each have distinctive policy and curricula in relation to Early Childhood Education and Care (ECEC). This new textbook offers a comprehensive look at early years education in England, Northern Ireland, Scotland and Wales, bringing the curriculum frameworks for each country together in one place.

Drawing on the cultural and practical pedagogy of each curriculum, this book aims to develop students' understanding of development, care, education, health, well-being and upbringing of young children across the UK in a social, pedagogical and policy context.

Divided into two sections, the first four chapters examine each country's learning and teaching requirements in detail within a policy context. The last chapter then explores the similarities and differences between the curricula, focusing on key areas such as play, the indoor and outdoor learning environment, the family and assessment. Accessible and engaging, this book will help students to analyse and question practice both in their own country and across all four home nations. Features include case studies to illustrate practice, a frequently asked questions section in each chapter to clarify key points and opportunities for reflection and debate.

Including contributions from expert practitioners in each country, this text is essential reading for all students studying early childhood and will help them to understand the impact of policy on children and families across the UK.

Diane Boyd is Senior Lecturer in Early Childhood Studies and Education Studies at Liverpool John Moores University, UK.

Nicky Hirst is Programme Leader for Early Childhood Studies at Liverpool John Moores University, UK.

Understanding Early Years Education across the UK

Comparing practice in England, Northern Ireland, Scotland and Wales

Edited by
Diane Boyd and Nicky Hirst

Routledge
Taylor & Francis Group

LONDON AND NEW YORK

First published 2016
by Routledge
2 Park Square, Milton Park, Abingdon, Oxon OX14 4RN

and by Routledge
711 Third Avenue, New York, NY 10017

Routledge is an imprint of the Taylor & Francis Group, an informa business

© 2016 Diane Boyd and Nicky Hirst

British Library Cataloguing in Publication Data
A catalogue record for this book is available from the British Library

Library of Congress Cataloging in Publication Data
Boyd, Diane.
   Understanding early years education across the UK : comparing practice in England, Northern Ireland, Scotland and Wales / Diane Boyd, Nicky Hirst.
      pages cm
   1. Early childhood education—Great Britain.   2. Early childhood education—Curricula—Great Britain.   3. Early childhood education—Great Britain—Case studies.   4. Comparative education.   I. Hirst, Nicky.   II. Title.
   LB1139.3.G7B69 2015
   372.210941—dc23   2015011857

ISBN: 978-1-138-02271-3 (hbk)
ISBN: 978-1-138-02272-0 (pbk)
ISBN: 978-1-315-77689-7 (ebk)

Typeset in Bembo
by Keystroke, Station Road, Codsall, Wolverhampton

Printed and bound by CPI Group (UK) Ltd, Croydon, CR0 4YY

Contents

About the contributors

Editors

Diane Boyd is currently a senior lecturer at Liverpool John Moores University (LJMU) teaching across Early Childhood Studies and Education Studies and Early Years. Diane is a practitioner at heart. Her qualifications include a BEd (Hons) in Primary Education and Drama, an MA in Early Years Education, a Certificate in Advanced Studies in Education (CASE) in Early Years and a CASE in Mentoring. Diane was a classroom teacher in Early Years for nearly 20 years before becoming a lecturer at LJMU. She was also an Early Years specialist support teacher for settings on the Wirral for three years. Her research interests lie within Early Years practice considering, for example, the outdoor environment and different pedagogical and historical approaches, which she embeds into her university practice.

Nicky Hirst is the programme leader for the undergraduate BAH Early Childhood Studies degree at Liverpool John Moores University (LJMU). She worked in the Early Years sector for over 15 years and moved into higher education and worked extensively teaching and mentoring students on the various pathways for Early Years Professional Status (now referred to as Early Years Teacher Status). Nicky worked closely with students on the foundation degree in Early Years Practice, and she keeps abreast of changes in the Early Years sector as a member of the Early Childhood Studies degree forum. Her qualifications include an Early Childhood Studies BA (Hons) from Manchester Metropolitan University and an MA in Academic Practice in Higher Education.

Contributors

Linda Davidge-Smith is currently the interim Associate Head of School (Initial Teacher Training) at the University of South Wales. Her qualifications include BEd (Hons), NPQH and Forest School Level 3. Having taught for 22 years in the primary sector, Linda has specialised in Foundation Phase practice and in 2008 she was seconded to Newport Local Education Authority as a Foundation Phase Teacher Adviser. Whilst based with the local authority, Linda participated in Welsh government working parties to ensure the successful implementation of the Foundation Phase. More recently, Linda has become the lead for the implementation of literacy (University of South Wales) as part of a Task and Finish group for Literacy and Numeracy established across the South East Wales Centre for Teacher Education and Training (SEWCTET). She has been invited to join the Foundation Phase Expert Group working with the Minister for Education and Skills in Wales to focus on a ten-year strategic plan for the Foundation Phase.

Andrea Doherty is a lecturer in Early Years Education at Stranmillis University College, Belfast. She specialises in Science, Technology, Engineering and Maths (STEM) within the early years, with research interests in the fields of playful pedagogy, cultural-historical theory, science education and coteaching in teacher education. With a BEd in Primary Science and a PhD in Play Theory and Practice in Northern Ireland, Andrea's research interests fuel, and are fuelled by, her work with undergraduate, postgraduate and practising teachers. She is currently a director of the Primary Science Teaching Trust Hub at Stranmillis University College, leading the Playful Approaches to Science project, and the Playful Technology project which focus on teacher education and curriculum development.

Lynn McNair is Head of Cowgate Under Fives Centre in Edinburgh and is a teaching fellow at the University of Edinburgh. Lynn is also a final year PhD student. Lynn has more than 30 years experience working in Early Years Education and was awarded an OBE for services to early education in 2009. She is an award-winning author. Finally, Lynn would say her passion for egalitarianism, emancipation, democracy and a belief that children are rich, active, resourceful beings came from being a mother to Kurt and Mischa and what she learned as she observed them playing freely as children. This way of being with children, trusting them in their abilities and capabilities is what she puts her energy into in her work with children today.

Alison Prowle has extensive experience of Early Years provision and family interventions as an academic, a practitioner and a manager. She began her career as a primary school teacher where she began to see the effects of multiple disadvantages on children's outcomes. This sparked a passion for early intervention with families with young children, working within the voluntary sector and local government. As Integrated Services Manager for Children for Blaenau Gwent, a post held until April 2012, Alison was responsible for managing a range of services for children, young people and families. Since April 2013, Alison has been teaching and researching in the area of Early Years, Parenting and Families at the University of Worcester.

Glenda Walsh is Head of Early Years Education at Stranmillis University College, Belfast. Her research interests focus on quality issues in Early Childhood Education, particularly in the field of pedagogy and curriculum. She played a significant role in the longitudinal evaluation of the Early Years Enriched Curriculum Project in Northern Ireland that has guided the course of the Foundation Stage of the revised Northern Ireland Primary Curriculum. Her interests in curriculum and pedagogy also involved her heading a project on examining pedagogy in Early Childhood Education for the Department of Education in the Republic of Ireland. Her PhD thesis, journal articles and book chapters reflect her interest in curriculum and pedagogy, particularly regarding the early years of primary schooling.

Claire Warden's approach to Nature Pedagogy has earned her international recognition as a pioneer in educational thinking. Her respect for children and families is very clear as they run through the Floorbook approach that is used within Nature Pedagogy to incorporate children's voices into intentional teaching. Claire is one of the world's leading consultants and writers on the use of consultative methods in education. The centre for excellence she has set up in the UK is renowned for Auchlone Nature Kindergarten and the consultative Floorbooks used there. Her own learning pathway as a teacher involves working in a wide variety of settings (2–18 years), mentoring and advisory work, authoring over 11 books and designing resources and landscapes. Lecturing at Strathclyde University in Glasgow and being a research fellow at Federation University in Victoria has allowed the vision of qualifications in nature pedagogy to become a reality. Claire is on the international advisory board for Children and Nature Network, the World Forum Foundation and the School Grounds Association.

Introduction

This book is intended for students studying degrees with a focus on early childhood or practitioners studying at undergraduate/graduate level at a university across the four home nations. This book will provide four different perspectives from across the home countries to enable students and practitioners to understand how the different countries recognise and support the early years. Additionally, the text was needed to offer a view of these different curriculum frameworks as a comparative tool for discussions and lectures, which later can build into students developing a greater awareness of international early years practice.

The idea for this book came from a recognised void in the early years market. The majority of literature considers and recognises the English perspective of early years and therefore students from Northern Ireland, Scotland and Wales do not have texts that seek a 'home' perspective. Students are encouraged to recognise and engage with alternative curriculum frameworks.

There are numerous texts and journals written from a theoretical perspective recognising different disciplines that students can access in their writing. Additionally, there are books that consider the influences and history of social policy in decision-making. However, there is no supporting literature, drawing on the cultural and practical pedagogy of each curriculum, available for students. This is the current gap in literature that this book aims to address.

Each chapter is written by two experienced early years practitioners. They draw upon the current and past curriculum, policies that have impacted upon them and links to practice. There are theoretical and historical links embedded within each chapter, as well as key supporting literature each country has developed to support practitioners in their practice. There are boxes within each chapter with questions to consider, reflect upon and discuss. There are some case studies, but all chapters have embedded practical examples and pictures to support them.

1 A perspective from England

Diane Boyd and Nicky Hirst

Introduction to the English context

This chapter is written by two experienced early years practitioners and offers a review of the English framework with an overview of the principles, themes and areas of learning and development. The English Early Years Foundation Stage (EYFS) (DfE, 2012, 2014) draws on multiple theories and contemporary research and at the heart of the framework, practitioners working with babies and young children from birth to five are regularly reminded of the uniqueness and individuality of each child. The research underpinning the original EYFS (DfES, 2007) was revisited in 2009 with 'Early Years Learning and Development: Literature Review' by Evangelou et al. and it was no surprise that the findings focused on the Vygotskian social constructivist account of learning, Bronfenbrenner's ecological domains and more recent research from neuropsychology where findings around brain development have influenced early years policy and practice. A notable observation by Brock et al. (2013:54) claims that whilst the child is seen to be placed at the centre of the EYFS (DfE, 2012, 2014), the Bronfenbrenner model situates the child as a passive recipient of cultural processes with 'little power or agency' that is dominated by the cultural context. It is worth considering Bandura's (1977) social learning theory where he stated that children are not simply passive recipients and practitioners need to consider the idea of reciprocal determinism (where cognition, environment and behaviour interact). Rogoff critiques the ecological model and 'argues that the model is still a hierarchical one, with the larger, outer contexts constraining the smaller, inner ones' (2003, cited in Brock et al., 2013:55). Practitioners draw on various pedagogical theories to inform and support their practice and 'many draw on a range of theories of learning and development, some based on the work of researchers and thinkers and others based on their own experience of children and childhood' (Pugh & Duffy, 2013:117). However, this sense of *agency* also translates to early years practice where practitioners need to consider a 'critical pedagogy' where they question and challenge ideologies and practices that exist in early years education and care (MacNaughton, 2005; Brock, 2014). For example, the earlier versions of the English EYFS (DfES, 2007; DCSF, 2008) were considered by many to be a playful pedagogy where the strapline, 'learning through play' was a familiar refrain in early years settings; however, this idea of 'play' has been challenging for early years practitioners who 'link their beliefs about the importance of play with the reality of meeting curriculum demands' (Keating et al., 2002, cited in Brock et al., 2013:89). This is even more pertinent with the revised EYFS (DfE, 2012, 2014) and the Statutory Framework which foregrounds the adult role as promoting teaching and learning 'to ensure children's "school readiness" and give children the broad range of knowledge and skills that provide the right foundations for good future progress through school and life' (DfE, 2014:5). Many within the early years sector have baulked at the repetition of the term 'school readiness' and it is sometimes linked to an indication of a top down perspective with pressure on practitioners to develop a more academically grounded programme of activities rather than a play-based pedagogy. 'Providers must guide the development of children's capacities with a view to ensuring that children in their care complete the EYFS ready to benefit fully from the opportunities ahead of them' (DfE, 2014:7). The semantic connotations associated with the ideas of 'completion' and 'readiness' imply that practitioners must rush children through their learning, advocating the image suggested by Dadds of 'a hurry along curriculum' (2002, cited in Ang, 2014:27).

The English early years framework did not materialise out of thin air, rather it is the result of many years of change within the early years sector and some practitioners who have been part of the early years community for a long time have worked with 'desirable learning outcomes' (SCAA, 1996a, 1996b), which were introduced as part of the national funding voucher scheme where parents and carers could, in effect, *purchase* early years education which Palaiologou (2013:14) refers to as 'the marketization of education'. The Curriculum Guidance for the Foundation Stage (QCA and Department for Education and Employment, 2000), with its 'Stepping Stones' and the 'Birth to Three Matters' (Sure Start, 2003), offered comprehensive guidance for those working with babies and young children from birth to three. As part of the ten-year strategy 'Choice for Parents, the Best Start for Children' (HM Treasury, 2004), the 2008 version of the EYFS (DCSF, 2008) was introduced to provide a seamless continuity with statutory guidelines for working with babies and children from birth to five. The statutory nature of the original EYFS was driven by the discourse around quality and uniformity where all settings, including child minders caring for children in their own homes, were required to adhere to the statutory requirements of the curriculum framework. The EYFS originated under the New Labour government and the intention to review the framework was articulated during its inception. Therefore, with the new Coalition government in 2010, Dame Clare Tickell was asked to conduct a review of the curriculum and the results of the research were published in the 2011 document 'The Early Years: Foundations for Life, Health and Learning' (Tickell, 2011). Many of the recommendations resulted in familiar discourses, for example the value of parental partnerships alongside some less familiar rhetoric related to the reduction of paperwork and perceptions of bureaucracy. The government responded with the publication of 'Supporting Families in the Foundation Years' (DfE, 2011) with a focus on 'early intervention', the promotion of children's development and the now familiar refrain around the concept of 'school readiness'. Subsequently, the Department for Education (DfE) invited a response to their report with the publication of 'Conception to Age 2: The Age of Opportunity' (WAVE Trust, 2013, in collaboration with the DfE – an addendum to the Government's vision for the Foundation Years). This report was produced by a special interest group supported by officials from the DfE and the Department of Health (DoH) with the remit to explore how best to promote effective implementation of the principles set out in 'Supporting Families', with specific emphasis on children under the age of two and their parents and families. The report focuses on the arguments based around early intervention and 'investment'.

This chapter offers the reader the opportunity to consider the English EYFS and what this may mean for practice. There are references to theory and to alternative perspectives and the reflective questions are designed as a prompt to support a developing understanding of some of the reasons for policy changes; thus, as Baldock et al. (2013:1) suggest, 'practitioners can do more than just cope'. The authors draw on theory and practice with some examples woven into the discussion and the reader is invited to question some of the contradictions in the way that the framework views the child, for example:

> The EYFS refers to each child as a unique individual and Development Matters states that children develop at their own rates, and in their own ways.
>
> (Early Education, 2012:6–46)

> However, there is also an expectation that by June of the academic year in which they become 5, all children will reach the early learning goals, despite some being 5 years 10 months and others not yet having reached their fifth birthday. Does this expectation reflect evidence of the actual achievements of children from a wide range of backgrounds and if it does not may the unintended consequence be that some children are viewed as failing before they have even started statutory schooling?
>
> (Pugh & Duffy, 2013:120)

The final report and recommendations of the Cambridge Primary Review in 2009 recommended a consolidation of EYFS and it was suggested that this important phase was extended to age six; however, in a recent keynote speech (2013), Robin Alexander vented his frustrations with the current government responses to questions raised about the English education system:

> Those who in March this year (2013), proposed an alternative national curriculum vision were denounced as 'enemies of promise' and 'Marxists hell bent on destroying our schools'; and those who this month raised perfectly legitimate questions about the kind of early years experience that will help children to thrive educationally were accused of 'bleating bogus pop-psychology', dumbing down and lowering expectations.

The Early Years Foundation Stage (DfE, 2012, 2014)

In the EYFS (DCSF, 2008:8) it stated that the principles must 'guide the work of all practitioners'. They were grouped into four 'distinct' principles but with complementary themes. The four principles were:

*   A Unique Child,
*   Positive Relationships,
*   Enabling Environments and
*   Learning and Development.

The guidance stipulated that the principles should 'provide a context for the requirements and describe how practitioners should support the development, learning and care of young children' (DCSF, 2008:9). Additionally, these four principles were broken down into a further 16 underpinning commitments. Practitioners were encouraged to utilise the EYFS Principles into Practice cards to support their everyday practice and as opportunities to reflect and discuss issues in training sessions. The overarching principles of the EYFS in the 2008 version remained in both the 2012 and 2014 versions; however, there was more focus on *how* young children learn with renewed emphasis on the Characteristics of Effective Learning.

At the time of writing, information from the national charity '4 Children' presented information on the revised EYFS which was launched in September 2014. However, the revisions reflect changes which apply to section 3 on safeguarding and welfare only and there are no changes to the learning and development including the Early Learning Goals.

A Unique Child

In the EYFS (DCSF, 2008:9) for 'A Unique Child', it states that 'every child is a competent learner from birth who can be resilient, capable, confident and self-assured'. It focused on four commitments (child development; inclusion; safety; and health and wellbeing). In the revised versions (DfE, 2014:6) there is a slight adaptation to the language: 'every child is a unique child who is constantly learning and can be resilient, capable, confident and self-assured.' Interestingly, there was no mention of the accompanying commitments.

Positive Relationships

The EYFS in 2008 recognised 'how children learn to be strong and independent from a base of loving and secure relationships with parents and/or key person' (DCSF, 2008:9) and it focused on four commitments (respect; partnership with parents; supporting learning; and the role of the key person). In the renewed versions there is a defined change within the language to: 'children learn to be strong and independent through positive relationships' (DfE, 2014:6). There remained no mention of the role of either the parent or key person in the life of the young child which is a significant point. Additionally, again there was no mention of any accompanying commitments.

Enabling Environments

The EYFS (DCSF, 2008:9) suggested 'that the environment plays a key role in supporting and extending children's development and learning'. It focused on four commitments (observation, assessment and planning; support for every child; the learning environment; and the wider context-transitions, continuity and multiagency work). In the renewed versions (DfE, 2014:6) it states that 'children learn and develop well in enabling environments, in which their experiences respond to their individual needs and there is a strong partnership between practitioners and parents/or carers'. Interestingly, the relationship between parents and practitioners is now moved into this principle. Additionally, there was no mention of any accompanying commitments.

Learning and Development

The EYFS (DCSF, 2008:9) 'recognises that children develop and learn in different ways and at different rates: and that all areas of learning are equally important and interconnected.' This language is also recognised in the statutory guidance (DfE, 2014:6) as 'children develop and learn in different ways and at different rates' with the additional statement: 'The framework covers the education and care of all children in early years provision, including children with special educational needs and disabilities.'

REFLECTIVE QUESTIONS

A Unique Child

Consider how an effective practitioner can consider the uniqueness of all children when planning for learning and teaching opportunities.

Positive Relationships/Enabling Environments

Consider the significance in the Statutory Framework (DfE, 2014:6) of the removal of 'partnerships with parents and carers' from the principle Positive Relationships into Enabling Environments.

Learning and Development

Tensions and challenges

Conduct your own personal research to support your response to the following:

*   The Development Matters in the EYFS was revised and presented as 'non-statutory guidance material to support practitioners in implementing the statutory requirements of the EYFS' (Early Education, 2012).
*   Early Years Outcomes is presented as a 'non-statutory guide for practitioners and inspectors to help inform understanding of child development through the early years' (DfE, 2013).

Now consider the following:

*   How are practitioners signposted to these documents?
*   What do you notice about the accessibility of the documents?
*   How are the principles of the EYFS translated within each document?
*   What are the implicit messages gleaned from the use of language within each document?

Characteristics of Effective Learning

The EYFS in 2008 provided handy Principles into Practice cards which were meant to be used to support practitioners as a reflective resource in staff meetings or training sessions. However, many practitioners seemed to focus on the six areas of learning (4.4) and this was often exemplified by displays within early years settings offering visual representations of these areas as 'holistic development'.

With the initial revised version in 2012, the cards were replaced with a greater emphasis on the three commitments 4.1, 4.2 and 4.3, now classified as the Characteristics of Effective Learning. Nancy Stewart (2011:17) commented in her supporting book to the Development Matters guidance that practitioners are still failing to recognise the deeper levels of child development in the early years. Instead of focusing on the end product, she advises practitioners to focus on the process of learning. For example, imagine a reception class with 30 identical Christmas cards hanging across the room on a piece of string. The Christmas tree shapes have been pre-cut by an adult and a practitioner has guided young fingers to ensure the children stick them in the right place but is there a 'right' place? In 2010, Sir Ken Robinson presented his now famous TED Talk, 'Changing Education Paradigms', and in this talk he presented the idea of *divergent thinking*, which, he claimed, whilst different from creativity, is an essential capacity for creativity. This way of thinking is articulated as the ability to see lots of possible answers, what Edward De Bono would call lateral thinking, and this non-linear process was captured in a longitudinal study and written up in a book entitled *Breakpoint and Beyond: Mastering the Future Today* (Land & Jarman, 2000, cited by Sir Ken Robinson in RSA Animate, 2010). In this study 1,500 kindergarten children were 'tested' to ascertain their level of divergent thinking and the results presented a startling realisation that the young, preschool aged children scored highly (98 per cent) and were therefore considered to be at 'genius level'; however, the scores reduced dramatically as they got older (aged 8–10, then again at 13–15). Sir Ken asserts that 'we all have the capacity for lateral thinking' but as children move through the English education system this capacity deteriorates substantially.

Now reconsider the uniqueness, individuality and creativity involved in production line activities such as the one noted earlier. Practitioners need to understand that early years education 'can help children to become confident, creative, motivated do-ers and thinkers'

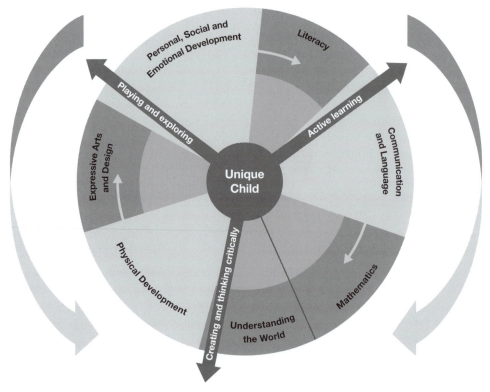

Figure 1.1 The four overarching themes and principles of the EYFS must work together.
Source: Early Education (2012:2)

as this will 'build flexible minds and an enquiring spirit' (Stewart, 2011:17). The four aspects or commitments of the Learning and Development principle are interconnected and the characteristics of effective learning support the unique child as if rotating through all prime and specific areas continuously. The statutory document EYFS (DfE, 2014:7) recognises that these Learning and Development requirements 'promote the learning and development of all children . . . to ensure they are ready for school.'

Interestingly, it then expects practitioners to guide the 'development of children's capabilities with a view to ensuring that children in their care complete the EYFS ready to benefit fully from the opportunities ahead of them' (DfE, 2014:7). However, the Development Matters non-statutory guidance (Early Education, 2012) places greater emphasis on the characteristics in a holistic manner rather than simply as preparation for school. Nancy Stewart (2011) expands upon these characteristics, stressing the importance practitioners must place in ensuring children have open ended opportunities that ignite curiosity, engage their brains, motivate them to ask questions and find answers, whilst providing challenges to think divergently with the support of a knowledgeable other (Vygotsky, 1978). The three columns in the guidance demonstrate the interconnectedness of the principles and the characteristics, whilst providing examples of what an adult *could* do and *could* provide. For practitioners, the importance of children developing the traits of resilience, self-efficacy, self-belief and motivation to achieve regardless of the circumstances is crucial. There is growing evidence that these traits impact on their adult lives, which resonates with the title of the Tickell review (2011), 'The Early Years: Foundations for Life, Health and Learning'.

Observation and assessment in the EYFS

The Statutory Framework notes the requirement for practitioners to observe 'children to understand their level of achievement, interests and learning styles, and to then shape learning experiences for each child reflecting those observations' (DfE, 2014:13). In the Development Matters guidance (Early Education, 2012) this is broken down into three aspects within a cycle of formative assessment as highlighted in Figure 1.2.

Summative assessments

The emphasis on early intervention is exemplified in the statutory requirement for practitioners to complete a summative progress check between the age of two and three. This report is a 'short written summary of the child's development in the prime areas. This progress check must identify the child's strengths and any areas where the child's progress is less than expected' (DfE, 2014:13).

The original EYFS suggested a 'summing up of each child's development and learning achievements at the end of the EYFS' (DCSF, 2008:16) and the Early Learning Goals (ELG) should be 'observations of consistent and independent behaviour pre-dominantly a child's self-initiated activities' (DCSF, 2008:11). It further stated that the summary must be based solely on those self-initiated activities, not adult led, which was a positive feature. Moylett and Stewart highlight the need for a 'best fit', rather than a 'checklist' approach with the former representing a more rounded view that 'acknowledges that there will be many individual variations within an overall typical pattern' as learning is not a linear process 'but occurs in overlapping waves, with stops and starts, reverses, plateaus and spurts' (2012:45).

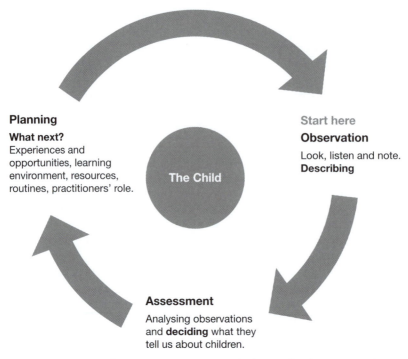

Figure 1.2 Ongoing formative assessment is at the heart of early years practice.
Source: Early Education (2012:12)

For children at the end of reception (the first formal year of school), providers should report in the early years profile:

- whether children are meeting expected levels of development, or if they are exceeding the expected levels, or not yet reaching the expected level (emerging) for each early learning goal;
- a commentary on each child's skills and abilities in relation to the three characteristics of effective learning;
- arrangements for discussing the report between reception and year one teachers and with parents.

(DfE, 2014:14)

The subjective nature of the terminology needs to be interpreted by practitioners and the renewed emphasis is on *how* the child learns and not simply *what* they have achieved.

Areas of learning

In the 2008 version of the EYFS, 4.4 of the Commitments had six areas of Learning and Development. They were:

- Mathematical Development;
- Communication, Language and Literacy;

- Physical Development;
- Creative Development;
- Personal, Social and Emotional Development; and
- Knowledge and Understanding the World.

These Learning and Development requirements (DCSF, 2008:11) were connected to one another and were seen as 'equally important'. Practitioners needed to 'support a rounded approach to child development,' implying a more spherically whole approach to holistic development especially when practitioners delivered through planned, purposeful play, with a balance of adult led and child initiated activities. Within the supporting Practice Guidance for the EYFS (DCSF, 2008:11) these six areas were split into four columns that 'represent the ongoing cycle of thinking about development and assessing children's progress'. These were Development Matters, replacing the original Stepping Stones in the Curriculum Guidance for the Foundation Stage QCA 2000: Look Listen and Note: Effective Practice and Planning and Resourcing. However, it was considered that ultimately practitioners only concentrated on the linear aspects of the Development Matters, cutting and pasting individual steps onto planning and possibly contributing to a tick box culture.

With the initial revised EYFS (DfE, 2012), there was a change in 4.4 Areas of Development. Following the Tickell review in 2011 there was recognition of the considerable neurological developments and research with the resulting separation of the six areas of learning (DCSF, 2008). Tickell (2011:6) proposed three prime areas (Physical Development; Communication and Language; and Personal, Social and Emotional Development) as being particularly important. In her review she stated they were 'essential foundations for children's life, learning and success'. Early Education (2012:4) described them in Development Matters as 'fundamental'. Research increasingly recognises that these three areas are time sensitive and universal. The Government acknowledged that practitioners have a short window of opportunity to ensure all children have access to quality early years education to develop children's 'ability to learn and develop healthily' (DfE, 2011:24) and the changes have been seen as 'crucial for igniting children's curiosity and enthusiasm for learning' (DfE, 2014:7).

The prime areas

Physical Development

The prime area Physical Development is divided into two categories – Moving and Handling, and Health and Self-Care – with the following early learning goals:

- **Moving and Handling**: Children show good control and coordination in large and small movements. They move confidently in a range of ways, safely negotiating space. They handle equipment and tools effectively, including pencils for writing.
- **Health and Self-Care**: Children know the importance for good health of physical exercise, and a healthy diet, and talk about ways to keep healthy and safe. They manage their own basic hygiene and personal needs successfully, including dressing and going to the toilet independently.

The EYFS (DfE, 2012, 2014) is also linked to the Healthy Child Programme (DoH) and the development review by the health visitor. In her review, Tickell (2011:9) suggested 'a renewed emphasis on healthy development for all children' with strong links between early years practitioners and health professionals, stressing the need to 'signpost the inter-relationship'. The introduction of these prime areas is a welcome development, as many historical pioneers, such as Margaret McMillan (1860–1931) and Maria Montessori (1870–1952), advocated the importance of movement and being physical in the early years. Montessori said movement was 'the basis for the development of personality. The child, who is constructing himself, must always be moving' (cited in Standing, 1998:230). She also recognised the importance of self-care developing her practical life materials, for example 'The Dressing Frames'. These frames provide opportunities for children to practice real life skills such as buttons, zippers and laces where cognition and physical activity go hand in hand. Whilst these frames are a Montessori material, the concept is transferable with everyday resources. Practitioners need to provide plenty of opportunities to scaffold children's development related to self-care and independence thus promoting intrinsic motivation, where they persist with difficult tasks and feel a sense of achievement and a 'can do' attitude (active learning).

McMillan also recognised the importance of a healthy child. Giardiello (2014) reminds us of the lasting legacy and philosophy of McMillan's open-air nursery. She stated that the 'driving force behind McMillan's methodology was that children needed to be healthy before learning could take place' (Giardiello, 2014:73). She further opines that McMillan built upon Locke's (1692) philosophy that 'a healthy body and a healthy mind went hand in hand'. This healthy child links to the importance of practitioners utilising their entire environment, especially the outside space and in all weathers.

Figure 1.3 The Montessori dressing frames with buttons, buckles, poppers and laces.

Figure 1.4 A child minder's home environment. The photograph illustrates the interconnectedness of the areas of learning.

Sensorial experiences offer children opportunities to develop both aspects of Physical Development. Children should be encouraged to care for their environment whilst recognising it supports their growth. Friedrich Froebel (1782–1852) in his first kindergarten provided each child with a garden plot. This may not be possible in most settings, but there is the potential, even on a smaller scale. For instance, planters or small areas created for growing allow children to develop holistically. It also encourages an awareness of a healthy diet. The practitioners/carers and parents can encourage children to talk through why certain foods are healthy and support this aspect of Physical Development.

Through the aspect Moving and Handling, the children would be using spades, rakes and hoes to care and tend to the land, utilising their gross motor skills. As it states in the Development Matters, practitioners must 'Teach children skills of how to use tools and materials effectively and safely and give them opportunities to practise them' (Early Education, 2012:24). A sense of community develops as the children recognise that there is a collective need to care and ensure the plants/seeds grow. Children would also gain an awareness of the rhythms of the seasons as advocated by Rudolph Steiner (1861–1925) and the interconnectedness of the whole (Froebel), gaining a better understanding of their world (one of the four specific areas). They could gather the fruits of their labour, chopping, slicing, peeling and mashing (all practical life skills as advocated by Maria Montessori, developing fine motor skills in a natural way) and finally cook the produce. This will not only provide aspects of health and self-care, but also support the characteristics of effective learning. Imagine the feelings of satisfaction and motivation as the child is sitting outside

Figure 1.5 Handling tools showing control and coordination through intrinsic motivation.

eating a mug of freshly made carrot soup which they had cooked! These sensorial experiences impact upon the child, physically, emotionally and cognitively forming the child. Oldfield (2012:101) suggests that this is 'sensory nutrition' describing it as 'a form of nourishment, a soul nourishment, as real as the physical nourishment provided by food', embracing the Steiner philosophy.

The Development Matters (Early Education, 2012) guidance recognises the importance of early mark making as an aspect of Physical Development rather than as Literacy. This is a welcome addition to the EYFS 2012 document, transferring early writing/marks from Literacy (previously the area Communication, Language and Literacy in 2008) into Physical Development. Early Education (2012:30) non-statutory guidance stresses that 'Early mark making is not the same as writing. It is a sensory and physical experience for babies and toddlers, which they do not connect to forming symbols which can communicate meaning.' Maria Montessori in her series of London Lectures (2012:168) defines this sensory aspect of development in young children as 'I see it with my hands.' She recognised it as the 'movement of the hands together with the inner power of the intellect'. In the 2008 EYFS there was an acknowledgement of early years pedagogy with 'sensory experiences' noted. This was, however, not included within the revised EYFS 2012 document.

This is especially relevant when considering the finer details of the prime area Physical Development. In the statutory guidance statement on Physical Development it returns to the 'readiness for school' discourse, with children being able to 'handle equipment and tools effectively, including pencils for writing' (DfE, 2014:10). The statutory nature of the

Figure 1.6 Making marks in the sand with a pebble.

guidance reiterates the hierarchical status that has been attributed to 'school literacy' and writing, therefore practitioners need to consider the emergent writing process and offer young children challenging opportunities to develop their gross and fine motor skills before they are encouraged to hold a pencil. Creating large strokes with a heavy bucket of water and paint brushes on the ground or the side of a brick wall and observing the subtle changes in the colour of the brick (cause and effect) and threading cotton reels or beads onto string encourages concentration and intrinsic motivation. Sally Neaum (2012:147) notes how a:

> number of researchers have highlighted the fact that discussion around, and assessment of literacy at home is dominated by school based literacy. School based literacy, they argue is so dominant in how we understand literacy that it is regarded as the 'real one' and all other literacies (community literacy, literacies of popular culture, intergenerational literacy and family literacy) are regarded as less important or less valid.

In early adulthood the responsibility to establish, maintain and further physical literacy is in the hands of the individual. The motivation to do this will be a direct result of the quality of the experiences that have been encountered in the preceding years. These experiences need to have developed a positive attitude to physical activity. Specifically, they need to be enjoyable, and should develop movement competence and promote confidence and self-esteem (Whitehead, 2006).

Children need to be offered opportunities to engage in challenging environments whilst using rich language (Communication and Language) and the development of self-esteem (Personal, Social and Emotional Development). Neaum refers to the findings from the research, suggesting that 'this, it is argued, disadvantages children who arrive in school with different literacy experiences' (2012:147). There is some excellent practice within early years settings and with the introduction of the EYFS (DCSF, 2008) practitioners were more aware of the need for open ended opportunities for young children and the historical practice of writing over dots or adult scribed writing decreased; however, it is worth remembering the Vygotskian (1978) notion of play where children act a head taller than their age by being mindful of the adult/child interactions that can suggest a demarcation between work and play and this is considered by Ang (2014:15) with the suggestion that attitudes like this will simply embed 'a culture of compliance in children'. Literacy is discussed further in the 'Literacy' section under 'Specific areas' (see p. 38).

Cathy Nutbrown (2012:5), in an executive summary of her review on qualifications in early years, stresses the importance of high quality practitioners needing a wealth of knowledge to be able to interpret these documents to provide the appropriate activities for young children. She states that:

> High quality early education and childcare can have a positive long term impact on children's later learning and achievements. . . . Quality is the key to that positive impact, and staff with the necessary skills, knowledge and understanding is a crucial element of that quality.

The revised EYFS for September 2014 places an expectation on managers, senior practitioners and head teachers to ensure that there are opportunities for staff development and training. In Section 3 of EYFS (DfE, 2014) – The Safeguarding and Welfare Requirements – it states under 'Staff qualifications, training, support and skills' that providers should ensure that staff have opportunities to 'discuss any issues concerning children's development or well-being' and 'to receive coaching to improve their own personal effectiveness' (3.22:20). These training sessions could discuss recent research, different pedagogical approaches and observations of practice to ensure all practitioners understand that development is not linear, but it weaves in and out allowing children to grow in their own ways and at their own pace. Practitioners, managers and head teachers also need to embrace the outdoor environment, offering children different textures, levels and challenges that will develop their sense of self. The environment is called the 'Enabling Environment' within all versions of the framework. Practitioners need to offer an appropriate, stimulating and rich environment that will encourage children to be adventurous, investigative and little explorers. Practitioners need knowledge of how children develop in a general sequence of movements and therefore provide the necessary enhanced and enriched provision.

However, within this prime area there seems to be a lack of the finer details of movement and the development of gross motor skills, a precursor to fine motor development. 'Children show good control and co-ordination in large and small movements' (DfE, 2014:10). This could be interpreted as a Physical Education lesson in the hall once a week on big equipment, rather than the rough and tumble play needed for development of the inner senses. Children need to develop both their inner and outer senses. The five outer senses (auditory, visual, touch, taste and smell) are external and provide the brain with information about stimuli received from outside the body, as Montessori stated over a hundred years ago advocating sensorial experiences. The inner senses are balanced through the vestibular system and proprioception. Proprioceptors in muscles, tendons and joints and the vestibular system send messages to the brain to inform about the body's position in space, movement and acceleration. Children need opportunities to develop these inner senses with resources such as monkey bars, tyres, beams, ropes and pulleys in the outside area, and the adult's role is to support. At an excellent local early years setting, several children were trying to gain access to the top of the monkey bars. Rather than offering a solution verbally, the practitioner suggested that the children utilise the resources available to them. After a short while the group had dragged over several tyres, built them up to an appropriate level to reach the bar and climbed up. This was achieved after several attempts to climb and balance on the wobbling tyres. The practitioner was there in a supporting role and the children were secure in their belief of their own ability to achieve. Through this activity children had demonstrated the elements of the characteristics of effective learning (engagement, motivation and thinking) as well as developing their inner senses, and in the context of 'playing and exploring', the children were initiating their own activity, seeking their own challenges, taking risks and demonstrating a 'can do' attitude (Stewart, 2011). In a tar-macked yard with some plastic pre-designed resources, this would not have happened. In the Development Matters guidance (Early Education, 2012:6) it states that practitioners could 'encourage children to try new activities and judge risks for themselves. Pay attention to how children engage in activities – the challenges faced, the effort, thought, learning and enjoyment.' This is only possible in the right circumstances and outside heuristic play provides the opportunities to support this requirement. In a 'blame' culture this can be worrying for early years practitioners and it is worth considering the subjectivity around the concept of 'risk'. Gill (2007) argues that risk and challenge are essential for a healthy childhood and this resonates with features of recognised early years pedagogy. He offers credible arguments that in order to manage certain types of risk children need to 'encounter' them first (Gill, 2007:15). He also cites the importance of 'feeding' children's appetite (Gill, 2007:16) to develop resilience and self-worth and this translates within Physical Development, Health and Self-Care thus: 'Shows understanding of the need for safety when tackling new challenges, and considers and manages some risks' (Early Education, 2012:27 and DfE, 2013:14).

When considering the EYFS there are different emphases shown in regard to utilising the outside space. In the EYFS statutory document (DCSF, 2008:35) it stated, 'There should be adequate space to give scope for free movement and well-spread activities.' Also ensuring there should be 'wherever possible . . . access to an outdoor play area'. If this was not possible, 'outings should be planned and taken on a daily basis'. It also recognised that children need 'adequately ventilated and well lit' environments, noting the importance of 'daylight' as the main source of light. As Joyce (2012) notes, this resonates with the ideals of Margaret McMillan as she designed her open air nursery in Deptford, London, to give children who lacked well ventilated homes and fresh air a healthy disposition. However, in the EYFS (DfE, 2014:28) it only stipulates the same access requirements on a daily basis. There is no regard shown to sensory experiences, adequate light and ventilation and promoting opportunities for free movement.

Goddard Blythe (2011) in her neurological research opines that these internal and external senses have to learn to work in coordination together. She states that the child needs countless opportunities to practise, repeat and refine through movement at

Figures 1.7, 1.8 and 1.9 Children need the time and space to develop an awareness of their own physical capabilities.

different speeds, conditions and positions. Enabling environments should provide a range of textures, levels and contours. Additionally, babies must be given access to floor play to develop postural abilities by being placed on either their front or their back. For example, by lying on their back on a firm floor surface, the baby can kick, stretch and move, developing their muscles safely. Additionally, these movements will send messages to the brain about their position in space too, developing the inner senses. Babies need opportunities for free movement rather than being constantly placed in baby chairs and rockers. They may be useful for short periods of time to allow practitioners to do something, but they restrict the *range* of movements available. Compare the range of movements a baby can do whilst lying on a mat. They can develop 'truncal' movements such as rolling, twisting and as Goddard Blythe (2011:23) states, facilitate 'efficient cooperative use of upper and lower sections of the body'.

The outdoor environment offers such possibilities if accessible and planned appropriately. Goddard Blythe states that this is why physical activity is so important and why it is now recognised as a prime area of development. She believes that 'practice not only improves performance over time, but also reduces the amount of mental energy required to carry out the task, increasing flexibility of response and adaptability of the changing conditions' (2011:14). Consider the children again on the monkey bars. The children engaged in the task will now have new information to accommodate in their brains. Some children might have just watched the others gathering the tyres together and will utilise the stored memories later when they feel more able to try. Having opportunities to watch, repeat (refine) and return to an activity is crucial in the developing child.

Figure 1.10 Babies need opportunities to crawl, roll and develop their strength.

Tickell, in her detailed rationale for physical development, reminds practitioners of the need to ensure opportunities for touch, movement and the senses to combat sedentary lifestyles at home or in settings. Children need to be investigative explorers who can confidently move, manipulating their bodies in time and space, whilst 'understanding and managing risk through lively play' (2011:95). Through this play they will recognise how physical activity and healthy choices are important to their growth and development.

Practitioners need to plan a range of diverse activities that will support the holistic development of the child.

Reflection – Moving and Handling

- What activities could you plan to support the development of the gross motor skills?
- Does the environment impact upon the development of the inner senses?
- What activities could you utilise drawing on historical pioneers to aid fine motor skills (in preparation for writing)?

Health and Self-Care

- Through sensorial experiences how can practitioners encourage children's awareness of a healthy diet whilst supporting the environment?
- How could you encourage children to manage their own bodily needs?
- Utilise different opportunities to draw attention to the children's bodies during exercise. Can they feel their heart beat faster? Are their cheeks rosy and glowing? Do they need a drink of water? These questions will help children to make connections between their reactions and changes in their body, exercise and a healthy diet.

Tensions and challenges

How can practitioners ensure that the goal-orientated nature of the EYFS curriculum does not encourage adults to rush children through the 'stages' towards more formal writing?

Researchers have linked obesity to a lack of physical development and with sedentary lifestyles associated with the twenty-first century; how can practitioners contribute to children's reengagement with nature in a physical and spiritual way?

The ELG for the aspect Moving and Handling suggests that children 'need to move confidently, safely and handle equipment and tools effectively'. Consider the tensions involved when adults are expected to support children to explore their world physically and compare the following:

- an early years setting with plastic resources, artificial grass and 'safe' play areas;
- an early years setting providing natural resources with open ended opportunities;
- an early years setting using real tools in their activities.

The aspect Health and Self-Care notes the need for children to 'tackle' new challenges and 'manage' risk, and the statutory requirement (3.63:25) cites the need for settings to have a 'clear and well-understood policy' and 'procedures for assessing any risks to children's safety'. Discuss the challenges that this may pose when providing children with opportunities for exploration and the development of resilience.

Communication and Language

The prime area Communication and Language is divided into three categories with the following early learning goals:

- **Listening and Attention**: Children listen attentively in a range of situations. They listen to stories, accurately anticipating key events and respond to what they hear with relevant comments, questions or actions. They give their attention to what others say and respond appropriately while engaged in another activity.
- **Understanding**: Children follow instructions involving several ideas or actions. They answer 'how' and 'why' questions about their experiences and in response to stories or events.
- **Speaking**: Children express themselves effectively, showing awareness of listeners' needs. They use past, present and future forms accurately when talking about events that have happened or are to happen in the future. They develop their own narratives and explanations by connecting ideas or events.

In the 2014 statutory document, Communication and Language is described as 'giving children opportunities to experience a rich language environment: to develop their confidence and skills in expressing themselves: and to speak and listen in a range of situations' (DfE, 2014:6). In the original EYFS (DCSF, 2008), Literacy was also included in the same area of learning as Communication and Language. However, in the revised EYFS (DfE, 2012), Literacy was moved into one of the specific areas. The statutory document states that practitioners 'must also support children in the four *specific* areas through which the prime areas are strengthened' (DfE, 2014:7). Tickell (2011:98) separates the literacy aspect from this prime area because it is 'experience dependent' and is also 'culturally constrained'. A huge leap in our understanding is the idea that 'recent research has been concerned to explore not just the capabilities, but the particular interests of the infant brain' (PEEP, 2009:45) and this 'interest' needs to be stimulated with the promotion of conversations where children are encouraged to question. This was highlighted by Evangelou et al. (2009) where they suggest a deficit in the number of 'why' questions in early years settings compared to the bombardment that parents and carers receive from young children in the home environment.

Communication and Language is divided into the three aspects, as listed above: Listening and Attention (formerly Language for Communication, DCSF, 2008); Understanding (formerly Language for Thinking, DCSF, 2008) and Speaking (again formerly Language for Thinking, DCSF, 2008). These aspects were a consequence of the excellent work through the National Strategy, Every Child a Talker (ECAT 2008) Programme. ECAT (2008) was a supportive programme that could be implemented either in a setting with a child minder or even in the child's home. It was marketed as a tool to help encourage early language development through fun and interesting activities. It was also a training resource encouraging practitioners to reflect and think about practice within the setting. Practitioners were encouraged to focus on the communication skills and attributes of the children in their setting utilising the four overarching principles of the EYFS (DCSF, 2008). Unfortunately this programme has now since concluded but was recognised by Clare Tickell in her review. She stressed the importance of separating receptive language (understanding) from expressive language (speaking), noting that it had been effective in supporting practitioners to understand language development better. Receptive language is having the ability to understand language that is either heard or read. Expressive language is having the ability to translate thoughts into words and then sentences. Practitioners need to consider how they can capture children's thinking and the theoretical ideas associated with scaffolding (Vygotsky, Bruner) resonate in the 'Effective Provision of Pre-School Education' (EPPE; Sylva et al., 2004) longitudinal study as 'sustained shared thinking'. This idea is reflected in the Development Matters guidance (Early Education, 2012) as one of the Characteristics of Effective Learning under 'creating and thinking critically' where practitioners are guided with ideas about 'what adults *could* provide'.

The focus on staff qualifications and the need for knowledgeable adults has been highlighted in the Nutbrown review (2012) and further reiterated in the 'Conception to Age 2' report (WAVE Trust, 2013, the Government Addendum vision to Supporting Families in the Foundation Years 2013:15). It also supports the 'wider context' of the original EYFS (DCSF, 2008:3.4) with working with multiagency partnerships and the Healthy Child

Figure 1.11 'Plan linked experiences that follow the ideas children are really thinking about' and 'Use mind maps to represent thinking together'.

Source: Early Education (2012:7)

Programme (DoH, 2009) in identifying children earlier with language delay. Identifying difficulties with either receptive or expressive language is crucial in the early years. There is an expectation that practitioners must 'identify the child's strengths, and any areas where the child's progress is less than expected' (DfE, 2014:13). This 'check' is based on all three prime areas and is fundamentally meant to be a supportive measure and 'parents and carers should be involved at all stages' (Tickell, 2011:23).

In her rationale, Tickell (2011:98) recognised that babies are communicators from birth drawing upon research stating that 'the development of communication and language skills happens during an optimum window of brain development'. Babies and young children need to be surrounded by a rich language-filled and spoken environment. The importance of Personal, Social and Emotional Development is crucial here as a child's learning stems from rich interactions with warm and encouraging adults. Practitioners and parents must provide time and patience to interact, explain points and describe what they can see and hear, and to recognise that engaging in new contexts supports brain development. Babies are communicators from birth and non-verbal language is an early sign of communicating. Picture a new born baby in the arms of his mother minutes after birth. The baby will gaze intently, watching her, scanning her face for details. Research by Murray and Andrews (2005) demonstrated that even babies who are 15 minutes old can imitate facial expressions. 'Ethan', the baby in their study, was able to watch his father totally absorbed for several minutes while his father slowly but clearly protruded his tongue. Ethan then 'appears to be concentrating completely on his mouth as he frowns and shuts his eyes ... then he looks back at his father as he protrudes his own tongue' (2005:29). This is without him even seeing his own face and knowing that he too had a tongue! Both the parent and the carer must develop the confidence and ability to engage in these non-verbal 'conversations'. An opportune moment for these 'conversations' could be baby changing time when the practitioners can imitate the baby, emphasising their facial expression or tone, thus providing valuable feedback for the baby. Murray and Andrews stated that Donald Winnicott, a highly respected paediatrician, believed these 'mirroring' responses are an important function in the baby developing a strong sense of 'self'. They consider, 'the experience of having her own actions and feelings reflected back in the behaviour of someone else affirms, enriches, and gives greater coherence to the baby's original experience' (2005:49). In the Development Matters guidance (Early Education, 2012:15) it reminds practitioners of ways they *could* support listening and attention: 'Being physically close, making eye contact, using touch or voice all provide ideal opportunities for early conversations' for the very young baby. Nutkins et al. (2013) also recognise this ability to imitate as a potential opportunity in the development of social cognition.

Supporting children's communication skills is highly dependent on practitioner awareness and understanding of child development and a high degree of self-reflection is needed to support the recognition of the impact that provision will have on individual babies and children. It is also dependent on the relationship between the parent and carers. Nutbrown (2012:13) consistently returned to the point of a knowledgeable practitioner, stressing that 'high quality provision matters and that poor and mediocre provision will not benefit children'. The WAVE Trust report, 'Conception to Age 2: The Age of Opportunity', also stresses the importance of parental attachments and how it impacts upon brain development: 'The developing brain of the baby adapts itself to the quality of the relationship with parents and the home learning environment, creating neural circuits that mirror his/her experiences' (2013:15). The home learning environment is crucial for communication and language development. Practitioners and parents need

Figure 1.12 The importance of early communication.

to 'bridge' the home and the setting as advocated by Froebel, who recognised the crucial role of mothers. In 1844 Froebel published his book of the 'Mother Songs'. He recognised that from birth interactions were fundamental and this is reflected today in settings where children should be singing nursery rhymes, alphabet songs and doing movement games with significant adults. Froebel, like Jean Piaget (1896–1980) recognised the importance of sensory–motor activities between the child and mother/carer. Liebschner (1992) reflected that to Froebel, mother and 'baby in arms' opportunities of physical movements and rhymes lead to abstract thinking.

Within the Development Matters guidance it suggests that as children develop and grow, practitioners *could* play listening games, make up rhymes, 'choose stories with repeated refrains, dances and action songs' (Early Education, 2012:17). In 2013, a small-scale research project (Powell et al.) funded by the Froebel Trust considered how singing is utilised in settings. They found that singing did not necessarily happen during routine activities but they did notice that most singing was 'upbeat' or 'fun'. Observations also supported neuro-scientific research of babies' capabilities in regard to songs. Babies under one moved their heads or other parts of their bodies to join in, whilst others sang or made some relevant accompanying sounds, such as 'wa-wa'. In their research, Powell et al. noted the lack of lullabies utilised when practitioners were soothing the babies in their care, thus the majority of practitioners remained silent, although they did rock as they soothed.

This also has implications for a child's developing cultural identity. In the child's setting parents, carers and extended families could be invited in to share traditional songs and movement games supporting the child's cultural identity. Therefore by sharing their own

Figure 1.13 A toddler 'in arms' with a familiar adult in a warm and caring environment.

cultural identity with their peers through these interactions, it will enhance the individual child's own awareness of their individuality as well as deepening other cultural identities around them in the setting. This is the very essence of Vygotsky's (1978) social cultural thinking and later Rogoff's (2008) work. Through communication and language babies and young children will experiment, play and tease, ultimately being involved and enjoying a sense of theatre involving movement and clapping games. Professor Colwyn Trevarthen, a renowned psychologist, was quoted on the Education Scotland Early Years website stating that the 'main purpose of communication is to belong to a world with other people, with common understanding' (Trevarthen, n.d.). Bronfenbrenner (1979) advocated that holistic practice should place the child at the centre of an ecological model of interconnecting layers of families and communities, all influencing the developing child.

When considering the importance of cultural identity and therefore opportunity within the EYFS, Ang (2014:23) suggests there is an 'implicit assumption' of a 'level playing field' and practitioners should be able to 'ignite' all children's curiosity through inclusive practice. The statutory requirement (DfE, 2012:26) stated that all practitioners 'should promote and value diversity and difference'. However, in reality this 'inclusive practice' and promoting diversity and difference could be challenged. Ang (2014) opines that there is no acknowledgement within the EYFS (DfE, 2012) of these very differences that practitioners need to celebrate. Young children enter early years settings with a wide range of experiences and family situations and therefore bring different levels of cultural and social capital with them. There is recognition of this in the early learning goal for the specific area Understanding the World (Early Education, 2012:38) when it states: 'They know similarities and differences between themselves and others, and among families, communities and traditions.' Ang (2014), however, considers that the middle class culture is perhaps the dominant discourse of the EYFS (DfE, 2012) and practitioners must be able to ensure all cultural and social diversity is respected, even recognising the slight differences that are within the same cultural groups in communities.

The longitudinal study EPPE (Sylva et al., 2004:1) supports the viewpoint advocating the importance of interactions within the home environment, stating, 'For all children, the quality of the home learning environment is more important for intellectual and social development than parental occupation, education or income. What parents do is more important than who parents are.' The research utilised an index to measure the quality of the home environment and the results demonstrated that simple basic activities supported the holistic development of young children. For example, within a quality home environment, the activities that parents or carers were engaging in included several that supported the prime area of Communication and Language. They were reading with the child, teaching songs and nursery rhymes, visiting the library and providing other opportunities to engage with the wider world. These were all associated with higher scores for intellect and social behaviour. A simple walk to the post office to post a letter provides a wealth of language opportunities for the growing child. Questions could be asked on the way: How many buses do you think we will see? What shape are the windows on our bus? If we needed some carrots which shop shall we visit?

Zeedyk (2008) conducted a small-scale study for the National Literacy Trust into the effect of either forward facing (towards the adult) buggies or buggies designed to face away from the adult. It was noted that the majority of buggies were 'away' facing and that these were associated with a reduction in communication with both adult and baby. The reduction rate for the baby in speaking to the parent/carer was one-third, whilst with the adults the rate of opportunity of speech halved. It was also recognised that in the 'away' facing buggies, the babies were twice as likely to go to sleep and therefore not engaging with the world around them. OFSTED emphasised the importance of daily outings with young children, not just as a physical development opportunity, but for valuable talking and sharing memories. The benefits may simply include more opportunities for clapping hands together excitedly as they watch the ducks on the pond on the way to the shops, but eventually it will lead to knowledge of their world, deeper thinking and intellect.

Hart and Risley's (1995) research into language development found that although children typically develop language skills around the same age, the growth rate of their vocabulary can be determined by the influences of how much their parents/carers talk to them. The research concluded that children from professional families tend to talk to their children and engage in language-orientated activities more than children from disadvantaged socio-economic backgrounds. This was furthered consolidated in research conducted by Hartshorne in 2006 ('The Cost to the Nation of Children's Poor Communication') which supported the importance of a quality social and emotional environment in the early years. It recognised that up to 50 per cent of children have poor language skills and in some socio-economically disadvantaged areas the figure was as high as 84 per cent. But the report stresses that the majority of these difficulties are *transient* rather than *persistent*, recognising that with the correct communication strategies employed in settings they are likely to catch up with their peers. Additionally, the EPPE research (Sylva et al., 2004) stated that if children from disadvantaged socio-economic backgrounds were attending high quality provision with good social and emotional support and mixing with children from a diverse

Figure 1.14 Opportunities to communicate with people and nature.

range of cultures and communities, this helped close the communication gap. This reaffirms the importance of both quality practice and knowledgeable practitioners in the early years as they need to provide a rich language-communication friendly environment. The settings could implement strategies to support this: for example, visual timetables displayed so that children can understand the consistent routines and structures of the day; ensure staff understand the stages in language development and can effectively provide relevant information to parents; know how to identify difficulties and who is the designated practitioner for support; model good communication skills themselves as this is how children learn. Additionally, the settings could have designated quiet spots in the indoor and outdoor environment, with fewer distractions so children can spend quality listening and talking times with their key person. Evidence recognises the importance of the enabling environment to support valuable, rich and warm interactions in developing language with time for reflection and thinking.

In the Child Health Promotion Programme (DoH, 2008) there is a suggestion that parents/practitioners need to promote language development utilising book sharing, singing, music and interactive activities as a means to support this. Settings should ensure that they utilise all opportunities to support the development of language and communication. Sir Jim Rose (2006:3), in his review for the National Literacy Trust, recognised that learning is a social construct and that settings should create time for children to interact with their peers to engage 'frequently in worthwhile talk and attentive listening, build a good stock of words, explore how language works, understand what is said to them and

Figure 1.15 'Allow time to follow young children's lead and have fun together while developing vocabulary, e.g., we're jumping up and going down.'

Source: Communication and Language-Speaking in Development Matters (Early Education, 2012:19)

respond appropriately'. The Development Matters non-statutory guidance (Early Education, 2012:21) consolidates this by stating that practitioners could 'Give thinking time for children . . . set up collaborative tasks . . . provide opportunities for talking for a wide range of purposes', as some examples of practice.

Steiner advocated that story, puppetry and drama should fire and motivate a child's imagination. Through the power of creativity children should develop and learn co-operatively, enriching their language. Sir Jim Rose (2006) also recognised the importance that imaginative opportunities would have to promote language. The Development Matters non-statutory guidance (Early Education, 2012:18) suggests that practitioners could introduce 'story props, such as puppets and objects, to encourage children to retell stories' or to 'provide for, initiate and join in imaginative play and role-play, encouraging children to talk'. In a Steiner kindergarten the youngest children have no pressure to read, write or perform worksheets in preparation for reading and writing. There is a huge emphasis upon children moving freely in their choice of play, movement and activity. For example, when it is clearing up time, the practitioner would begin to sing a tidying up song. All the children tidy up the materials whilst singing along with the teacher if they wish. There is no pressure to 'perform'. The teacher leads them from free play into a teacher led ring time. The children imitate the practitioner with the carefully chosen rhyme or action of the season. If it was autumn, for example, the children would be miming shaking apples from the trees, gathering them, becoming squirrels that are 'scampering' and 'nut collecting'. Through these rhyme time activities children learn the words of the songs effortlessly and with no anxiety. Oldfield (2012:7) states that through creative and imaginative experiences all prime areas are reinforced:

> Speech and language development are strengthened, fine and gross motor skills addressed, knowledge and understanding of the world extended. Socialisation and attentiveness is encouraged. They feel the pleasure and security of being caught up in their imagination and the ease of being led by the teacher's example – all within the comfort of a shared, communal experience.

The statutory document (DfE, 2014:6) states that through Communication and Language, settings must have a 'rich language environment' both inside and out. Through the interconnecting prime areas, practitioners will support children's Personal, Social and Emotional development and Physical Development alongside Communication and Language, by allowing babies and children to 'develop their confidence and skills in expressing themselves'. This can be achieved only if the knowledgeable practitioner understands how language develops and provides opportunities for them to 'speak and listen in a range of situations'. That is how effective settings support babies and children to become rich and competent communicators.

Practitioners need to plan and reflect upon a range of activities to support the holistic development of the child.

Listening and Attention

- How does an environmental sound walk support a child's developing language skills?
- Consider the many different ways a practitioner can 'tell' a story rather than just reading it. Why is it important for children to engage in creativity and oracy?
- What strategies could you implement to support good listening skills? Be aware that it is sometimes a child's inability to pay attention that is impaired, not their understanding.
- Emphasise the importance of the practitioner modelling thinking, questioning and listening.

Understanding

- How can a practitioner support a child's developing receptive language skills in the setting?
- Why is it important to give clear instructions and not overload children with instructions? How can a pictorial time line of activities support a child's understanding?
- How can practitioners use stories to help children answer 'how' and 'why' questions?

- How can a story chair be used to support the development of narratives?
- How can you ensure that all staff model language and thinking skills?

Speaking

- How can practitioners help children to understand the conventions of language and conversations?
- Powell et al. (2013) noted a lack of singing with very young babies. How can singing support early communication skills and be embedded into practice? How would you support adults to feel comfortable in their communications with very young babies?

Tensions and challenges

There is a statutory requirement for practitioners to provide parents with a summary assessment of their children's progress (at age two) in the three prime areas (Communication and Language; Physical Development; and Personal, Social and Emotional Development). In light of this requirement, consider the following statements from the Statutory Framework for the EYFS (revised for 2014).

> Practitioners must discuss with parents and/or carers how the summary of development can be used to support learning at home.
>
> (DfE, 2014:2.4:13)

> In group settings, the manager must hold at least a full and relevant level three qualification and at least half of all other staff must hold at least a full and relevant level 2.
>
> (DfE, 2014:3.23:20)

Personal, Social and Emotional Development

The prime area Personal, Social and Emotional Development (PSED) is divided into three categories with the following early learning goals:

- **Self-Confidence and Self-Awareness**: Children are confident to try new activities, and say why they like some activities more than others. They are confident to speak in a familiar group, will talk about their ideas and they will choose the resources they need for their chosen activities. They say when they do or don't need help.
- **Managing Feelings and Behaviour**: Children talk about how they and others show feelings, talk about their own and others' behaviour and its consequences, and know that some behaviour is unacceptable. They work as part of a group or class, and understand and follow the rules. They adjust their behaviour to different situations and take changes of routine in their stride.
- **Making Relationships**: Children play cooperatively, taking turns with others. They take account of one another's ideas about how to organise their activity. They show sensitivity to others' needs and feelings, and form positive relationships with adults and other children.

PSED is one of the three prime areas and this focus is a welcome reminder of the primacy of these three interrelated areas from one of six areas of learning (DCSF, 2008). In 2010 Marion Dowling argued that there were 'grounds for optimism' and:

> there is a pervasive acknowledgement from research, which is being carried into practice, that we are educating and caring for more than a child's intellect. If early years settings foster children's personal, social and emotional qualities they are surely opening doors for them to live a life of personal fulfilment whatever their other achievements. However, it is unrealistic and unfair to place this requirement on settings alone. Society as a whole must take ultimate responsibility for children's personal development.
>
> (2010:8)

At the time of writing, in the fourth edition of her book, Dowling asserts that 'despite the brevity' of the revised EYFS, 'the framework continues to be based on the themes and principles established in the previous framework and affirms the significance of children's personal, social and emotional development' (2014:2).

The acceptance that practitioners need to nurture and support PSED is now firmly associated with effective pedagogy in the early years; however, as previously noted, some spectators see the revisions to the EYFS as a simplification which simply focuses 'much more directly on preparing children for school' (Baldock et al., 2013:34). The rationale for the changes is embedded in the Tickell review (2011) and there are some subtle adaptations to the vocabulary in this particular area which resonate with speculations around the idea of school 'readiness'. According to Tickell, changes in this area are overtly linked to 'research and the lessons learned from the implementation of the National Strategies programme, Social and Emotional Aspects of Learning (SEAD)' (2011:9).

Initial scrutiny suggests little change from the original EYFS (DCSF, 2008), although the focus on educational achievement is firmly situated as Tickell asserts: 'recent literature identifies the centrality of personal, social and emotional capabilities for children's later learning and development' (2011:99). There are undoubtedly very few people who would argue against this centrality and as Palaiologou (2013) reminds us, at policy level, the PSED of young children remains a government priority with previous Labour government strategies resonating in the initial revised version of the EYFS (DfE, 2012). Supplementing the research around the value of early intervention in the early years, the WAVE Trust's 'Conception to Age 2: The Age of Opportunity' clearly focused on the 'wide range of research which now shows that conception to age 2 is a crucial phase of human development and it is the time when focused attention can reap great dividends for society' (2013:3). This report is well worth further exploration as the emergence of young children's PSED is scrutinised from many perspectives including valuable psychological and neurological research and the socialisation of children into 'our society' tacitly suggests a nation wide ownership of children as future citizens who have the potential to make a valuable contribution (resonating with the ambition to 'make a positive contribution' in the Every Child Matters agenda (HM Treasury, 2003)) or conversely, to contribute to the substantial drain on government spending.

Personal, Social and Emotional Development are universally recognised areas; however there are cultural differences that need to be addressed if children's individual responses are to be truly understood. It is also important to acknowledge how feelings and emotions play a key role in our ability to interact and coexist with others and special attention has been focused on understanding and recognising feelings, not least through the much-lauded work around emotional intelligence by Daniel Goleman (1996). The EYFS (DfE, 2012, 2014) is a child centred, developmental and goal-orientated framework and as the principle of the 'Unique Child' remains, there is more emphasis on parental involvement and the key person. The rationale for changes articulated within the Tickell review (2011) highlight the familiar rhetoric around parental influence on children's holistic development. In fact, Tickell (2011) highlights the need to provide parents with clear information to support this partnership thus reflecting the tag line in the Curriculum Guidance for the Foundation Stage with its proclamation that parents are 'children's first and most enduring educators' (QCA and Department for Education and Employment, 2000:9). The suggested support for children's PSED has been viewed through an ecological lens where health and education are inextricably linked (DoH and DfE), resonating with Margaret McMillan's and Rudolph Steiner's philosophy of the development of 'healthy will activity' (Nicol & Taplin, 2012:14) where children are 'not educated in order to imprint learning on the child' but where they are left to be 'as free as possible to develop as individuals. It is only through this freedom that human beings can realize the impulses that they bring with them before birth' (Nicol & Taplin, 2012:35).

PSED has come under substantial scrutiny in recent years and Ecclestone and Hayes (2009:371) claim that this emphasis:

> mirrors calls by international bodies such as UNICEF for indicators of children's well-being, where children feel loved, safe and respected, to be the hallmark of civilized societies and similar claims by the Organisation for Economic Cooperation and Development for well-being to be a key outcome of learning in progressive societies.

Tina Bruce examines the influence of some of the pioneers of early childhood education and whilst these 'bedrock principles' can be seen in the EYFS, it is worth remembering that 'each has an international reputation and influence' (2011:15). The very idea of well-being is enshrined in the United Nations Convention on the Rights of the Child and Bruce (2011) offers an accessible and thought provoking review of early pioneers to support personal translations of pedagogical practice. Oliverio (2013) reminds us of the 'education of emotions' and how Maria Montessori valued a pedagogy that 'favours the development of a personality that is able to participate in society and to contribute to its organization. This is in line with the concept of a "just society"', but he reiterates that, 'for Montessori, the child's individuality and autonomy are not synonyms for egoism, but a condition for growth' (2013:98). Oliverio's claim that 'a just society is able to settle conflicts in a rational way without resorting to a struggle between the strong and the weak, which mirrors the conflict between adult and child' (2013:99), can be related to the pioneering philosophy of Loris Malaguzzi. The world-renowned Reggio Emilia Approach was conceived as an antidote to fascism and from a philosophical position, children would be supported to think for themselves and develop the confidence to question, rather than blindly follow instruction (Moss, 2013). This also resonates within early years practice where less confident practitioners have been confused by some of the messages within the original EYFS (Tickell, 2011). Dowling notes that there are times where adults are reluctant to use their initiative for fear of doing the 'wrong thing'. She argues for 'strong leadership' to support a confident workforce to enable practitioners to 'recognize that rather than blindly following dictates from above, they still have a degree of autonomy in their work based on their secure knowledge of what is right for young children' (Dowling, 2010:5). The quality and stability of a child's relationships in the early years lay the foundation for a wide range of developmental outcomes that really do matter, therefore practitioners may wish to consider how they can support young children to develop self-confidence, self-awareness, manage their feelings and behaviour and make relationships in the context of the EYFS (DfE, 2014). In her independent report on the EYFS, Tickell asserted that the conscious decision to replace the term 'self-esteem' with 'self-awareness' was justified on the basis that they 'blend the SEAD self awareness capability with the concept of agency' and this replaced the 'idea of global self-esteem which is not as clearly supported by research as confidence and agency' (2011:99). Instead of the language of introspection, fragility and vulnerability, it could be argued that the promotion of PSED is more about self-efficacy and the type of confidence that is linked to a sense of purpose reflected in the Characteristics of Effective Learning (DfE, 2012, 2014).

The development of confidence is a valued characteristic, defined by the Centre for Confidence and Well-being (www.centreforconfidence.co.uk) as, 'not simply a feeling that things will go well, but also a judgement of our own or others' abilities', and Marion Dowling (2010:12) acknowledges the confident person as being, 'comfortable with them-selves' and as having 'insights into their own strengths and weaknesses' and she notes the distinguishable feature of confident versus over confident people, with the latter catego-rised as lacking 'self-insight' with a 'false sense of optimism'. Within the Characteristics of Effective Learning (Early Education, 2012:6) the guidance for 'positive relationships' notes what adults could do to support *active learning and motivation*: 'be specific when you praise, especially noting effort such as how the child concentrates, persists, solves problems, and has new ideas'. It is worth thinking about how young children can be supported to develop this motivation and adults play a key role with their responses to children. Stewart (2011:62) notes:

> If children are intrinsically motivated by a need for autonomy which includes setting their own goals, when adults convey a message through rewards and praise that the goal actually has been chosen by the adult then children identify less with the activity and become less motivated to participate.

This resonates with the philosophy of Maria Montessori and the concept of self-discipline and self-correcting materials. In essence, practitioners need to consider the use of extrinsic rewards such as stickers and 'golden time'.

Palaiologou notes, 'the principle that states every child as unique cites the characteristics of resilience, capability, confidence and self assuredness as ideals for children, all of which come through effective provision for PSED' (2013:228). These 'ideals' suggest a view of the child as an individual who seeks to understand their place in the world and in terms of early years practice it is worth considering how effective pedagogy can support young children to understand and interpret the early years setting/classroom rules so that they can form and maintain positive relationships. Whilst the EYFS (DfE, 2014) states the understanding of 'rules' as an early learning goal within PSED, Maria Montessori advocated an ethos of respect and the idea of a prepared environment. Practitioners need to ensure that the setting ethos supports a respectful attitude from both adults and children, for example by encouraging children during tidy up time to work together and ensure that resources are replaced so that the next person can use them. The journey towards the goals stipulated in the EYFS (DfE, 2014) can be negotiated rather than seen as a summative goal.

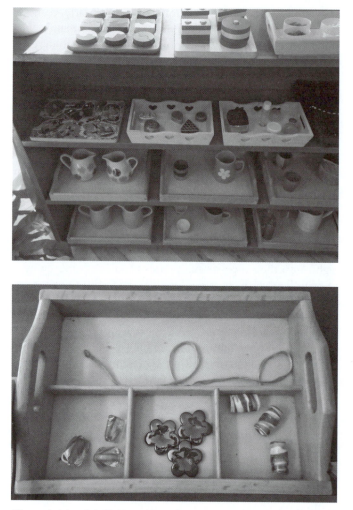

Figures 1.16 and 1.17 Examples of an aesthetically pleasing and prepared environment in a
Montessori setting.

Children develop a capacity to cope with a range of feelings and emotions and this is
often at the same time as more visible skills in mobility. Therefore it is no surprise to see
the correlation between PSED and Physical Development as two of the three prime areas
of the current EYFS (DfE, 2014). There were no changes to the principles and commitments, therefore the emotional environment remains firmly catalogued with the 'outdoor'
and 'indoor' environments and the familiar requirement for adults to scaffold children's
development of empathy and regulation of emotions. As noted in the section on Physical
Development, the documented statutory requirement for adults to facilitate 'access to the
outdoors on a daily basis' (DfES, 2007:35) remained in the 2012 and 2014 versions of the
EYFS and due to the vast amount of research highlighting the value of outdoor provision
to support the development of personal, social and emotional aspects of learning, the
current guidelines (DfE, 2014:28) note that 'providers must provide access to an outdoor

play area' and 'if that is not possible, ensure that outdoor activities are planned and taken on a daily basis'. Adverse weather conditions are deemed to be an appropriate reason for a relaxation of these requirements and writing in 2011, Sarah Knight, a prolific writer on the benefits of outdoor experiences for young children, cites how policy makers seem to need to formalize the contact with the outdoor environment. This is worth thinking about in the context of PSED as mental health problems, including anxiety in young children, continue to rise. Practitioners need to consider using the outside environment and remember that rain does not constitute 'adverse weather conditions'. This is nothing new, as Johann Pestalozzi (1746–1827) noted the need for an emotional environment within his 'general method' and Joyce (2012:48) notes how Pestalozzi valued the creation of 'a secure and loving environment where the child's self esteem and confidence were fostered and were of central importance to learning'.

The Special Interest Group (WAVE Trust, 2013) explored and considered how best to promote effective implementation of the principles set out in 'Supporting Families', and the recommendations for the early years workforce include explicit reference to understanding attachment and child development, particularly from birth to three, to include an understanding of:

- social and emotional development
- age-appropriate expectations
- early brain development
- cultural, social and emotional factors that contribute to common behavioural problems in young children
- the importance of a preventative approach (recognizing the need to intervene early to prevent escalation of concerns and/or maltreatment).

(WAVE Trust, 2013:64–65)

The overarching principles of the EYFS did not change and the idea of the Unique Child, who is 'born ready, able and eager to learn' (Early Education, 2012:2), is dependent on the child having opportunities to interact within the context of positive relationships and enabling environments. There is also more emphasis on the learning and development principles where it is recognised that young children need opportunities to play and explore, actively learn and create and think critically in order to support their learning across all areas. Within this principle there is more emphasis on parents as partners (2.2) and the key person (2.4), and whilst the key person role was already a statutory requirement in the 2008 version of the EYFS, the 'safeguarding and welfare requirement' has been strengthened with the *supervision* of all staff as a welcome addition to this statutory requirement. In March 2009, Lord Laming presented 'The Protection of Children in England: A Progress Report' where he noted the need for strong leadership, accountability and supervision, 'making sure there is a supervisor constantly assessing the decisions being made and the action being taken' (2009:28). This supervision is sold within the EYFS Statutory Framework as opportunities for professional conversations about children and the emphasis on early intervention is tacitly noted with reference to opportunities to 'discuss any issues, particularly concerning children's development or well-being', 'identifying solutions to address issues as they arise' and 'receive coaching to improve their personal effectiveness' (DfE, 2014:20). As noted in Physical Development, the term 'coaching' may be a little misleading with its suggestion of *training* rather than the reflective conversations required with a supervisor who has developed sufficient self-awareness to support coaching and mentoring conversations. Such conversations are a vehicle for meaningful dialogue and Jerome Bruner suggests that *meaning* is both individually and culturally constructed but these discussions can be learning opportunities 'to lead, shape and build changing attitudes, behaviours and performance in the work place' (cited in Garvey et al., 2009:99) to support children's personal, social and emotional wellbeing. Babies and young children will build a picture of themselves as a separate person and this self-awareness will be highly dependent on how others respond to them, thus the need for safe and secure attachments is exemplified in the statutory requirement (3.26) for a key person to be assigned to each child and their remit is to ensure that every child's care is tailored to meet their individual needs, to help the child become familiar with the setting and to offer a settled relationship for the child and build a relationship with their parents (DfE, 2012:18). There is a swathe of research (see Trevarthen, 2001; Elfer et al., 2011) suggesting that the key person role is so important for children in their preschool years. The key person role includes the requirement to 'seek to engage and support parents and/or carers in guiding their child's development at home' (DfE, 2014:8), however practitioners need to be supportive and work with parents and carers to avoid the perception of an amateur/ professional dialogue where the 'professional' knows best. Marion Dowling suggests that despite the uniqueness of the parental role and the time that parents spend getting to know their children,

> parents are at least very modest about their influence, and in some cases still remain unaware of how essential they are to their children's personal growth. Perhaps the one most important thing that staff, particularly key persons, can offer all parents is to help them recognise this.
>
> (2010:203)

Interestingly, Bruce (2011) cites the work of Antonio Damasio (2004) who argues that feelings and emotions can be categorised differently with the consequence that 'emotions lead to feelings' (2011:42). With the elevation of PSED to one of three prime areas it may be worth taking the time to reflect on the pedagogical implications of Damasio's work and consider how, as early years practitioners, adults often insist on eliciting responses from children, for example, 'tell me how you feel?' In a review of New Zealand's Te Whariki approach, Lee et al. (2013:47) consider:

> relationships with 'people', 'place' and 'things' and in terms of early child-hood provision, objects provide props for dramatic play and the taking on of a new identity … and material objects cross boundaries, connecting home and early childhood centre: photographs, food, works of art and the stories that are attached to them.

Young children need support to manage strong feelings and emotions and this is captured in the non-statutory Early Years Outcomes guidance under 'typical behaviour': 'Can express their own feelings such as sad, happy, cross, scared or worried' (DfE, 2012:17).

The importance of relationships and the development of sustained shared thinking with an important 'other' has been highlighted by the EPPE longitudinal study in the UK (Sylva et al., 2004) and the correlation between the quality of provision and PSED referred to the importance of supporting children to develop and maintain friendships. Palaiologou notes how practitioners can explore 'emotional language through story' (2013:239–240)

Figure 1.18 Children in a child minder's home – 'Create areas in which children can sit and chat with friends, such as a snug den and cosy spaces'.

Source: PSED Making Relationships in Development Matters (Early Education, 2012:9)

and she offers an example of a child who exclaims that if he met the bear from the bear hunt (*We're Going on a Bear Hunt* by Michael Rosen and Helen Oxenbury, 1989), he would 'feel funny'. She further notes how this child has not yet acquired the language to fully express his emotions, and this awareness of adult–child interactions is an important one, although the nuances involved in the English language are also worthy of contemplation. Adults can sometimes assign meaning to the utterances of young children without further scrutiny and the development of trusting relationships, where children can experiment with their thoughts, feelings and vocabulary needs to be facilitated. The enabling environments section suggests that adults could, 'provide books stories and puppets that can be used to model responding to others' feelings and being helpful and supportive to them' (Early Education, 2012:13). There is an enormous industry dedicated to the development of children's PSED, including persona dolls, puppets and mood charts, and circle time has become a familiar experience associated with the development of PSED in early years settings. Jenny Mosley (2005) promotes its use as an opportunity to use puppets and persona dolls to support children to develop strategies to develop their feelings and behaviour, and the Development Matters document guides practitioners to use these resources within PSED and Understanding the World. Dewey (1959) argued that young children do not think in subjects, so activities like circle time need to be considered

Figure 1.19 Puppets, referred to as 'the formed doll' (stuffed fabric with wool and no features) used in a Steiner setting.

holistically rather than as an attempt to squeeze in one of the prime areas of the EYFS (DfE, 2014).

Mosley claims that children are able to suspend disbelief with puppets so that the characters become real and the interactions become meaningful in a social context, however, it is also worth considering the authenticity of the experiences being offered and acknowledge that very young children are impressionable and often want to please adults with a 'correct' response. In this sense, children who are unsure about how to articulate their feelings may simply resort to mimicry. Palaiologou (2013) and Bruce (2011) explicitly reference the impact of the pioneers and the recognition that young children need support to make relationships with those around them. Bruce considers the principles of the pioneers and transposes these to view how 'the relationships with other people (both adults and children) are of central importance in a child's life, influencing emotional and social well-being' (2011:34). The traditional view of the English nursery teacher's role is that he or she is not an expert or authority, but an advisor and facilitator, and the legacy of not intervening in the child's discovery comes from Froebel, Montessori and Dewey. However, with the repetitive refrain around 'school readiness', a term that has now acquired a place within everyday parlance, it is incumbent on those working with the youngest children to negotiate a shared understanding of the term.

Practitioners need to plan and reflect upon a range of activities to support the holistic development of the child.

Self-Confidence and Self-Awareness

- How can you foster the development of self-concept and self-esteem with babies and young children?
- How do the interactions you have with babies and young children help them to feel safe and secure?
- What do you think about the removal of 'self-esteem' in favour of 'self-awareness' as advocated by Tickell in her review in 2011?

Managing Feelings and Behaviour

- How do you support children to emotionally refuel when they are feeling tired, stressed or frustrated?
- How do you support children to negotiate their understanding of boundaries and behavioural expectations in the early years setting?
- Why is knowledge of attachment theory considered to be so important when working with babies and children in the early years?

Making Relationships

- How can you use your knowledge and understanding of child development to support children to cooperate and form positive relationships with adults and other children?
- Consider Figure 1.19 and compare and contrast the featureless 'formed doll' used within Steiner settings and the use of 'persona dolls' promoted in the Development Matters guidance (Early Education, 2012, PSED & UW).

Tensions and challenges

The economic case for investing in the early years and the omnipresent promotion of young children's social and emotional development is exemplified in the revised EYFS (DfE, 2012). However, is it also worth investigating alternative positions, for example, Peter Moss equally proclaims that it may help to consider alternative narratives other than the dominant messages from policy documents around 'investment' and the 'human capital argument' (Moss, 2013:370).

Consider the argument that there is a national fear that parents may be abdicating responsibility for their children's behaviour and consider how this has influenced the most recent revisions to early years policy.

The key person role is exemplified within the statutory guidance of the EYFS (DfE, 2012:3.26) and the statement (albeit lean in terms of wordage) captures the idea that relationships are important. What is the message about the child's position in this web of relationships?

Specific areas

Literacy

The specific area Literacy is divided into two categories with the following early learning goals:

- **Reading**: Children read and understand simple sentences. They use phonic knowledge to decode regular words and read them aloud accurately. They also read some common irregular words. They demonstrate understanding when talking with others about what they have read.
- **Writing**: Children use their phonic knowledge to write words in ways which match their spoken sounds. They also write some irregular common words. They write simple sentences which can be read by themselves and others. Some words are spelt correctly and others are phonetically plausible.

Tickell aimed to reverse the 'school readiness' debate with her reference to the idea of 'school unreadiness' (2011:19). The presentation of this argument captures the idea of literacy as an essential 'life' skill, and whilst she makes a conscious decision to avoid the more ambiguous and emotive connotations of 'school readiness', she further notes that, 'balanced against this, some feel that we do children no favours if we fail to prepare them for the realities of the school environment, where skills such as literacy are at a premium' (Tickell, 2011:19). However, the term remains a contentious issue within the early years sector and beyond, and the emphasis on the teaching of synthetic phonics as the Holy Grail to literacy attainment has been repeatedly challenged. The current debates are multifaceted and in her review of qualifications within the early years sector, Nutbrown justifies her argument that practitioners working with babies and young children should hold a formal qualification in English and demonstrate confidence in their own communication skills if they are to support children to 'discover a world of books, stories and rhymes and where they are challenged and supported to explore and question' (2012:36). Literacy is assigned as one of the four 'specific' areas, however it is important to remember that whilst this presents as a separation from Communication and Language (one of the three prime areas) the 'threads of literacy; reading and writing are interwoven and build upon a child's early development as a communicator' (Head & Palaiologou, 2013:269).

The EYFS Statutory Framework notes that: 'Literacy development involves encouraging children to link sounds and letters and to begin to read and write. Children must be given access to a wide range of reading materials (books, poems and other written materials) to ignite their interest' (DfE, 2014:8).

Linking sounds and letters are subsumed into reading and writing and as noted in the section on Physical Development, the reference to hand writing has been incorporated into this prime area with the following statement embedded into the early learning goal: 'They handle equipment and tools effectively, including pencils for writing' (DfE, 2013:8).

The specific areas are dependent on the prime areas and are linked to a specific body of knowledge and skills, and Literacy is strongly dependent on children's language development and their ability to communicate, thus, the Development Matters guidance (Early Education, 2012) for Literacy exemplifies the importance of reading with babies and young children. We now know that very young babies communicate from birth (refer to Communication and Language) and the early interactions associated with singing songs, repeating rhymes and reading support brain development, the acquisition of language and provide an emotional environment to support the bonding and attachment process. This recognition is highlighted within the context of the three principles, to support learning and development, which subsequently support and foster the characteristics of effective learning and the writing section is clearly signposted to the prime area of Communication and Language (Early Education, 2012).

> The demonstrable brilliance of babies at tapping in to the human voice and, further, one voice, in particular, supports subsequent developmental experiences. That is, intimate interactions with significant adults in their environment ensure that children's speech sounds imitate those of the speech sounds around them.
>
> (Goouch, 2014:6)

Whilst at first glance the choice of reading material in Figure 1.20 may seem inappropriate for such a young baby, it is worth considering the playfulness and tenderness that marks such interactions. When we speak our speech is organised into prosodic units, marked by intonation contours and this has a powerful effect on

Figure 1.20 Reading to baby Finley, aged 12 weeks – *Precautionary Tales for Grandparents: Some of which may be read to the young for their moral development* by James Muirden (2008).

interaction, thus, you can convey meaning using the same words but changing the pro-sodic structure (Neaum, 2012) and you only have to look at the concentrated stare of the baby in Figure 1.20 at the printed text to acknowledge the 'tapping in' to the rhythmic intonation of a special voice. This personal experience is reflected in the Development Matters guidance for the 'birth to 11 months' age range in the context of the principles of the EYFS and is translated thus, 'Enjoys looking at books and other printed material with familiar people' (Early Education, 2012) and this is similarly repeated in the Early Years Outcomes guidance as 'typical behaviour' for this age range (DfE, 2013:20). Making sense of the relationship between literacy development and the needs of young babies, Kathy Goouch (2014) presents a wonderful chapter entitled, 'Baby rooms' where she uses examples from 'The baby room' project (Goouch & Powell, 2013) with a summary:

> acknowledging the incredible sophistication and brilliance of the first years of life may help teachers of older children to realise that they are only influencing one part of a child's literacy 'life course project' and the more connections are made, with and for children, the more transitions can be managed.
>
> (Goouch, 2014:15)

Whilst the notion of learning to read and write remains an undisputed goal for all chil-dren, Hutchin (2013:81) argues that 'literacy involves more than technical skills of linking sounds to letters and EYFS only gives a partial definition of what it takes to read and write'. At this juncture it is probably worth remembering that practitioners are not a homogenous group of people and alternative pedagogies are often adopted for philosophical and ideo-logical reasons. Steiner education have argued that the statutory nature of the EYFS (DfE, 2014) has led to 'bureaucratic processes of having to apply for exemptions to those learning and development requirements which they could not meet because of difference of edu-cational approaches and ethos', and they note these *differences* as 'those relating to reading, writing, letter and number formation and the requirements to have electronic gadgetry in the room' (Nicol & Taplin, 2012:152). Moylett and Stewart (2012) remind us of the key differences between the prime and specific areas; for example, specific areas, such as Literacy, are not universal, but are culturally dependent on the priorities within communi-ties and cultures. Early literacy develops within a social context and young children are surrounded by print in the environment and their exploration of writing and drawing needs to be encouraged and celebrated.

Reading and Writing

Reading involves two skill sets, the first of which is comprehension and the second con-stitutes the ability to technically decode text, and this requires a knowledge of phonics and knowledge about the rules of written language. The rationale for Communication and Language as a prime area is pretty clear as children need to have a rich vocabulary and an understanding of verbal language (Neaum, 2012).

The single adoption of systematic synthetic phonics as an approach has proved to be very controversial and practitioners are advised to read the 'Independent Review of the Teaching of Early Reading', often referred to as 'The Rose review' (Rose, 2006), and conduct some personal research related to different perspectives (a good chapter is 'Phonics in the early years' by Sally Neaum, 2012). Neaum highlights that expressions of concern resonate in the early years where the emphasis on phonics 'is narrow, limited and dry' (2012:155) and Hutchin (2013:81) suggests that there is a distinct emphasis on phonics within the revised EYFS but as noted by many authors, 'children need to know that the squiggles we call writing convey a message and they need to want to find out what the message is'.

Emergent literacy is the term used to describe the gradual acquisition or 'emergence' of the knowledge, concepts and skills through, and about, communication from birth (Neaum, 2012:139). Children do not simply arrive at school into the reception class as empty vessels waiting to be filled with literacy, nor are they passive recipients being stuffed with literacy by adults (Hall, 1987) and practitioners need to adopt a pedagogical approach that models positive literacy practices within the setting. Neaum talks about 'teachable moments' (2012:149) where practitioners observe when a child is 'ready' to learn something and grasps that opportunity to scaffold this learning. This resonates with Maria Montessori's 'sensitive period' where practitioners are encouraged to intervene and support children to centre their attention on specific aspects of the environment, for example practitioners can facilitate the playfulness attached to early mark making (see Physical Development) – how often do we see children recognising the first initial of their name and proudly proclaim ownership of the letter?! The EYFS (DfE, 2014) notes that adults should 'ignite' children's interest to ensure that they are motivated to find out and this motivation is a much-lauded attribute to support children to become lifelong learners.

Children need skills as they learn to write, for example they need to make a decision to write and have an audience for their composition. They also need to transcribe their thoughts and develop the physical dexterity with which to hold a pencil and this is now placed within the Physical Development area as literacy is dependent on the physicality needed to manipulate and control writing implements. However, there are many who would argue that the emphasis on the transcriptional skills in the early learning goal for Writing ignores the idea that children should actually comprehend and write with a sense of authenticity. This idea is captured eloquently by Nigel Hall in 1989 where he disassociates the idea of authorship with what he describes as 'a final printed product'. Rather, he portrays the complexity surrounding the process of authorship and he defines this succinctly in the title of his book as 'writing with reason' (Hall, 1989) and Moylett and Stewart (2012) remind us that literacy in its broadest sense should not be left to later stages of the EYFS.

Practitioners need to plan and reflect upon a range of activities to support the holistic development of the child.

Reading

- How often do you read aloud to very young babies and why is this important?
- *Telling* stories is very different to *reading* stories. Consider how oracy and story telling is valued within some cultures and why this is a valuable aspect of literacy with young children.

- Bower and Barrett (2014:131) suggest that learning nursery rhymes 'is a valuable way for pupils with English as an additional language to learn the cadences of the English language'.
- Rhyme, rhythm and repetition are noted as crucial components for reading. Consider the opportunities offered for children to have fun with words.

Writing

- Consider why the Development Matters guidance (Early Education, 2012) sign-posts practitioners to early mark making within the physical development section.
- Many authors have noted how the focus of schools has been related to the writing *product* as this is easy to assess; however, Barrett (2014:185) notes 'the process approach constructs children primarily as authors with a focus on meaning making, rather than as "secretaries" (Latham, 2002)'. How can practitioners ensure consistent formative assessment of children's early literacy attempts?

Tensions and challenges

Providers of early years education in England must adhere to the EYFS Statutory Framework (DfE, 2014), however many settings also adopt a specific philosophy, for example, The Steiner Waldorf Approach, and Tickell suggested the following:

> All providers of early years education and care may apply for exemptions from the EYFS learning and development requirements if a majority of parents agree that an exemption should be sought because the established principles of learning and development that govern the provider's practice cannot be reconciled with the EYFS learning and development requirements.
>
> (Tickell, 2011:53)

Research different philosophies such as The Steiner Waldorf Approach or Montessori education and discuss the tensions related to the focus on the teaching of synthetic phonics within the EYFS (DfE, 2014).

A spokesperson for the DfE recently stated that,

> We are determined to eradicate illiteracy and our phonics check is a key part of this objective. In the past far too many children left primary school unable to read properly and continued to struggle in secondary school and beyond.

Reflect on the rationale for the phonics check in the early years and consider the arguments.

Mathematics

The specific area Mathematics is divided into two categories with the following early learning goals:

- **Numbers**: Children count reliably with numbers from one to 20, place them in order and say which number is one more or one less than a given number. Using quantities and objects, they add and subtract two single-digit numbers and count on or back to find the answer. They solve problems, including doubling, halving and sharing.
- **Shape, Space and Measures**: Children use everyday language to talk about size, weight, capacity, position, distance, time and money to compare quantities and objects and to solve problems. They recognise, create and describe patterns. They explore characteristics of everyday objects and shapes and use mathematical language to describe them.

Attainment in mathematics has been the subject of increasing national angst for a number of years and various reviews have shone the spotlight on attitudes to personal attainment at GCSE level. In June 2008, Sir Peter Williams presented his 'Independent Review of Mathematics Teaching in Early Years Settings and Primary Schools' for the Department for Children, Schools and Families and he noted: 'The United Kingdom is still one of the few advanced nations where it is socially acceptable – fashionable even – to profess an inability to cope with the subject' (Williams, 2008:4). At the time his review followed, and was complementary to, the Rose review of the teaching of early reading. Following a review of the 2008 version of the EYFS, Tickell presented her independent report which noted the conflation of the former aspects, 'numbers as labels' and 'for counting and calculating ... in order to reflect the same experience and processes as that for linking sounds and letters, reading and writing' (2011:103). Furthermore, the recommendation by Williams to include 'time and capacity within the Early Learning Goals' (DCSF, 2008:33) resonates in the Tickell review:

> The aspects of mathematics contain some of the key mathematical skills that children will use throughout the rest of their lives, including telling the time. A significant factor in children's understanding of mathematics is the ability to talk about and apply their knowledge in ways that make sense to them.
>
> (Tickell, 2011:104)

The characteristics highlight the importance of the child's disposition and attitude to learning and ability to engage in exploration, play and creativity across all areas of learning and the previous title of 'Problem solving, reasoning and numeracy' are reflected in these characteristics. It is therefore pertinent that practitioners need to facilitate play and exploration, active learning and opportunities for children to create and think critically (DfE, 2014). Interestingly, Tickell noted that 'Evidence from EYFS profile results in recent years illustrates that many children are able to recognise numbers and numerals but the same picture of attainment is not reflected in the application of this knowledge to solving problems with numbers' (2011:104).

The photograph in Figure 1.21 is used to consider the development of mathematical concepts noted within the EYFS and aims to provide early years practitioners with confidence to make connections between the holistic nature of the principles. Tickell noted

Figure 1.21 A child independently picking, sticking and counting leaves.

that there appeared to be considerable confusion surrounding the role of play as a vehicle for learning, as some practitioners 'advised that any element of adult direction or teaching would contravene the requirements of the EYFS' (2011:28–29). This is a serious mis-conception and the theoretical positions within developmental psychology (Piaget, Vygotsky) can support practitioners to sensitively scaffold children's development to support more advanced modes of thinking.

The child in Figure 1.21 illustrates an interaction between the individual and the environment that has led to spontaneous but purposeful activity. This activity simply devel-oped in an environment where the adults and her peers were all actively involved. The adults allowed her the space and time to develop this interest and there was no pressure on her to perform and 'count the leaves' in the initial stages of her own meaningful con-struction. This principle is also reflected in alternative pedagogies, for example in Steiner education, where 'the two main things that play needs are time and space and children need time within a healthy rhythm for their own self initiated play' (Nicol & Taplin, 2012:73).

The child in Figure 1.21 is learning to count and from a psychological perspective, Jean Piaget's stage theory could be used to define her learning within what he defined as the preoperational stage of development. In this 'stage' children use symbolic representation and the EYFS (DfE, 2014), which reflects a developmental 'age stage' approach, suggests an 'outcome' within two overlapping age ranges (22–36 and 30–50 months) that children may 'recite some number names in sequence' and 'use some number names and number language spontaneously' (DfE, 2013:23). Whilst Piaget's ideas are still relevant today, subsequent research indicates that children learn within a social context and the manipulation of the leaves, characterised as 'concrete materials' (Haylock & Cockburn, 2013:7) supports the child to make connections. More importantly, the child is finding out and exploring, involved and demonstrating considerable concentration and intrinsic motivation. Understanding how these characteristics influence pedagogy in the early years is not to discount the value of adult interactions but to consider how play experiences can be 'capitalised upon to deepen children's thinking and understanding through promoting self regulation and metacognition' (Brock, 2014:98).

In his review of mathematics in primary and the early years, Peter Williams explicitly noted the unique differences in the early years and the need for 'tailored pedagogies and a highly sensitive approach' (2008:4) and the review laid great store by play-based learning of a mathematical nature, with specific reference to early mark making as a precursor to abstract mathematical symbolism.

Bruce (2011) considers Piaget, Vygotsky and Bruner and how practitioners need to value the 'personal, highly individual symbols that children develop to make something stand for something else' (2011:119) and Figure 1.22 illustrates how sensitive conversations are an integral part of the learning process and give definition to the meanings that children and practitioners give to particular activities. The Early Years Outcomes (DfE, 2013:23) suggest that 'typical behaviour' for a child at around 22–36 months would include the ability to 'create and experiment with symbols and marks representing ideas of number' and this idiosyncratic representation of a number line using 'green leaves from the bush' was further pursued with the application of a paint brush to 'camouflage' the number line and in this sense the curriculum and the environment become one!

The idea that children do not artificially demarcate their learning has been captured in the rationale for the prime and specific areas and, as clearly noted by Tickell (2011), Literacy and Mathematics are natural bedfellows with mathematical language often defined as 'confusing' or context specific. The use of stories with a mathematical theme often provides a narrative with numerical language and well-loved stories like Eric Carle's *The Very Hungry Caterpillar* and *10 Little Rubber Ducks* are timeless and useful examples. The latter uses positional language (first, second, etc.), which is not often used in everyday parlance and the development of story sacks are an interactive way for children to develop their literacy and numeracy skills. Mathematical and scientific knowledge is not a simple accumulation of facts and most young children can articulate some factual 'knowledge', for example that big boats can sail on top of the water, however their thinking is governed by the idea that heavy things will sink rather than float on top of the water. Meaningful experiences enhance learning and children will develop the mathematical skills necessary to 'double, halve and share' with the

apple that needs to be divided into the correct number of pieces so that everyone may have some. Sometimes scales and measuring jugs are used, and all the time this is in

Figure 1.22 A child's idiosyncratic representation of symbolic representation.

response to the needs of daily life not as an exercise contrived to test a specific skill or teach a specific point.

(Nicol & Taplin 2012:100)

Whilst this commentary is taken from a book advocating the Steiner approach to early years practice, practitioners can note the practical application of Bruner's (2012) Spiral curriculum by offering opportunities to revisit mathematical concepts in different social contexts.

The photographs in Figures 1.23 and 1.24 show how children subsequently described the objects, discarded pieces from the block construction, as 'big pieces of cheese' that needed to be 'grated'. The objects, imbued with social significance from their understanding of the social context, became a symbolic representation within their play. This open ended play opened up a plethora of mathematical explorations and Vygotsky would remind us not to see the children 'as simply a passive recipient of culture's tools, but also as a creative builder of their own thinking' (Oates & Grayson, 2004:310). In general terms, children were thinking creatively and were given the time and space to extend their understanding related to the tessellation of shapes and the cause and effect whilst using a piece of block to grate the 'cheese' on the cheese grater (a builders rasp).

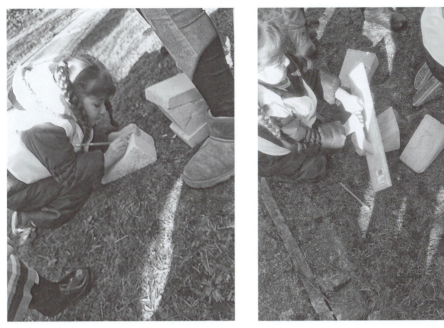

Figures 1.23 and 1.24 Symbolic representation within play.

Practitioners need to plan and reflect upon a range of activities to support the holistic development of the child.

Numbers

Number is an abstract concept; therefore young children need to be supported to make sense of mathematical ideas through the provision of a range of meaningful experiences.

Young children need to be provided with opportunities to count in meaningful situations. Consider opportunities in day to day routines that offer these opportunities in a social context.

Shape, Space and Measures

Babies encounter mathematical patterns from a very early age so consider talking about the mathematical properties of objects with children to help them to understand how things work.

The early years setting offers many opportunities for problem solving and cannot be assigned to one area of learning in isolation. Consider opportunities to solve problems by using a questioning rather than a didactic approach, for example, 'how many children are staying for lunch?'

Tensions and challenges

There are many books dedicated to the learning and teaching of mathematical concepts and whilst teachers are expected to have a comprehensive grasp of the subject, Derek Haylock (with Manning, 2014:2) argues that there are 'long term effects on children's confidence in mathematics resulting from teachers' own mathematical misconceptions and limited understanding of the subject'.

He cites the necessity of understanding as a goal for both teachers and learners. Nunes and Bryant (2004:262) argue that 'The learning of mathematics and science can sometimes be mistakenly characterised as the mastery of facts and procedures.'

Reflect on these statements and consider why practitioners need to demonstrate confidence with mathematical ideas.

Understanding the World

The specific area Understanding the World is divided into three categories with the following early learning goals:

- **People and Communities**: Children talk about past and present events in their own lives and in the lives of family members. They know that other children don't always enjoy the same things, and are sensitive to this. They know about similarities and differences between themselves and others, and among families, communities and traditions.
- **The World**: Children know about similarities and differences in relation to places, objects, materials and living things. They talk about the features of their own immediate environment and how environments might vary from one another. They make observations of animals and plants and explain why some things occur, and talk about changes.
- **Technology**: Children recognise that a range of technology is used in places such as homes and schools. They select and use technology for particular purposes.

This specific area presents a renewed emphasis on a 'concentric approach to learning and is a recognition that children learn first about themselves and the people and things that are important to them' (Tickell, 2011:104), and the title reflects the position that this area is less about the acquisition of *skills* and more about the application of the Characteristics of Effective Learning. With this in mind, practitioners need to consider how to help young children make sense of their world to support them to 'play a full role as autonomous participants in their social and cultural worlds' (McDowall Clark, 2013:111). The idea of a 'concentric approach' noted by Tickell reminds us that learning is not a linear event in a child's life and children need to be offered opportunities to revisit ideas in many different contexts.

This metaphoric reference to a 'concentric approach' also reflects Bronfenbrenner's (1979) ecological model of childhood where many young children spend considerable time in an early years setting, including their first formal year in a reception class, and this microsystem acts as a major site of socialisation (McDowall Clark, 2013:13). Children live their lives as members of different communities and:

> children's development, in all its aspects, is a social process but that different communities of practice will lead to the development of particular skills and understandings. In this sense, learning and development are situated in the particular community of

practice in which they occur and the development of ways of being in one context does not necessarily transfer to another.

(Barron, 2005:201)

With this in mind it is worth considering the messages that are tacitly transferred to young children and their families and how daily interactions about learning are translated within the current EYFS (DfE, 2014). As noted in the introductory section, there was always an intention to review the EYFS (DCSF, 2008) and there was a comprehensive review of research literature in the Early Years Learning and Development study (Evangelou et al., 2009) with the rationale that given the rapid growth of research related to children's development an update was necessary. Some grand theories (those that are well established) are closely associated with learning and development in the early years and whilst there are many criticisms of Piaget, his ideas related to 'schema' have been a useful vehicle when observing children making sense of their world. Children tend to make sense of the world by seeking out patterns that connect different objects and experiences and these patterns become elaborated into schema:

> and the elaboration of these schema, in turn, become templates for looking at, acting in and explaining the world. However, schema are not just ways of framing experience as it comes along; they provide a focus of interest for the child's intellectual energy, and the search for objects and experiences which fit the child's schema and confirm their expectations, seem to be highly motivating.
>
> (Evangelou et al., 2009:44)

Of course, as the authors suggest, 'this search for pattern, what Piaget calls "assimilation", also results in disconfirmation when something doesn't seem to fit the current schema and expectations are confounded' and this 'intellectual crisis, referred to by Piaget as disequilibrium, has to be resolved through an elaboration or redefinition of mental organisation, which Piaget refers to as "accommodation"' (2009:45) and practitioners are encouraged to consider Donaldson's (2006) concept of embedded and disembedded thinking and support children to make 'human' sense of the world around them.

As noted in the section on Communication and Language, the research by Evangelou et al. (2009) highlights the lack of 'why' questions and this recognition calls for a reflective stance from practitioners and an examination of the value of mutual conversations. Carlina Rinaldi suggests the need to use any theory as a 'tool' rather than a 'prison which tells you what the end result will be' (2006:181). The Statutory Framework for the EYFS (DfE, 2014) recognises how the application of the Characteristics of Effective Learning are visible and how adults can support children to understand and interact in the world through opportunities for play and exploration, actively learning and creating and thinking critically, and transitions are considered within the context of an 'enabling environment' (Early Education, 2012:38). The idea of 'guided discovery' and Vygotsky's (1978) zone of proximal development offer a pedagogical platform for practice, however, it needs to be acknowledged that the evaluation of children's 'understanding' may also create a 'micro-culture' of assessment and testing with very young children.

> It is important to avoid any prediction. In the exhibition 'The Hundred Languages of Children' there are some words of Loris about a concept of being. He says this exhibition is against all pedagogy whose purpose is in some way to predict the result, which

is a sort of predictor that predetermines the result, and that becomes a sort of prison for the child and for the teacher, and for the human being.

(Rinaldi, 2006:181)

Figure 1.25 The heavy blocks *should* sink in the bucket of water, but they remain afloat. Opportunities for the development of 'why' questions.

The world-renowned 'Reggio Approach' considered above may seem a world away from the goal-orientated EYFS (DfE, 2014); however, Gary Beauchamp (2013) reminds practitioners that whilst they should not teach 'Understanding the World' within discrete subject areas, (history, geography, science and ICT), it is helpful to use a 'subject lens' (2013:288) and:

> for each investigation and exploration practitioners need to consider how they are going to assess the outcomes and ensure that adequate challenges are built in to extend children's learning. When considering assessment, the importance of looking at situations through, for example, a 'scientific lens' is crucial, as this may offer unique insights. For instance, the processes of exploration and investigation (including the so called 'process skills' identified by Harlen (2003 [cited by Beauchamp]) as observing, raising questions, hypothesising, predicting, planning, interpreting and communicating) are in themselves outcomes and are just as important as the end product of the investigation.

(2013:290)

The Development Matters guidance reiterates the importance of early attachments and the development of relationships, and the cohesion between this specific area and the prime areas of PSED and Communication and Language is clear (Early Education, 2012:37). Interestingly, practitioners are guided to 'provide opportunities for babies to see people and things beyond the baby room, including the activities of older children' (Early Education,

2012:37); thus, this acknowledgment of babies as competent learners who learn from interacting with those around them was a welcome recognition. In the 2008 version of the EYFS, learning about cultures and beliefs was situated within PSED, as well as knowledge and understanding of the world and the emphasis on learning about 'similarities and difference' is exemplified in 'Understanding the World' with guidance for practitioners to support children to understand and develop empathy through the use of 'puppets and dolls to tell stories about diverse experiences, ensuring that negative stereotyping is avoided' (Early Education, 2012:37). The 'Birth to school' study (Evangelou et al., 2005) considers how young children need to be encouraged to develop empathy for others, and Laible and Thompson (2007) suggest that one effective method may be to engage young children in conversation about feelings, both their own and those of others, and of societal expectations. They suggest that an elaborate narrative style involving open questions, for example, is likely to be most effective. The Piagetian idea of 'assimilation' is referred to within Vygotskian theory as 'appropriation' and this is important as this term refers to the taking on and use of 'cultural tools' which may be a physical resource such as a persona doll/puppet, or a psychological one, such as language. These resources are referred to as *cultural tools* because their characteristics or physical properties tell us little about how they might be used and it is our culture and social history that 'explains' how to use them (Oates & Grayson, 2004:294). The Early Years Outcomes (DfE, 2013) notes (overlapping) ages and stages and reference to 'developmental milestones' and 'typical' behaviour that is tempered with regular reminders of the principle that 'all children develop and learn in different ways and at different rates, with all learning and development considered equally important and interconnected'; however, it is worth remembering that:

> Cultural contexts influence learning trajectories, children's brains are designed to adapt to the contexts in which they find themselves and domains of learning are prioritised accordingly. International comparisons of observations of adults' responses to children's developing musicality illustrate such diverging contexts. For example, a child in a Kenyan village bangs on his metal mug and the rest of the family join in to create a musical event, whilst a child behaving similarly in a UK context is rebuked. Children's interests also determine the time and intensity of engagement in particular domains.
> (Evangelou et al., 2009:59)

Understanding the World relates to the understanding of scientific concepts where young children engage and interact with the natural world around them and the use of technology is referred to with broad reference far removed from the initial focus on 'computers' and Tickell suggested that this was to reflect 'the fact that through continuing developments in technology young children are often conversant with a broader range of applications and technological devices than formerly' (2011:104).

Practitioners need to plan and reflect upon a range of activities to support the holistic development of the child.

People and Communities

Sustainable development is considered by Siraj-Blatchford (UNESCO, 2008) and the need for children to be supported to understand similarities and differences has been captured in this specific area. Consider how practitioners can promote an anti-discriminatory and anti-bias approach to early years care and education.

The World

Moylett and Stewart (2012) suggest this aspect focuses on children being able to recognise the difference between the natural and the manmade 'world'. Consider how this can be applied in practice.

Technology

Define what technology is. Beauchamp (2013:291) reminds practitioners to both 'embrace and facilitate' new technology, giving children 'openness to explore, or play'. With this in mind, consider the everyday technology children are surrounded by in their homes, communities and settings.

Tensions and challenges

Consider what this powerful statement (from the 1997 UNESCO report, *Educating for a Sustainable Future*) means in the context of early years education: Education is humanity's best hope and most effective means in the quest to achieve sustainable development.

Expressive Arts and Design

The specific area Expressive Arts and Design is divided into two categories with the following early learning goals:

* **Exploring and Using Media and Materials**: Children sing songs, make music and dance, and experiment with ways of changing them. They safely use and explore a variety of materials, tools and techniques, experimenting with colour, design, texture, form and function.
* **Being Imaginative**: Children use what they have learnt about media and materials in original ways, thinking about uses and purposes. They represent their own ideas, thoughts and feelings through design and technology, art, music, dance, role-play and stories.

This area replaced the previous Creative Development reducing four aspects to two where the practitioner is encouraged to sing songs and rhymes which are an essential part of early language development (Communication and Language). Again the latter part of this aspect (safely exploring a variety of tools) explores requirements closely aligned within Physical Development in the moving and handling section. Therefore the practitioner needs to ensure children are engaging with 'a variety of materials, tools and techniques, experimenting with colour, design, texture, form and function' (DfE, 2014:12), reflecting the Reggio Emilia hundred languages that children possess. As with Understanding the World this area should be considered using a thematic lens, encompassing all elements of the prime and specific areas alongside the characteristics of effective learning.

In early childhood, children should have access to many sensorial activities that are not subject orientated. Whilst playing outside children will explore the textures, forms and colours that nature provides. Practitioners can introduce very young children to 'a wide range of music, painting and sculpture' (Early Education, 2012:44); for example, Mondrian, Kandinsky and Klee are all used to experiment with shape, line and form. Consider the holistic learning involved in designing and creating an original 'Andy Goldsworthy'

Figure 1.26 A two-year-old child's artistic representation of natural materials.

Figure 1.27 A four-year-old child's artistic representation using natural materials.

creation using natural open ended materials in an 'unhurried environment', noted in Steiner education as the key to understanding and recognising the 'child's sensory sensitivities' (Steiner Waldorf Education, 2009:6).

Expressive arts must not be restricted to 'doing Reggio' as opportunities for creativity and divergent thinking need to be embedded in practice. Peter Moss (2013) reports how Loris Malaguzzi contemplates the value of practitioners asking children: 'What has made you wonder today?' In the poem *The Hundred Languages of Children*, Malaguzzi talks about the school 'cutting off the head' and just concentrating on the cognitive academic activities and learning to the detriment of creativity and divergent thinking. This creativity can be facilitated in numerous ways, for example providing children with large roller brushes and chalks outside on the ground would be recognised through the prime area Physical Development. This is reflected in Development Matters (Early Education, 2012) when it explicitly directs the practitioner towards the prime areas and characteristics of effective learning. Practitioners need to support children to think in original ways and this reinforces 4.3 creating and thinking critically which challenges children to 'have their own ideas, make links and choose ways to do things' (Early Education, 2012:5), or as Bruner (2012:xviii) notes:

> Cultivating imagination is the first thing, but it isn't enough to read fairy tales. It is imagination that saves us from all the obvious and banal, from the ordinary aspects of life. Imagination transforms facts into conjecture. Even a shadow cast onto the floor is not only a shadow: it is a mystery. Try drawing one and you will realise.

Ken Robinson makes the point that schools and early years settings should let children 'discover the Element in them (selves) and in their way' (2009:xiii). Robinson asserts that

Figure 1.28 Splashing in puddles, "My shadow is moving".

this 'Element' is within everyone, it just needs the right environment and practitioner to unlock the potential. He believes that practitioners, by sticking rigidly to the cognitive expectations and check lists, do not utilise all capacities of young children. He suggests that practitioners should encourage the capacities of imagination, feelings and intuition, spirituality, physical and sensory awareness.

Practitioners need to plan and reflect upon a range of activities to support the holistic development of the child.

Exploring and Using Media and Materials

Consider the Reggio philosophy of 'The Hundred Languages of Children' and reflect on how practitioners can develop 'a repertoire of techniques for artistic expressions and representation of their experiences' (Moylett & Stewart, 2012:29).

Being Imaginative

Consider how role play can support children to represent their ideas, thoughts and feelings. Reflect on how children's cultural identity is reflected in the choice of role-play within early years settings.

Tensions and challenges

The Cambridge Primary Review (Alexander, 2010:13) noted: 'Creative activities, the decline of which concerned many witnesses to the Review, raise the quality and capacity of children's thinking, perseverance and problem-solving abilities, as well as fuelling their imaginations.' What are the messages embedded in the current EYFS in relation the idea of creativity?

The concerns highlighted in the review could also relate to how practitioners appear to limit creativity to artistic activities rather than divergent thinking. Reflect on this statement.

Children need time and space to be creative. Consider the idea of the 'unhurried environment' advocated by Steiner education and the tensions within the EYFS as a goal-orientated early years framework.

References

Alexander, R. (ed.) (2010) *The Cambridge Primary Review Research Surveys*. London: Routledge.

Alexander, R. (2013) *The Best That Has Been Thought and Said by Robin Alexander*, Forum, Volume 56, Number 1 [online]. Available at: www.wwwords.co.uk/forum [accessed October 2014].

Ang, L. (2014) *The Early Years Curriculum: the UK Context and Beyond*. London: Routledge.

Baldock, P., Fitzgerald, D. & Kay, J. (2013) *Understanding Early Years Policy* (3rd Ed.). London: Sage.

Bandura, A. (1977) *Social Learning Theory*. Upper Saddle River, NJ: Prentice Hall.

Barrett, S. (2014) Empowering Young Writers. Chapter 12 in Bower, V. (Ed.), *Developing Early Literacy 0–8: From Theory to Practice*. London: Sage, pp. 184–199.

Barron, I. (2005) Understanding Development in Early Childhood. Chapter 15 in Jones, L., Holmes, R. & Powell, J. (Eds), *Early Childhood Studies: A Multiprofessional Perspective*. Maidenhead: Open University Press, pp. 194–203.

Beauchamp, G. (2013) Understanding the World. Chapter 20 in Palaiologou, I. (Ed.), *The Early Years Foundation Stage: Theory and Practice* (2nd Ed.). London: Sage, pp. 286–298.

Bower, V. & Barrett, S. (2014) Rhythm, Rhyme and Repetition. Chapter 8 in Bower, V. (Ed.), *Developing Early Literacy 0–8: From Theory to Practice*. London: Sage, pp. 118–134.

Brock, A. (2014) Curriculum and Pedagogy of Play: A Multitude of Perspectives? In Brock, A., Jarvis, P. & Olusoga, Y. (Eds), *Perspectives on Play: Learning for Life* (2nd Ed.). London: Routledge, pp. 70–102.

Brock, A., Jarvis, P. & Olusoga, Y. (2013) *Perspectives on Play: Learning for Life*. London: Routledge.

Bronfenbrenner, U. (1979) *The Ecology of Human Development*. Cambridge, MA: Harvard University Press.

Bruce, T. (2011) *Early Childhood Education* (4th Ed.). London: Hodder Education.

Bruner, J. (2012) Reggio: A City of Courtesy, Curiosity, and Imagination. Preface in Edwards, C., Gandini, L. & Forman, G. (Eds), *The Hundred Languages of Children: The Reggio Emilia Experience in Transformation*. Santa Barbara, CA: ABC-CLIO, LLC.

Carle, E. (2002) *The Very Hungry Caterpillar*. London: Puffin.

Carle, E. (2010) *10 Little Rubber Ducks*. New York: HarperFestival.

DCSF (Department for Children, Schools and Families) (2008) *The Early Years Foundation Stage*. Nottingham: DCSF Publications.

Dewey, J. (1959) *Dewey on Education*. New York: Bureau of Publications, Teachers College, Columbia University (Issue 3).

DfE (Department for Education) (2011) *Supporting Families in the Foundation Years*. London: Department for Education [online]. Available at: www.gov.uk/government/uploads/system/uploads/attachment_data/file/184868/DFE-01001-2011_supporting_families_in_the_foundation_years.pdf [accessed December 2014].

DfE (Department for Education) (2012) *Statutory Framework for the Early Years Foundation Stage: Setting the Standards for Learning, Development and Care for Children From Birth to Five*. Runcorn: DfE Publications.

DfE (Department for Education) (2013) *Early Years Outcomes: A Non-Statutory Guide for Practitioners and Inspectors to Help Inform Understanding of Child Development Through the Early Years*. London: DfE Publications.

DfE (Department for Education) (2014) *Statutory Framework for the Early Years Foundation Stage: Setting the Standards for Learning, Development and Care for Children From Birth to Five*. Runcorn: DfE Publications.

DfES (Department for Education and Skills) (2007) *The Early Years Foundation Stage*. Nottingham: DfES Publications.

DoH (Department of Health) (2008) *The Child Health Promotion Programme: Pregnancy and First Five Years of Life* [online]. Available at: www.education.gov.uk/publications/. . ./DH-286448.pdf [accessed August 2014].

DoH (Department of Health) (2009) *Healthy Child Programme*. London: Department for Children, Schools and Families.

Donaldson, M. (2006) *Children's Minds*. London: Harper Perennial.

Dowling, M. (2010) *Young Children's Personal, Social and Emotional Development* (3rd Ed.). London: Sage.

Dowling, M. (2014) *Young Children's Personal, Social and Emotional Development* (4th Ed.). London: Sage.

Early Education (2012) *Development Matters in the Early Years Foundation Stage (EYFS)* [online]. Available at: www.early-education.org.uk/development-matters-early-years-foundation-stage-eyfs [accessed May 2015].

Ecclestone, K. & Hayes, D. (2009) Changing the Subject: The Educational Implications of Developing Emotional Well-Being, *Oxford Review of Education*, 35(3): 371–389.

Elfer, P., Goldschmied, E. & Selleck, D. (2011) *Key Persons in the Nursery and Reception Classes: Building Relationships for Quality Provision*. London: David Fulton.

Evangelou, M., Brooks, G., Smith, S. & Jennings, D. (2005) *Research: Birth to School Study – A Longitudinal Evolution of the Peers Early Education Partnership (PEEP) 1998–2005*. Nottingham: DfES Publications.

Evangelou, M., Sylva, K., Kyriacou, M., Wild, M. & Glenny, G. (2009) *Early Years Learning and Development: Literature Review* (Research Report DCSF-RR176). Oxford: DCSF Publications.

Garvey, R., Stokes, P. & Megginson, D. (2009) *Coaching and Mentoring: Theory and Practice*. London: Sage.

Giardiello, P. (2014) *Pioneers in Early Childhood Education: The Roots and Legacies of Rachel and Margaret McMillan, Maria Montessori and Susan Isaacs*. London: Routledge.

Gill, T. (2007) *No Fear: Growing Up in a Risk Averse Society*. London: Calouste Gulbenkian Foundation.

Goddard Blythe, S. (2011) *The Genius of Childhood: Secrets of a Thriving Child*. Stroud: Hawthorne.

Goleman, D. (1996) *Emotional Intelligence*. London: Bloomsbury.

Goouch, K. (2014) Baby Rooms. Chapter 1 in Bower, V. (Ed.), *Developing Early Literacy 0–8: From Theory to Practice*. London: Sage, pp. 3–17.

Goouch, K. & Powell, S. (2013) *The Baby Room: Principles, Policy and Practice*. Maidenhead: Open University Press.

Hall, N. (1987) *The Emergence of Literacy*. Portsmouth, NH: Heinemann Educational Books Inc.

Hall, N. (1989) *Writing with Reason: The Emergence of Authorship in Young Children*. London: Hodder Education.

Hart, B. & Risley, T.R. (1995) *Meaningful Differences in the Everyday Experience of Young American Children*. Baltimore, MD: Brookes Publishing.

Hartshorne, M. (2006) *The Cost to the Nation of Children's Poor Communication*. (I CAN Talk Series issue 2) [online]. Available at: www.ican.org.uk/~/media/Ican2/Whats%20the%20Issue/Evidence/2%20 The%20Cost%20to%20the%20Nation%20of%20Children%20s%20Poor%20Communication%20 pdf.ashx [accessed November 2014].

Haylock, D. & Cockburn, A. (2013) *Understanding Mathematics for Young Children* (4th Ed.). London: Sage.

Haylock, D. with Manning, R. (2014) *Mathematics Explained for Primary Teachers* (5th Ed.). London: Sage.

Head, C. & Palaiologou, I. (2013) Literacy. Chapter 18 in Palaiologou, I. (Ed.), *The Early Years Foundation Stage: Theory and Practice* (2nd Ed.). London: Sage, pp. 256–270.

HM Treasury (2003) *Every Child Matters*. Norwich: The Stationery Office.

HM Treasury (2004) *Choice for Parents, the Best Start for Children: A Ten Year Strategy for Childcare*. Department for Education and Skill, Department for Work and Pensions and Department for Trade and Industry. Norwich: HMSO.

Hutchin, V. (2013) *Effective Practice in the Early Years Foundation Stage: An Essential Guide*. Maidenhead: McGraw-Hill.

Joyce, R. (2012) *Outdoor Learning Past and Present*. Maidenhead: Open University Press.

Knight, S. (2011) *Forest School and Outdoor Learning in the Early Years* (2nd Ed.). London: Sage.

Laible, D. & Thompson, R. (2007) Early Socialization: A Relationship Perspective. Chapter 7 in Grusec, J. & Hastings, P. (Eds), *Handbook of Socialization: Theory and Research*. New York: Guilford Press, pp. 181–207.

Laming, H. (2009) *The Protection of Children in England: A Progress Report*. London: The Stationery Office.

Latham, D. (2002) *How Children Learn to Write: Supporting and Developing Children's Writing in School*. London: Paul Chapman.

Lee, W., Carr, M., Soutar, B. & Mitchell, L. (2013) *Understanding the Te Whariki Approach*. London: Routledge.

Liebschner, J. (1992) *A Child's Work: Freedom and Guidance in Froebel's Educational Theory and Practice*. Cambridge: Lutterworth Press.

McDowall Clark, R. (2013) *Childhood in Society for the Early Years* (2nd Ed.). London: Sage.

MacNaughton, G. (2005) *Doing Foucault in Early Childhood Studies: Applying Poststructural Ideas.* London: Routledge.

Montessori, M. (2012) *The 1946 London Lectures* (Volume 17). Amsterdam: Montessori-Person.

Mosley, J. (2005) *Circle Time Handbook for the Golden Rules Stories: Helping Children with Social and Emotional Aspect.* Trowbridge: Positive Press Ltd.

Moss, P. (2013) Beyond the Investment Narrative, *Contemporary Issues in Early Childhood*, 14(4): 370–372.

Moylett, H. & Stewart, N. (2012) *Understanding the Revised Early Years Foundation Stage.* London: Early Education.

Muirden, J. (2008) *Precautionary Tales for Grandparents: Some of Which May be Read to the Young for Their Moral Development*: Chichester: Summersdale Publishers Ltd.

Murray, L. & Andrews, L. (2005) *The Social Baby* (2nd Ed.). Richmond: C.P. Publishing.

Neaum, S. (2012) *Language and Literacy for the Early Years.* London: Sage.

Nicol, J. & Taplin, J. (2012) *Understanding the Steiner Waldorf Approach: Early Years Education in Practice.* London: Routledge.

Nunes, T. & Bryant, P. (2004) Mathematical and Scientific Thinking. Chapter 7 in Oates, J. & Grayson, A. (Eds), *Cognitive and Language Development in Children.* Oxford: Blackwell and The Open University, pp. 261–301.

Nutbrown, C. (2012) *Foundations for Quality: The Independent Review of Early Education and Childcare Qualifications.* Final Report June 2012 [online]. Available at: www.gov.uk/government/uploads/system/uploads/attachment_data/file/175463/Nutbrown-Review.pdf [accessed November 2014].

Nutkins, S., McDonald, C. & Stephen, M. (2013) *Early Childhood and Care: An Introduction.* London: Sage.

Oates, J. & Grayson, A. (2004) *Cognitive and Language Development in Children.* Oxford: Blackwell and The Open University.

Oldfield, L. (2012) *Free to Learn: Steiner Waldorf Early Childhood Care and Education* (2nd Ed.). Stroud: Hawthorne Press.

Oliverio, A. (2013) Development of the Child's Mind and Values of Solidarity in Double Theme Issue on Peace Through Education. *AMI Journal*, 1(2): 98–100.

Palaiologou, I. (Ed.) (2013) *The Early Years Foundation Stage: Theory and Practice* (2nd Ed.). London: Sage.

PEEP (2009) *Parents Early Education Partnership Project* [online]. Available at: www.peep.org.uk [accessed December 2014].

Powell, S., Goouch, K. & Werth, L. (2013) Seeking Froebel's Mother Songs in Daycare for Babies. In: TACTYC Annual Conference 2013, 1–2 November, The ICC Birmingham.

Pugh, G. & Duffy, B. (2013) *Contemporary Issues in the Early Years* (6th Ed.). London: Sage.

QCA and Department for Education and Employment (2000) *Curriculum Guidance for the Foundation Stage.* London: QCA [online]. Available at: www.smartteachers.co.uk/upload/documents_32.pdf [accessed December 2014].

Rinaldi, C. (2006) *In Dialogue with Reggio Emilia: Listening, Researching and Learning.* London: Routledge.

Robinson, K. (2009) *The Element – How Finding Your Passion Changes Everything?* New York: Penguin.

Rogoff, B. (2008) Observing Sociocultural Activity on Three Planes: Participatory Appropriation, Guided Participation and Apprenticeship. In Hall, K., Murphy, P. & Soler, J. (Eds), *Pedagogy and Practice: Culture and Identities.* Milton Keynes: Open University Press, pp. 58–74.

Rose, J. (2006) *Independent Review of the Teaching of Early Reading: Final Report.* Nottingham: DfES Publications [online]. Available at: www.ioe.ac.uk/study/documents/Study_Teacher_Training/Review_early_reading.pdf [accessed August 2014].

Rosen, M. & Oxenbury, H. (1989) *We're Going on a Bear Hunt.* London: Walker Books.

RSA Animate (2010) *Changing Education Paradigms* [Adapted from RSA Lecture by Sir Ken Robinson June 2008] [online video]. Available at: www.youtube.com/watch?v=zDZFcDGpL4U [accessed August 2014].

SCAA (School Curriculum and Assessment Authority) (1996a) *Looking at Children's Learning: Desirable Outcomes for Children's Learning on Entering Compulsory Education*. London: SCAA.

SCAA (School Curriculum and Assessment Authority) (1996b) *Nursery Education: Desirable Outcomes for Children's Learning on Entering Compulsory Education*. London: SCAA and Department for Education and Employment.

Standing, E.M. (1998) *Maria Montessori: Her Life and Work*. London: Penguin Plume.

Steiner Waldorf Education (2009) *Guide to the Early Years Foundation Stage in Steiner Waldorf Early Childhood Settings*. Forest Row: Steiner Waldorf Schools Fellowship [online]. Available at: http://dera.ioe.ac.uk/2387/1/780cec736755cbe8ae2756917f4e732d.pdf [accessed December 2014].

Stewart, N. (2011) *How Children Learn: The Characteristics of Effective Learning*. London: Early Education.

Sure Start (2003) *Birth to Three Matters: Framework to Support Children in Their Earliest Years*. Nottingham: DfES Publications.

Sylva, K., Melhuish, E., Sammons, P., Sirja-Blatchford, I. & Taggart, B. (2004) *The Effective Provision of Pre-School Education (EPPE) Project: Effective Pre-School Education: A Longitudinal Study Funded by the DfES 1997–2004* (Research Brief No. 61). Nottingham: DCSF.

Tickell, C. (2011) *The Early Years: Foundations for Life, Health and Learning (Tickell Review)*. London: DfE.

Trevarthen, C. (2001) Intrinsic Motives for Companionship in Understanding: Their Origin, Development and Significance for Infant Mental Health, *International Journal of Infant Mental Health*, 22(1–2): 95–131.

Trevarthen, C. (n.d.) *Communication* [transcript of video] [online]. Available at: www.educationscotland.gov.uk/video/p/video_tcm4637501.asp [accessed December 2014].

UNESCO (2008) *The Contribution of Early Childhood Education to a Sustainable Society*. Paris: UNESCO.

Vygotsky, L. (1978) *Mind in Society*. Cambridge, MA: Harvard University Press.

WAVE Trust (2013) *Conception to Age 2: The Age of Opportunity*. Croydon: WAVE Trust.

Whitehead, M. (2006) *Physical Literacy and Physical Education: Conceptual Mapping* [online]. Available at: www.physicalliteracy.org.uk/conceptualmapping2006.php [accessed November 2014].

Williams, P. (2008) *Independent Review of Mathematics Teaching in Early Years Settings and Primary Schools, Final Report*. London: DCSF.

Zeedyk, M.S. (2008) *What's Life in a Baby Buggy Like? The Impact of Buggy Orientation on Parent–Infant Interaction and Infant Stress* [online]. Available at: www.literacytrust.org.uk/assets/0000/2531/Buggy_research.pdf [accessed August 2014].

2 The Foundation Stage curriculum in Northern Ireland

An inside practical perspective

Andrea Doherty and Glenda Walsh

Chapter outline

This chapter sets out to detail and explain the ethos, manifestation and implementation of the Foundation Stage (FS) in Northern Ireland (NI). Initially it will examine the underlying principles and aims of the FS curriculum, making particular reference to how it was informed by a local intervention and research study, whilst simultaneously highlighting its underpinning theoretical perspective. It will then address the content of the FS curriculum, first in terms of the Areas of Learning and then from the standpoint of the cross-curricular themes. The next section of the chapter will report the challenges and tensions associated with the translation of the FS into practice and suitable solutions as to how such tensions can be overcome will be highlighted. The chapter will end with a short section entitled 'Future directions for the FS curriculum in NI' which will provide an insight into the way forward with early years (EY) education in the context of NI. References to cameo evidence and reflective questions will be made throughout the chapter to fully engage the reader with the current educational climate for NI 4–6-year-old children.

Underlying principles and aims: the context

In 2007, the FS was introduced in NI to reflect the changing outlook on learning and development in the early years. According to NI policy and documentation (for example the Early Years Draft Strategy (DENI, 2010) and the Learning to Learn Framework (DENI, 2012)) the early years range from 0 to 6 years. However it is essential to emphasise from the outset of this chapter that the FS in NI, since its implementation, has only targeted Years 1 and 2 of primary schooling, therefore being relevant to children aged 4–6 years.

Important to note at this point is the early school starting age in NI. Children are obliged to start primary school as young as four years and two months, younger than any of their European counterparts (Hunter & Walsh, 2014; Walsh et al., 2006). Prior to the introduction of the new FS a more formal, traditional curriculum was in place for these young children, a curriculum that was deemed to be subject-based and assessment-led, and which focused principally on academic achievement (Walsh et al., 2006). However, concerns about the appropriateness of this type of curriculum, and changing theoretical views of early child development, led to a shift in thinking towards a more child-centred, play-based curriculum in the early years of primary school (Hunter & Walsh, 2014). In September 2000, the Enriched Curriculum (EC) was initially introduced in six primary schools in a disadvantaged area of Belfast, as part of a local initiative. These schools identified tensions with the traditional curriculum in place at that time, particularly in terms of transitions between preschool and primary school and the over emphasis placed on the formal instruction of

Literacy and Numeracy at this early age. In NI there is no standard form of preschool provision – children enter primary schooling from a range of experiences, including nursery schools, playgroups, day care settings and in some cases directly from the home environment. The schools involved in the development of the EC identified that 'their school entry children tended to have poor oral language skills and were not always well prepared for school routines' (McGuinness et al., 2009:5). The development of the EC was a response by the participant schools to tailor provision to match the children's developmental stage, with another overarching aim being the enhancement of children's self-esteem in relation to their competences in school. Overall, the EC aimed to focus on a change of curriculum towards emergent learning skills. For example, rather than focus immediately on reading and writing, the EC concentrated on phonological awareness in Literacy, and in Numeracy the emphasis was placed on laying foundations in terms of numbers through sorting, matching and counting, rather than formal number recording (McGuinness et al., 2009). A major pedagogical change in the EC was the introduction of play- and activity-based learning for young children in order to enhance their dispositions to learning. In the two years following its introduction in Belfast schools, other schools and Education and Library Boards began implementing the EC. Inspired by the Belfast initiative and with similar outlooks on the original curriculum, a total of 120 schools across NI introduced the EC into their practice. During 2000, a research team from the School of Psychology at Queen's University, and Stranmillis University College, was commissioned by the Northern Ireland Council for Curriculum, Examinations and Assessment (CCEA) to devise and conduct an evaluation of the impact of the EC and related issues. A longitudinal study was conducted over a period of eight years looking at factors including curriculum development and implementation issues, classroom experiences and practices, parental perceptions and outcomes for children (McGuinness et al., 2009).

   This longitudinal and rigorous evaluation of the impact of the EC yielded mainly positive findings. According to McGuinness et al. (2009) the EC, with its focus on play and on social-constructivist theories of learning, provided children with a higher quality learning experience. It afforded children opportunities for independent learning and enhanced children's dispositions to learning. Children also demonstrated higher levels of emotional, social and physical well-being (Walsh et al., 2006). Teachers too responded positively to the EC, describing it as 'exhausting and challenging but very worthwhile'. In the main, Year 1 teachers were extremely enthusiastic, highly motivated and showed ownership of the development and implementation processes involved (McGuinness et al., 2009:25). Further positive comments from the teachers included:

> Playing is the medium by which young children learn best. Why would we want to squash young children's enthusiasm towards learning by making them complete low level worksheets?
>
> (Walsh et al., 2008:55)

> Play should go on for ever. There is a time and place for the formal teaching of reading and mathematics but only when children are ready.
>
> (Walsh et al., 2008:56)

> The Enriched Curriculum is all about individuals and on this premise future learning should be built.
>
> (Walsh et al., 2008:56)

Figure 2.1 Building Willy Wonka's Chocolate Factory.

Year 2 teachers were more 'measured' than their Year 1 counterparts, but were also positive towards the EC in terms of sharing ideas with colleagues and in employing playful approaches in formal work (McGuinness et al., 2009; Walsh et al., 2010). The change in curriculum towards more play-based activities in the early years of primary schooling proved to have implications beyond the Year 1 and 2 classrooms it was designed for and in some cases these knock-on effects were not anticipated. However, McGuinness et al. (2009) recommended whole-school support, collaboration with external agencies and involvement in clusters of schools also implementing the EC, for more successful translation into practice.

When asked directly about this new course of pedagogical direction in the early years of primary school, the children themselves appeared to welcome the emphasis placed on the more playful learning experiences available to them: 'Yes I love it. The work is better. You do experiments' (Walsh et al., 2008:50).

Children also attributed value to social relationships, including friendships and adult interactions, in their experiences of the EC. The EC classrooms in Year 1, specifically, provided continuity with children's nursery experiences and eased their transition to primary school (Walsh et al., 2008).

Despite the advantages, there were also challenges experienced in relation to the EC. Inadequate training for teachers, insufficient resources and unexpected knock-on effects throughout the whole school were some of the stumbling blocks identified in relation to the EC. The lack of training was particularly influential as different teachers with different theoretical outlooks used play in different ways – a lack of clarity about play therefore resulted in different experiences of the EC across school contexts (McGuinness at al., 2009).

However, the EC evaluation was predominantly positive and was comparatively more appropriate for young children in EY education. Following the success of the pilot and the lessons learned from its implementation, the 'Foundation Stage' was introduced, comprising Years 1 and 2 of the primary school. It was made compulsory in 2007 for all Year 1 classrooms (children aged 4–5 years) and in 2008 for all Year 2 classrooms (children aged 5–6 years).

The FS curriculum in NI recognises the importance of continuity and progression in children's learning. It acknowledges that children come from a range of preschool settings and identifies at its core the importance of an appropriate, broad and balanced learning programme which meets the needs of all young children. The centrality of skills and dispositions to learning being developed at this early stage of education are also highlighted, so as to support the child in transitioning to 'formal' schooling and to subsequent stages of education and life (CCEA, 2007). The FS curriculum, it would seem, has moved away from formal, teacher-led modes of instruction and instead focuses on a pedagogy of active participation by children in directing their learning, with adults who facilitate and guide, rather than lead. Teaching and learning, according to the FS curriculum, should be social, experiential and context and child sensitive, where teachers have a degree of flexibility to 'follow the interests of the children, encouraging them to see links in their learning and to appreciate that the skills they learn in one area can be applied elsewhere' (CCEA, 2007:14).

Figure 2.2 Displays of children's work.

Figure 2.3 Creative displays in the play environment.

In the FS, play is identified as the principal pedagogy for learning but also for development, and it is highlighted that children should 'experience much of their learning through well-planned and challenging play' (CCEA, 2007:9) with EY practitioners who are 'committed, sensitive, enthusiastic and interact effectively to challenge children's thinking and learning' (CCEA, 2007:16).

The overarching aims of the FS curriculum are summarised as follows:

- promote children's personal development;
- promote positive attitudes and dispositions to learning;
- promote children's Thinking Skills and Personal Capabilities;
- encourage creativity and imagination;
- enable children to develop physical confidence and competence;
- develop children's curiosity and interest in the world around them;
- enable children to communicate in a variety of ways;
- motivate children to develop literacy and numeracy skills in meaningful contexts.

(CCEA, 2007:15)

The FS curriculum, its pedagogical approaches and its underlying principles are rooted in the cultural-historical theory of Lev Vygotsky (1896–1934) (Walsh et al., 2011). Central to Vygotskian theory is the appreciation of the social and cultural contexts for young children's learning; children learn through interactions with adults, with their peers and with their environment. The adult role is perceived as central to children's learning and development, as they are the creators of the environment and of the ethos for learning. Adults also are mediators of the culture in which children grow and learn, and as such, are models of development for children. The FS curriculum stresses the value of adult interactions in the early years of schooling, and of the adult's responsibilities in planning, observing and reflecting on their practice in relation to children's learning. The focus on play as pedagogy in the FS is in line with Vygotsky's theory of child development where play is identified as the leading activity – the activity: 'in connection with whose development the most important changes take place in the child's psyche and within which psychic processes develop that pave the way for the child's transition to a new, higher level of development' (Leont'ev, 1981:369).

In cultural-historical theory, play is a distinct phase in mental development. Doherty (2013) details the staged model of child development, based on the work of Vygotsky and Vygotskian scholars, with play being a step in its own right in child development, *followed* by formal learning. According to Leont'ev (1981) there are three particular leading activities in society: play, school and work. Edwards (2011) extended Leont'ev's thinking, identifying more leading activities, but she reaffirmed play as the precursor to formal learning. Play is the leading activity of early childhood, and as such is the activity which aids most greatly in the development of the young child (Chaiklin, 2003). Without play and mastery of play in the early years, children face potential difficulties in relation to formal learning (the next leading activity) where abstract thought, self-regulation and memory (skills formed in play) are necessary.

In Vygotsky's (1933) paper 'Play and its role in the mental development of the child', Vygotsky explained that abstract thought develops via the use of objects such as toys, props and clothes in make-believe play. The use of these objects for pretend, rather than for real-life purposes serves as a bridge between sensory-motor manipulation of objects and fully developed logical thinking, when the child can manipulate ideas in their heads

(Murphy, 2012). Multifunctional and unstructured props as opposed to real-life props can be more effective in the development of abstract thought as children name and rename objects dependent on the play scenario, for example a cardboard box may be used initially as a car, then as a spaceship and even a shop. This extends and develops children's use of language greatly as they then need to explain and elaborate on specific details associated with the box. In this way children are encouraged to separate the 'meaning' of the object from the object itself, for example, to drive a block on a carpet as if it were a truck (gives the block 'truckness') and acts as a precursor to abstract thought. Vygotsky claimed that the repeated naming and renaming in play helps children to master the symbolic nature of words, which leads to the realisation of the relationship between words and objects, and then of knowledge and the way knowledge operates (Murphy, 2012).

Play also aids in children's development of self-regulation. In play, specifically role-play, children take on roles, for example that of a doctor, teacher or hairdresser, and in so doing, follow an implicit set of rules so as to talk in a certain way, and act in the way expected of their role. As they abide by these rules, they learn to self-regulate their physical, social and cognitive behaviours. These rules place restraints on a child's actions and force them to act 'a head taller' (Vygotsky, 1978). Vygotsky (1978:102) himself suggested that play creates a zone of proximal development (ZPD) for the child:

> This strict subordination to rules [during play] is quite impossible in life, but in play it becomes possible: thus, play creates a zone of proximal development of the child. In play a child always behaves beyond his average age, above his daily behavior; in play it is as though he were a head taller than himself.

Young children in role-play exhibit behaviours beyond their current level of development, and act at a higher level of development. For example, consider asking a child of three years to stand still whilst they get their hair cut – the child will not stand still for very long. In comparison, invite a three-year-old child to play 'musical statues' or 'hide and seek' – the child will stay still as long as the play situation requires. The employment of a playful scenario forces children to exercise self-regulation; they need to control their behaviour so as to prolong the pleasure of the playful experience.

Vygotsky (1933) posited that play also develops children's memory. He stated that play was more about 'recollection than imagination', describing it as memory in action, as opposed to a novel imaginary situation. Play is more about children acting out real situations that have taken place, i.e. a recollection of something that actually has happened. Vygotsky (1933) claimed that as play develops, we see a movement towards the conscious realisation of its purpose for the child.

Cultural-historical theory states that at school age (i.e. at age seven in Russia where cultural-historical theory is rooted) play does not disappear or die away. In actuality Vygotsky (1933) claimed that it permeates the child's attitude towards reality. Play creates a new relationship between the semantic and the visible, between situations in thought and real situations. In visible terms, play bears little resemblance to what it leads to (formal instruction), but it has its own inner continuation in school instruction and work (Vygotsky, 1933). Drawing on a Vygotskian perspective therefore, it would seem that by incorporating a more play-based approach in the FS, NI children should be better prepared for school instruction and work, as they develop their dispositions to learning and education.

REFLECTIVE QUESTIONS: UNDERLYING PRINCIPLES AND AIMS: THE CONTEXT

- Compare and contrast the underlying principles and aims associated with the NI FS curriculum with the other UK contexts. What are the similarities and differences?
- Reflect on the early school starting age in NI, where children as young as four years and two months are obliged to commence primary school. What in your opinion are the advantages and disadvantages of such an early school start?
- The NI FS has clearly been informed by the EC pilot initiative and research study. Reflect on the outcomes of the evaluation of the EC and consider how these appear to have informed the underlying aims and principles of the FS curriculum.
- Recap on the value placed on play from a Vygotskian perspective.
- The philosophy of the NI FS curriculum is firmly embedded in a Vygotskian perspective. In contrast, if the philosophy of the NI FS were to have been more Piagetian in focus, how might the underlying principles and aims change?

The content of the NI FS curriculum: the Areas of Learning

The statutory FS curriculum in NI incorporates six key Areas of Learning:

- **Language and Literacy** – including Talking, Listening, Reading and Writing;
- **Mathematics and Numeracy** – including Number, Measures, Shape and Space, Sorting, and Patterns and Relationships;
- **The Arts** – including Art and Design, Music and Drama;
- **The World Around Us** – including Geography, History, and Science and Technology;
- **Personal Development and Mutual Understanding** – including Personal Understanding and Health, and Mutual Understanding in the Local and Wider Community; and
- **Physical Development and Movement** – including Athletics, Dance, Games and Gymnastics.

Religious Education is also identified as an Area of Learning within the NI FS curriculum, however the detail and substance of this Area of Learning is not specified but rather is to be provided, according to the curriculum document, 'in accordance with the core syllabus drafted by the four main Christian Churches in Northern Ireland and specified by the Department of Education' (CCEA, 2007:16).

Despite the Areas of Learning being presented as discrete and segregated, teachers are encouraged to integrate learning through connected learning experiences. Providing such a 'joined up' experience promotes children's ability to see connections and relevance in what they are learning, and enhances their ability to transfer learning across contexts. In each Area of Learning, the FS curriculum also includes a box entitled 'Progression', taking into consideration the range of abilities in mainstream classrooms and providing ideas as to how teachers can extend teaching and learning appropriate to the needs and interest of the children involved.

Language and Literacy

Language and Literacy is integral to all other Areas of Learning as it enables children to understand and use language in both written and spoken forms. It is a vehicle that allows children to access the curriculum, promoting their interactions with one another and with the world around them, and enhancing their ability to express themselves creatively and to communicate confidently (CCEA, 2007). Language and Literacy focuses on the four modes of communication (talking, listening, reading and writing) and within the FS, teachers should promote all four, using the children's previous experiences of preschool as starting points. The FS curriculum highlights the value of interactions with both adults and other children in work and play for developing vocabulary and oral language, and for sharing and obtaining information. The curriculum emphasises the need for adults to question effectively, but also to listen to children and interact sensitively to extend their communication skills, whilst also facilitating children's thinking through providing appropriate oral language when necessary (CCEA, 2007). Again this idea of adults scaffolding learning and assisting in making children's thoughts verbal is in line with Vygotsky's cultural-historical theory both in relation to the role of the adult and in relation to the link between thinking and speech:

a) The role of the adult: In his theoretical construct, the ZPD, Vygotsky (1978) highlighted the potential in what, and how, we can learn through interactions with others. The ZPD is 'the distance between the actual developmental level as determined by independent problem solving and the level of potential development as determined through problem solving under adult guidance or in collaboration with more capable peers' (Vygotsky, 1978:86). The ZPD, in essence, suggests that with help from more competent others, the level of development or learning is accelerated. Bruner (1978) developed the term 'scaffolding' from Vygotskian theory to explain the role of the adult more explicitly. The adult provides children with the 'tools' to learn and introduces language and strategies to aid the child's performance. This assistance or 'scaffold' can then temporarily be withdrawn as the child learns to use this tool independently.

b) Thinking and speech: Vygotsky postulated that during the first two years of life, language and thought develop relatively independently. However, private speech soon develops and language and thought start to merge and influence each other (Verenikina, 2005). This fundamentally changes the nature of both thinking and speech in that language becomes intellectualised and thinking becomes verbal (Vygotsky, 1986). In Language and Literacy in the FS, the teacher aids in the development of the child's thinking skills and helps to extend the child's speech so as to extend their holistic development in the long term.

Within the Area of Learning entitled 'Language and Literacy', focal areas for development include attention and listening skills, phonological awareness, the social use of language, language and thinking, and the development of an extended vocabulary. Reading and writing are explicitly described as needing a role model in the form of the teacher to model both processes. The environment is also identified as invaluable in developing an ethos for reading and writing. An effective environment will allow children to recognise that print has meaning and that writing has a purpose and, as such, enhance learning dispositions in relation to these activities (CCEA, 2007). The curriculum specifies that: 'Reading experiences should be informal and enjoyable, with children learning in an environment where print is all around them. . . . They should have regular opportunities . . . to see modeled reading and to participate in shared reading' (CCEA, 2007:20). In addition it states that: 'Children should have opportunities to talk about why people write and be given opportunities to experiment with their own written communication. As the teacher writes in a range of situations, children should see him/her as a role model' (CCEA, 2007:20).

The FS curriculum also highlights the value of second language learning in the early years, not only for Language and Literacy but also for other Areas of Learning, such as The World Around Us and Personal Development and Mutual Understanding. Although not compulsory, specific resources have been designed and are available on the NI curriculum website to support primary teachers to develop and integrate language learning and teaching into the primary classroom and can be viewed at www.nicurriculum.org.uk/pl/.

REFLECTIVE QUESTIONS: LANGUAGE AND LITERACY

- The NI curriculum emphasises that the reading experience in the FS should be 'informal and enjoyable'. Consider how the teaching of reading can be delivered in such a fashion. Contrast the delivery of this experience with a much more formal approach to the teaching of reading and discuss the impact of such an experience on children's enthusiasm for reading and their overall progress.
- Promoting literacy through play-based activities can be perceived as a very challenging and complex task on the part of the teacher. Consider a playful environment and indicate how literacy can be fully infused into such a learning experience in a natural and spontaneous fashion.
- Sometimes teachers are accused of doing all of the talking in an EY classroom whilst children, who have already quite a limited concentration span, are expected to listen for lengthy periods at a time. The NI FS curriculum emphasises the importance of the adults listening to the children. Reflect on your own experience of an EY classroom and indicate how this might be effectively facilitated.
- The NI FS curriculum details the need for adults to effectively question children. In reality, however, evidence would suggest that on occasions questioning on the part of the teacher can sometimes translate into a form of interrogation of the child: 'What shape is this?' 'What colour is that?' 'How many cars do you have?' Children tend to respond much better to natural dialogue rather than intense questioning. Reflect on ways in which a natural dialogue between a teacher and child/ren can be promoted in an EY classroom.
- There has been much recent debate about the teaching of phonics in EY classrooms to promote effective reading skills. What are your views and perspectives on the teaching of phonics in the early years of schooling?

Mathematics and Numeracy

Within the Area of Learning entitled 'Mathematics and Numeracy', the development of mathematical language and mental mathematics are of fundamental importance. Through talking about their mathematical experiences children's understanding of the underlying concepts is enhanced. The FS curriculum promotes the use of play, games, exploratory activities and investigations to extend mathematical learning, but also highlights the value of embedding mathematics in the daily routine of the classroom. From as early as 1996, Van Oers was exploring the relationship between play and mathematics in this way:

• Mathematics made playful – in this scenario the primacy of maths is the starting point, and elements of maths are introduced to playful scenarios. Van Oers' (1996) diagrammatic representation of this situation is as follows:

• Mathematising elements of play activity – this situation originates in the primacy of play, with the educator attempting to introduce some mathematical elements. Van Oers (1996) represents this situation as such:

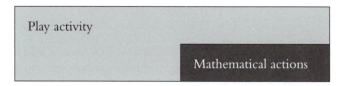

Van Oers (1996) proposed that opportunities for meaningful learning with young children may be maximised through employing the second method: mathematising elements of play. Play activity can be a teaching/learning situation for the enhancement of mathematical thinking in children, provided that the teacher is able to seize the teaching opportunities in an adequate way (Van Oers, 1996). The role of the adult is therefore vital in play, specifically in relation to mathematics.

Teaching mathematics in and through meaningful contexts offers children the opportunity to make sense of the concepts more easily and the use of stories, songs and rhymes are identified as valuable to this process. Finally, the curriculum highlights the use of physical objects and resources, as well as technology, in mathematics and numeracy to extend comprehension. Through having experiences with concrete materials children can develop understanding more quickly as these objects can be used physically to demonstrate mathematical ideas and actions. The focal areas at the FS for mathematics and numeracy include understanding numbers, counting and number recognition, understanding money, measures, shape and space, sorting, and patterns and relationships.

REFLECTIVE QUESTIONS: MATHEMATICS AND NUMERACY

• Mental maths is considered as integral to the teaching of Mathematics and Numeracy in the NI FS curriculum. Consider a range of approaches that might be used to allow mental maths to be developed in a playful fashion in an EY classroom with 4–6-year-old children.

- The FS curriculum in NI promotes the use of play, games, exploratory activities and investigations, and daily routines as ways to extend mathematical learning. Identify three activities that would allow maths to be developed through:

  - play
  - games
  - exploratory activities and investigations
  - daily routine of the classroom.

- Reflect on Van Oers' models for integrating playfulness into mathematics and for 'mathematising' play. Discuss activities appropriate to each model.
- Consider different concrete materials that can be employed in an EY classroom to promote the teaching of maths. Detail how these resources could be used effectively in context to ensure that the experience becomes more lifelike for the young children concerned.
- In your opinion, how could the use of the outdoor learning environment be effectively employed to encourage the development of mathematical knowledge and skills for young children?

The Arts

'The Arts' comprises art and design, music and drama. This Area of Learning is based on the outlook that a child's creative, expressive and physical development is closely linked with all aspects of their learning (CCEA, 2007). The Arts offers children the chance to explore and share their thoughts, feelings and emotions with others through a variety of media, including dance, art and design, and role-play. Gross and fine motor skills, children's confidence and their self-esteem are developed through children's participation in The Arts. Creativity too is enhanced, and expressed not just in the final product but also in the process of creating and learning (CCEA, 2007). Within art and design, children should have the freedom to play and explore with the elements of colour, line, tone, shape, form, texture and pattern in the development of visual, spatial and tactile awareness. An important aspect of art and design is that children are given time to explore, develop and explain their ideas, whilst also having time to observe and talk about their own and others' work. Teachers should actively encourage children to value their own and others' work as this is essential to understanding that everyone's work is unique.

Within music, children again can explore feelings and emotions and express themselves in a way that supports and extends verbal communication (CCEA, 2007). Music also develops children's listening skills and enhances their responses to pulse and rhythm. Children should be given opportunities to work creatively with sound, sing and play simple instruments, as well as listen to and respond to their own and others' music-making.

Drama, the third component of The Arts, is an Area of Learning linked closely to the overarching pedagogy of the FS: play. 'Play is the essence of drama and when children play, drama happens' (CCEA, 2007:34). As children mature their play develops, becomes more structured and becomes more social, until it resembles the 'play' of the theatre. Role-play and drama allow children to become someone else; they can live in a different world, have an entirely different personality and behave in a totally different way, and all in a safe and secure environment. Through taking on different roles and playing in different role-play scenarios, children internalise social and cultural norms, and act out the scenarios they experience in their everyday lives. Role-play allows them to deal with any concerns, feelings, thoughts or ideas and in the process develop emotional awareness, and self-regulation. Role-play is rooted in Vygotsky's cultural-historical theory. According to Vygotsky (1933) role-play is mature play. Mature play requires children to be involved in creating an imaginary situation. Second, within this play situation, the children should take on roles; these could be the different members of a family or perhaps animals in a zoo. Each role they create requires the child to act in different ways, wear different costumes and even use a specific type of language (Doherty, 2013). Vygotsky (1933) identified a third characteristic of mature play; that the children must follow the rules of their designated role. The child does not explicitly address these rules before or during the actual play but they are made visible through the way in which the child behaves. Considering the three aspects of Vygotskian play, Vygotsky considered imaginary, dramatic and make-believe play scenarios to be the most beneficial forms of play for development. During role-play, for example, the child takes a real object or situation, changes the meaning in their imagination and acts it out or uses it differently. Vygotsky (1933) described the child's use of a stick to represent a horse as an example of the child's first steps in severing meaning from the object. The stick acts as a pivot for the child to initially separate the meaning of horse from a real horse. In role-play, children develop abstract thought as they learn to separate meaning from objects. In role-play children also develop the skill of self-regulation. Play continually creates demands on the child to act against their immediate impulses. In role-play scenarios there are rules, and children act in accordance with these rules rather than their immediate impulses because when they follow the rules, play becomes more pleasurable for the child (Vygotsky, 1933). In the FS curriculum, drama opportunities should enable children to express their thoughts, ideas and feelings, develop their creativity and imagination, engage in dramatic play for learning and participate in drama games and strategies (CCEA, 2007).

REFLECTIVE QUESTIONS: THE ARTS

- An important aspect of art and design in the NI FS curriculum is that children are given 'TIME to explore, develop and explain their ideas'. Time is certainly of the essence in an EY classroom and finding adequate time for each and every child in a class of at least 30 is not an easy task. Consider ways in which The Arts might be given greater prominence in an EY classroom without overlooking the importance of the other Areas of Learning.
- Drama is considered to be an extension of young children's role-play. 'Vygotsky considered imaginary, dramatic and make-believe play scenarios to be the most beneficial form of play for development' (Doherty, 2013:33). Discuss how role-play and drama can be effectively employed in an EY classroom to promote all aspects of the FS curriculum.
- When we think about role-play in particular, our thoughts conjure up images of children taking on the role of mummy and daddy, the doctor or the dentist, the post person or the pilot. However, what, in your opinion, would the impact be on the learning experience if the teacher were to take on the role of someone else? View Drama in Maths on www.youtube.com/watch?v=GxDcr2Wx QQY and comment on the effectiveness of the adult adopting a different role.

The World Around Us

'The World Around Us' comprises geography, history, and science and technology. It is based on the premise of children's innate curiosity and the questions they have about themselves and about the environment and context where they live and learn. Sensory, experiential learning is the focus within this Area of Learning and teachers are encouraged to offer children experiences to promote independent learning where children construct their own knowledge. Based on constructivist theories of learning, enquiry-based teaching and learning is a strategy that allows the teacher to start with a question or problem and use children's ideas to solve this issue. Children plan, predict, experiment, explore, compare, carry out and review their work in the process. These skills are therefore developed continually within The World Around Us. There are four main strands to this Area of Learning: Interdependence, Place, Movement and Energy, and Change over time. Where possible, teaching and learning episodes should address the three curricular areas to present a more holistic experience.

An example of international practice that employs an innovative approach to teaching and learning science, geography and history is the Golden Key programme, based in Russia. These schools were formed based on the theories of Lev Vygotsky. In these schools, children from three to ten years are taught occasionally through role-play scenarios in mixed-age environments. These schools believe that children do not construct science generalisations or concepts until 12 or 13 years of age – as such the early years are vital to developing emergent skills and abilities. The Golden Key curriculum seeks to embed children in:

a) Space (or place) – When children start at the age of three, space is the first focus. They are 'oriented' first in a group space within the room, then in their own space within that group. They begin their exploration of space by working with the teachers to 'set up' the room (Kamen & Murphy, 2011). This continues until the children use maps to locate their village, town, province, country, continent and so on. Teachers support children's ongoing exploration of space by creating imaginary journeys connected to the playful events that serve as the core of the lesson. In participating in these events children practise skills of observation, communication, problem-solving and decision-making, and therefore build skills towards developing scientific, geographical and historic competency.

b) Time – Children are oriented within the concept of time by constructing timelines from the beginning of life, and then using these as a tool in subsequent classroom activities and investigations. For example, they can mark the times when dinosaurs roamed the earth, the discoveries of fire, the wheel, the solar system, electricity and the moon landings, etc. They can use the timeline to visualise life spans of large trees, humans and elephants, and to consider themselves in relation to older members of their family, ascendants and younger members (Kamen & Murphy, 2011).

c) Substance – In relation to the 'substance' concept, children use materials in different ways depending on their age. Early exploration of materials is important for speech development. As children get older they focus on manipulating a wide variety of materials and theorising on these experiences to arrive at logical explanations of phenomena (Kamen & Murphy, 2011).

d) Reflection – All children have partially formed scientific understandings – emerging concepts which become more complex as they get older (Kamen & Murphy, 2011).

Reflection allows children to discuss experiments with their classmates and share perspectives so as to develop and extend understanding.

The employment of these four themes resembles The World Around Us in NI, and provides teachers with ideas as to how to combine the geography, history, and science and technology elements effectively so that meaningful contexts for children are created.

REFLECTIVE QUESTIONS: THE WORLD AROUND US

- In the traditional NI curriculum geography, history, and science and technology were each considered as separate learning disciplines. In an effort to ensure a more connected learning experience, the FS curriculum has integrated these subject areas into one Area of Learning entitled The World Around Us. Reflect on the advantages and disadvantages of this decision on the quality of the young child's overall learning and development.
- Plan a range of learning experiences that allow these three curricular areas to be addressed simultaneously in a playful fashion. Consider the challenges involved in this planning process.
- In the traditional curriculum in NI science was not only a discrete subject area but was deemed as a core subject like English and mathematics and it was in these three subject areas that children were assessed at the end of Key Stage 1 and 2. Discuss the place of science in the new NI curriculum as part of the Area of Learning entitled The World Around Us. In your opinion should science deserve greater prominence or, from an EY perspective, is it better integrated into a connected Area of Learning to ensure a more cohesive and holistic experience for young children?
- The NI FS curriculum (CCEA, 2007) encourages teachers to offer children experiences to promote independent learning where children can construct their own knowledge. Discuss the challenges and opportunities that this may pose for young children's content knowledge and skill development.
- Reflect on the Golden Key programme and its relevance to teaching and learning within The World Around Us.
- Consider ways in which the pedagogy promoted in this Area of Learning might reflect aspects of the Montessori philosophy.

Personal Development and Mutual Understanding

This Area of Learning aims to enhance children's self-awareness, particularly in social and emotional terms. It is recognised in the FS that emotions are influential on the learning process and, as such, it is noted that children's awareness of their emotions and their ability to understand them is vital. Dispositions to learning and schooling develop at a young age so it is important for teachers to create an enjoyable and safe environment for learning, where children can express themselves, and their emotions, freely. Teachers should nurture children's motivation, perseverance, curiosity and creativity, and provide time for children to reflect on their learning and development so that they become more aware of themselves as learners. This also helps children to become aware of others, and of similarities and differences between individuals. Personal Development and Mutual Understanding (PDMU) is important for dealing with and attempting to remove any negative connotations or attitudes children may already hold in relation to other groups in their society. Its focus is ensuring that children respect themselves, and learn to respect others (CCEA, 2007). Tolerance and open-mindedness are key principles that teachers should seek to develop in children from the youngest age so that they learn to respect the differences in people and in communities. Strands within this Area of Learning include self-awareness, feelings and emotions, health and safety, relationships with families, and relationships in school and the community.

This Area of Learning is particularly relevant to the context of NI, a divided society, in terms of mutual understanding. Research in NI has highlighted the effect of this divided society on young children in schooling, for example Connolly (2009) presented anecdotal evidence of children playing at shooting games, re-enacting paramilitary-style funerals and striding around the playroom re-creating political marches. Children were playing and acting out activities they had observed in their society and culture through play, as a way of developing their understanding of them. Connolly's study (2009) suggested that by the ages of five and six, notable proportions of children in NI were explicitly recognising that they belonged to one community or the other and developing negative attitudes and prejudices on the basis of this. He also claimed that by the ages of three and four, children were already beginning to acquire and internalise the cultural preferences of their own communities. PDMU is invaluable as a strategy in dealing with these issues and building more positive images and relationships between the different communities.

REFLECTIVE QUESTIONS: PERSONAL DEVELOPMENT AND MUTUAL UNDERSTANDING

- NI suffers from a troubled past and even today research has shown that young children's social and emotional development has, in some cases, been impacted upon. This Area of Learning within the NI FS curriculum encourages teachers to promote tolerance and respect in young children in an effort to foster a more inclusive society. Consider some of the challenges that teachers may face, particularly from parents, when they try to deal with these issues in the classroom context.

- Strands within the PDMU Area of Learning include self-awareness, feelings and emotions, health and safety, relationships with families, and relationships in schools and the community. From your experience of working with young children do you feel it is important to tackle negative as well as positive emotions with children as young as four? If so, highlight appropriate ways that such feelings can be addressed in an EY classroom.

- The traditional curriculum in NI was deemed to be demotivating for young children, resulting in some children switching off learning much too soon. Think about the importance of promoting a learning experience for young children which is highly motivating and stimulating and discuss the impact that such an experience has on the overall learning and development of 4–6-year-old children.

Physical Development and Movement

'Physical Development and Movement' is an Area of Learning within the NI FS curriculum that influences children's overall well-being and long-term health. Children experience and develop 'a range of fundamental movement skills that enhance coordination, loco-motion, control, balance and manipulation' (CCEA, 2007:43). Physical activities can also promote emotional development as children gain confidence and self-esteem, whilst also feeling the benefits of being healthy and active. Social skills too are practised and developed as children take turns, share equipment and resources, and negotiate activities and games. Both fine and gross motor skills are developed in the FS not only through games, athletics, dance and gymnastics, but also through working with smaller-scale resources, such as peg boards, jigsaws, beads, play dough and clay.

The FS curriculum in NI places particular emphasis on the outdoors as a medium for developing children's physical skills in a fun way. An array of research evidence highlights the benefits of outdoor learning, not only for children's health and well-being benefits (Bird, 2007), but also for their holistic development in terms of knowledge and understand-ing, attitudes and feelings, values and beliefs, activities or behaviours and personal and social development (see e.g. Dillon et al., 2005; Murray & O'Brien, 2005; Nicol et al., 2007). However, recent evidence would suggest that in modern UK society many children's contact with the outdoors has been limited, as compared with their European counterparts, and that the vital experience of using the outdoors as an effective learning experience is being lost (Moss, 2012; RSPB, 2010).

NI's Education and Training Inspectorate (ETI, 2010) reports that out-of-classroom learning opportunities provide the learners with inspiring, sensory and memorable experiences that could bring the curriculum to life in an inclusive way and they recom-mend that schools should provide a range of opportunities for out-of-classroom learning.

Figure 2.4 Developing social skills in the outdoor environment.

**REFLECTIVE QUESTIONS: PHYSICAL DEVELOPMENT
AND MOVEMENT**

- The importance of young children's physical and emotional well-being has been prioritised from as early as the late nineteenth century by the McMillan sisters. Although the NI FS curriculum supports this position, like all other FS curricula throughout the UK, what challenges do teachers face in translating the rhetoric into reality?
- At present many schools in NI are becoming ECO schools, the aim of which is to foster greater environmental awareness and activity within the life and ethos of the school. Topics that are addressed include litter, waste, school grounds, energy, transport and healthy living, to name but a few. Choose one of these topics and plan a series of activities that would help promote young children's awareness of such an issue, ensuring effective integration with the Areas of Learning within the FS curriculum in NI.
- Identify the value of outdoor learning for young children's learning and development and consider ways in which getting outdoors and becoming closer to nature can endorse aspects of the NI FS curriculum.

The content of the NI FS curriculum: whole curriculum skills and capabilities

Alongside the Areas of Learning, the FS curriculum also highlights whole curriculum skills and capabilities to be infused into teaching and learning across the curriculum. Again, these skills and capabilities are relevant to progressing children's development, and to preparing them for subsequent stages of education and life.

Three cross-curricular skills are recognised:

- Communication;
- Using Mathematics; and
- Using Information and Communication Technology (ICT).

Figure 2.5 provides an overview of each of these skills as detailed in the FS curriculum (CCEA, 2007).

Schools are required to assess and report annually on each pupil's progress in each of the three cross-curricular skills. Levels of Progression frameworks have been designed to support teachers in leveling children's progress in each of the skill areas.

Although FS teachers are **not** required to assess using the Levels of Progression for Communication, Using Mathematics and Using ICT, they are required to report annually on each pupil's progress on each of the cross-curricular skills.

Five Thinking Skills and Personal Capabilities are also identified in the curriculum as skills that 'underpin success in all aspects of life' (CCEA, 2007:8). According to the curriculum, these should be fostered explicitly to develop children's self-management and interaction skills, alongside developing their cognition in relation to how they learn and how they can use knowledge. The Thinking Skills and Personal Capabilities are detailed more fully in Figure 2.6.

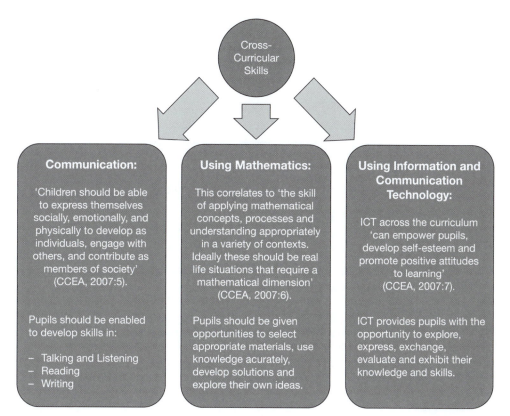

Figure 2.5 Cross-curricular skills in the NI curriculum.

A range of support materials have been designed and developed to support teachers in their efforts to deliver a more thinking curriculum in practice. These include posters, prompt sheets, case study exemplars and story books. Examples of these materials can be viewed on the NI curriculum website at www.nicurriculum.org.uk/TSPC/getting_started/foundation_stage/index.asp.

The three cross-curricular skills, and the five Thinking Skills and Personal Capabilities promote a holistic picture of development, where children will be developing all of these skills whilst also learning content and strategies within each Area of Learning. This aids in the vision of children too as holistic beings, who learn and develop in a multitude of ways undertaking various learning processes at any one time. In addition, the inclusion of play as pedagogy supports this holistic curriculum. Play develops the whole child. It is an end in itself (Piaget, 1962), and in contrast to non-play activities, the focus of play is on the means rather than on the ends. Children participate in play for the experience rather than working towards an outcome. As such, play is where young children learn how to learn. International practice, such as that in Montessori schools, in the Te Whāriki curriculum and in Golden Key schools (Russia), alongside research and theory in the field, highlight the need for play in EY education to ensure the all-round development of the young child. According to Hunter and Walsh (2014:22), 'the introduction of the FS curriculum signifies that EY policy in NI has moved in line with contemporary early childhood research; play is now viewed as pedagogy – "an art of teaching" which facilitates young children's learning and development.'

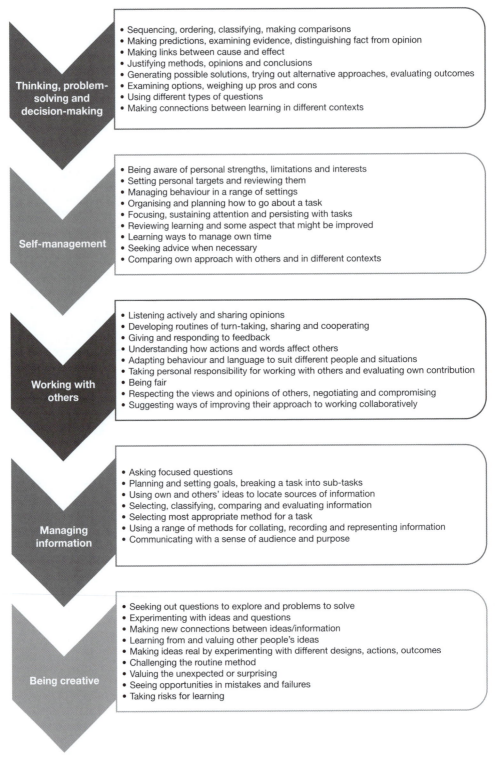

Figure 2.6 The Thinking Skills and Personal Capabilities Framework.

Source: adapted from CCEA (2007)

REFLECTIVE QUESTIONS: WHOLE CURRICULUM SKILLS AND CAPABILITIES

- Discuss ways in which you could develop the following in your classroom:

  - a thinking ethos;
  - a thinking environment.

- What teaching strategies might you use in order to promote thinking skills across the curriculum?
- If children were considered to be displaying high levels of thinking in a FS classroom, what actions in your opinion would the children be displaying? (Use the poster on the following website to enrich your discussions: www.ni curriculum.org.uk/TSPC/doc/getting_started/foundation/FS_thinking_skills_ poster.pdf.)
- Encouraging children to communicate, use mathematics and ICT across all of the Areas of Learning seems a somewhat daunting experience. The Level 1 descriptors for Talking and Listening within the cross-curricular skill include the following:

  - listen for information;
  - take on the role of someone else;
  - understand short explanations and simple discussions;
  - follow short, straightforward instructions;
  - ask and answer questions for specific information;
  - use vocabulary from within their experience to describe thoughts and feelings;
  - talk about their experiences;
  - speak audibly to be heard and understood;
  - make eye contact and take turns whilst engaging in conversation.

  Consider ways in which these skills might be fostered through the medium of play-based learning.

- Plan and discuss a playful activity that would encourage aspects of the cross-curricular skill 'Using Mathematics' to be developed for 4–6-year-old children. (To support your thinking view this website to provide detail on the descriptors associated with this cross-curricular skill for Levels 1 and 2: www.nicurriculum. org.uk/docs/skills_and_capabilities/cross_curricular_skills/new_levels/ UMaths/UMaths_levels1-5.pdf.)
- Reflect on ways 'Using ICT' might be infused into a play-based experience in a FS classroom. (See the following website for support: www.nicurriculum.org. uk/docs/skills_and_capabilities/cross_curricular_skills/new_levels/UICT/ UICT_levels_1-5.pdf.)

The content of the FS curriculum: assessment

Throughout the FS, teachers are noted as having a number of specific duties and responsibilities in the classroom. In addition to those mentioned previously (for example, developing a classroom environment conducive to learning, scaffolding learning and development

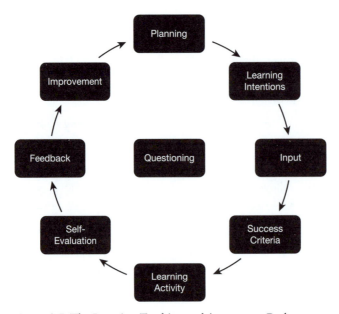

Figure 2.7 The Learning, Teaching and Assessment Cycle.
Source: adapted from CCEA (2012)

through interactions, and using children's previous experiences as starting points) teachers are encouraged to also engage in the 'Learning, Teaching and Assessment Cycle' (CCEA, 2012). This focuses on the interdependence of learning, teaching and assessment and the need for dialectical relationships between each of these so as to inform and develop best practice. Figure 2.7 displays this cycle more fully.

At the heart of the cycle is 'questioning'. According to the FS curriculum the FS classroom should reflect a culture of open communication so that questioning by both adults and children is promoted. Questioning by adults enables the collection of information to inform the Learning, Teaching and Assessment Cycle. Through initial questioning teachers can identify the interests and needs of the children, and can decipher their current stage of development, based on their previous experiences. This feeds into the planning process where teachers develop long-, medium- and short-term plans so as to provide a broad range of experiences for children that are developmentally appropriate, engaging and interesting. Teachers' plans should also involve children's input, and they should be flexible to ongoing assessment.

During teaching and learning in the FS, teachers will assess through observation (predominantly) although assessment strategies are open to the direction of the specific teacher. Observations can be made throughout the school day in different activities and contexts, and can create a comprehensive picture of each individual child. Observations are valuable for assessment *of* learning (summative) and in assessment *for* learning (formative). In summative assessment, observations can confirm what the child has already learned, and what they can now achieve. In contrast, in formative assessment, observations make the process of learning visible – learning is observed as it is happening.

Assessment for Learning (AfL) is a prominent area within the FS curriculum. According to CCEA (2012), AfL has four predominant key elements:

- focus on learning
- effective questioning
- formative feedback
- scaffolding reflection.

With a focus on learning, the learning intentions and success criteria of a lesson or activity are shared with the children. Children are therefore immediately active participants in the teaching and learning process. As children engage in the activity and with the teacher, effective questioning by the adult aids in assessment information being gleaned, but also allows the adult to clarify and, in some cases, extend the child's thinking. When teachers model effective questioning, children can also become questioners, developing their language skills and also becoming increasingly active in the learning process. Formative feedback is usually oral in the FS and it should give children information on their performance, as well as information on how they can improve or enhance their work. Finally, reflection provides children with the opportunity to think about what and how they learn. Peer- and self-evaluation are effective strategies in offering children opportunities to discuss their learning, share their understandings and see their mistakes as learning opportunities (CCEA, 2012).

Overall, assessment, in general, is viewed as an integral part of the learning process rather than the end-point. Children should be actively engaged in the process, and their learning should be challenged, as well as supported; teachers should have high expectations of children; and there should be a two-way flow of information with parents/carers. The information gleaned from assessment should directly inform planning and the reflective teacher uses this information to tailor their plans more accurately to their specific class. The cycle continues.

Despite assessment at the FS being non-statutory, the curriculum emphasises the value of assessment for developing a whole-school approach, whilst also recognising assessment as good practice. It is recommended that assessment at the FS is based on the Areas of Learning, but also on the three cross-curricular skills: Communication, Using Mathematics and Using ICT. There is no uniform type of assessment at the FS, but CCEA (2012) recommends that teachers use Developmental Stages in learning grids. These show potential steps of development children in the FS may take towards Level 1 of the statutory Levels of Progression, and can provide direction as to the types of activities and observations teachers can employ in assessment.

An AfL guide (CCEA, 2009) is available online for FS teachers in NI with examples of good practice. One such example of good practice is providing feedback. The advice given to practitioners is as follows:

1. Highlight success: find two or three successes referring to the learning intention or success criteria.

2. Identify an area for improvement: find something that could be improved (not always the worst part!).

3. Give an improvement suggestion: write a prompt that will help the learner make the improvement. Bear in mind that three levels of prompt can be used: Reminder: reminding the pupils of the learning intention/success criteria; – Scaffold: giving examples of what they could do or asking focused questions; and – Example: giving the pupil concrete examples or suggestions that they can use.

4. Give time: give the pupil an opportunity to read the improvement and make the changes.

Questioning

'I started quality marking with just one group of children at a time. I'm now in the way of writing prompts, and children are getting used to feedback from their talk partner, so it doesn't take so long.' (Teacher)

This booklet is entitled 'Assessment for Learning: A Practical Guide' and is available at the following link with further suggestions for practice: www.nicurriculum.org.uk.

REFLECTIVE QUESTIONS: ASSESSMENT

- Many FS teachers use acronyms such as WALT – 'We are learning to' and WILF – 'What I am looking for' to share learning intentions with young children. Discuss creative ways in which learning intentions can be shared with young children.
- Consider the importance of sharing learning intentions with young children. What advantages might this have for their overall learning and development?
- Observing and questioning are the principal ways in which young children are assessed in the FS. After completing a topic on, for example, 'Healthy Eating', what questions might you pose and what observations might you make to capture the learning that has taken place?
- Reflect on creative ways in which feedback can be provided to young children to ensure that the experience is both positive and worthwhile.
- Consider the importance of the teacher frequently reflecting on the learning and teaching available in the FS classroom. How might such reflections enhance the overall quality of the learning and teaching experience provided?

The FS curriculum in practice: challenges and tensions

The introduction of the FS in 2007, and its refinement since this date, 'marks a seismic shift in thinking within NI and stands in stark contrast to previous traditional curricula that emphasised knowledge acquisition and teacher-directed models' (Hunter & Walsh, 2014:21). However, with these advantages and leaps forward, a number of challenges and tensions have presented themselves over the past seven years. Based on evidence from classrooms, these challenges and tensions relate to the place of play in education, pedagogical issues in relation to play, promoting thinking skills through play, and also wider school issues such as transitions. This sections aims to explain the emergence of these challenges, and provide examples of each, in practice.

Place of play in education

In the past ten years EY education has been a growing priority on government agendas around the world (OECD, 2006). As research has evidenced, the country that invests in effective EY provision can benefit economically, socially and educationally (Hunter & Walsh, 2014) as well as morally (DfE, 2011). As a result, EY provision is constantly being revised and refined by educators, researchers and policy-makers who strive to identify new practical approaches, and theoretical constructs to improve their contribution to the EY field (Doherty, 2013). Much research indicates that too-formal a pedagogical approach is inappropriate for young children (Alexander, 2009; Bennett, 2005; Wylie & Hodgen, 2007) with a revived focus on the value and principles of play-based pedagogies. In actuality, some research has identified play and learning as inseparable domains in the early years of a child's development (Johansson & Pramling Samuelsson, 2006). In many countries this has caused a change to their policy contexts in relation to play. In the UK and Ireland, for example, this has manifested in the introduction of specific stages of education; the Foundation Phase in Wales, 3–7-year-olds (Welsh Assembly Government, 2008); the Early Years Foundation Stage in England, 0–5-year-olds (DfE, 2012); the Foundation Stage in Northern Ireland, 4–6-year-olds (CCEA, 2007); a Curriculum for Excellence in Scotland for 3–18-year-olds (Learning and Teaching Scotland, 2010); and Aistear: the Early Childhood Curriculum Framework in the Republic of Ireland (NCCA, 2009). According to Hunter and Walsh (2014), this development moves the UK and Ireland in line with their international counterparts as they recognise the value in articulating the specific needs and interests of the young child.

However, despite the changes in policy, EY practitioners around the globe today face the dilemma of allowing young children time to play, or teaching academic skills (Bodrova & Leong, 2007). Teachers are under pressure to deliver academically based curricula and as a result play can be disregarded or used in ways that compromise its value as a developmental activity. Bodrova and Leong (2012:34) criticised the use of play in many modern classrooms:

> Mature make-believe play is an important and unique context, providing opportunities to learn not afforded by other classroom activities. It should not be considered something extra that can be cut to accommodate more time for academic skills, nor should it be used as a means of adding 'entertainment value' for inherently boring and decontextualized drills.

As a result of the academic foundation inherent in many EY classrooms, play, too often, is used for purposes other than development and learning, and as a result, its value is lost or degraded. Bodrova and Leong (2007) and Kravtsov and Kravtsova (2010) criticised the supposed dichotomy between play and learning. They explained that play and education are not at odds with each other. Play does not prevent realistic learning but in actuality it contributes to it (Fromberg, 2002). In valuing play as developmental, Zaporozhets criticised the 'schoolification' process (OECD, 2006:62) that occurs in many EY settings as academically based curricula and activities are employed to further children's intellectual and academic abilities, rather than allowing time for children to participate in play, the activity which he claimed is more suited to their developmental stage.

In NI, where play is now the pedagogy of the FS, teachers too share, it appears, the outlook that play is appropriate for young children's learning and development, and therefore, that it has an essential position in education. The earliest research in this area by Walsh (2000) discovered that teachers did not value play, and were sceptical of having play in the curriculum. In 2006, research by Sproule et al., and by Walsh and Gardner, displayed a change in that teachers then accepted the emotional, social and dispositional elements of play, what Hunter and Walsh termed 'the mother and apple pie' benefits of play (2014:31). Teachers still, however, held their concerns about the academic value of play for learning at this stage. The most recent research (Hunter & Walsh, 2014) demonstrates a major development in teachers' views of play in EY education. The majority of FS teachers in 2014 appear to have embraced, and endorse play in education, as stipulated by the FS curriculum. Hunter and Walsh (2014) suggest that some Year 2 teachers are less disposed than their Year 1 counterparts, but on the whole FS teachers accept and value play at the heart of the FS classroom. However, the interpretation of play in practice reveals a more complex and pessimistic picture of play as learning. Evidence from the classroom suggests that FS teachers still struggle with the concept of playful learning per se and knowing how to infuse playfulness into learning and learning into play is something on which teachers require further training and professional development (Hunter & Walsh, 2014; Walsh et al., 2011).

Pedagogical issues in play

Despite the general acceptance of play as pedagogy by FS teachers in NI, and its inclusion in policy, the interpretation of play in practice reveals cracks and flaws. This may stem from uncertainty and differences in opinion as to what actually constitutes high quality play. Stephen (2012) stresses the range of ongoing debates about play within EY education, for example play being either the way of learning, or one way of learning; being either a rule-bound activity or a child-directed activity; and being either a structured activity or a spontaneous activity. These conflicting and varied views of play owe to the uncertainty held by FS teachers. With no 'extensive elaboration of what play as learning and play as pedagogy mean for the EY of primary schooling' (Hunter & Walsh, 2014:33), NI teachers are left to build their own subjective constructions of play in education. As a consequence, play has become widely varied across FS classrooms.

   Hunter and Walsh (2014) identified constraints in relation to the practice of play provision, adults' roles, parents' perceptions and top-down pressures: altogether affecting the 'frequency, duration and quality' of play in practice (Wood, 2004:21). In NI, observations completed by Hunter and Walsh (2014) in FS classrooms suggested that the predominant constraints for teachers were as follows:

*   lack of training and skills for planning play
*   interactions in play
*   progression in play.

A four-day period of training was offered to FS teachers upon the introduction of the FS curriculum, with one day specifically focused on play. Further guidance about play was made available in a booklet entitled 'Understanding the Foundation Stage' (CCEA, 2006), while some Education and Library Boards offered additional support through cluster group meetings. This limited period of training does not now appear sufficient in developing teachers' understandings of play. Hunter and Walsh's (2014:32) observations of FS classrooms indicated that there was 'somewhat impoverished and mundane play-based activity, particularly in Year 2 classes'. They acknowledged that teachers recognised the value of play but also identified that they lacked 'the skills needed to provide quality play experiences and that their efforts [were] mainly "tokenistic" in nature.' A major aspect of play in which FS teachers demonstrated apprehension was in relation to interactions i.e. when they should intervene and be play participants, and when they should let children play alone. This is supported by Hunter and Walsh's (2014) small scale study as evidenced by the following data: when FS teachers were posed with the statement 'during play, the teacher should always be interacting with the children', it resulted in an ambiguous response, with 45 per cent of the respondents agreeing (n=70), 50 per cent (n=78) disagreeing and 4 per cent (n=7) being unsure. There was no clear consensus among FS teachers in relation to adults actually being involved in play. In addition, when posed with the statement 'during play all interaction with the teacher helps children learn', 41 per cent (n=63) agreed, 37 per cent (n=58) disagreed and a sizeable proportion (22 per cent, n=34) were unsure. Again, there was no clear consensus among FS teachers about the value of their interactions with children for learning. This suggested that teachers were not aware of the learning potential in their interactions within play and were unsure of how, when and in what way they should be participants in children's play. The FS curriculum states that EY practitioners should 'interact effectively to challenge children's thinking and learning' (CCEA, 2007:16), but as identified through research, this has not translated well into practice. The concept of challenging and extending children's play, too, has proved more difficult in practice than in theory. Hunter and Walsh (2014:32) described play activities as 'mundane' particularly in Year 2 classrooms. From their observations of classrooms it was noted that higher levels of challenge and extension were not always evident and the teacher's perspective of play appeared to differ between the two classes. This introduces questions in relation to the transition from Year 1 and 2, but also about the transition from FS into Key Stage One. What pressures or issues does play introduce for Year 2 teachers who are preparing young children for Key Stage One?

Transitions

The FS comprises Year 1 and 2 of formal schooling. As such there are two transitions for FS children:

1.   Preschool to Year 1
2.   Year 2 to Key Stage One.

An EY curriculum that ensures continuity and progression across these transitions is beneficial for child development. When children experience an EY education with smooth, seamless transitions where similar teaching approaches and activities are employed to extend the child's abilities in a continuous manner, EY education is more effective (Doherty, 2013). Children's experience of education and their progression through it will be more harmonious and children will be more able to construct a solid learning foundational base.

Throughout the FS curriculum (CCEA, 2007), the transition from preschool to Year 1 is acknowledged. FS teachers should value and use children's preschool experiences as starting points for further development. The curriculum promotes flexibility for teachers in following children's interests within their teaching and, as such, these transitions may be eased in this way. However, without any uniform preschool provision in NI, this suggestion for practice becomes less effective. Children come from nursery schools, day care centres, and some directly from the home setting, meaning that teachers have a wide variety of previous experiences to recognise, and from which to build. These initial transitions from preschool to primary school can be viewed as opportunities for families and the education system to work together to build children's dispositions to engage with change, whilst sustaining their capacities to learn (Fabian & Dunlop, 2005). Margetts (2000) noted that transition programmes should be based on a philosophy that children's adjustment to school is easier when children are familiar with the situation, parents are informed about the new school and teachers have information about children's development and previous experiences. Therefore, interaction between the various participant groups involved in children's learning contexts is vital. Fabian and Dunlop (2005) suggested the employment of play-based transitional activities that create links between, and actively involve, children, parents, families, teachers, early childhood services, schools and the local community. Play's position in the FS is in line with theory in this respect.

The second transition FS children experience is from Year 2 into Year 3 (from FS into Key Stage One). There is little reference to this transition in the curricular documentation. Evidence from practice, however, indicates that this transition is as influential as the initial transition into the FS. A study by Walsh et al. (2008) collated child and teacher perspectives of transition from the FS into Key Stage One. Through interviews with children, prior to the transition, the research identified that children, in general, look forward to Year 3, and noted that they would feel more grown up, and the physical environment would be different:

"I can't wait for the big hard questions."
"You don't have to do baby things any more in P3, like having to colour-in all day."
"The classroom is much bigger."
"You get sitting at big tables."

In relation to issues the children identified as making them feel nervous about Year 3, responses focused on the ideas of hard work, friends and teachers:

"In P3 you have to write, write, write and my hand might get sore."
"If I sit at a different table next year, then J and S will not be my friends."
"In P3 the teacher will not allow you to talk or play."
"My friend K told me that when you move up the stairs the teachers don't smile any more."

In interviews with children in Year 3, it was noted by Walsh et al. (2008) that children valued friendships during the transition, and they welcomed playful and more challenging learning experiences, but disapproved of too much writing. The teaching approaches and the social environment therefore can be modified by teachers so as to aid in the transition from FS into Key Stage One.

In terms of teachers' views on this transition it was discovered by Walsh et al. (2008) that continuous pedagogies should be employed in Year 3 in the form of activity-based learning to support children and provide time for them to adjust to the more formal approaches in Year 3. Teachers highlighted, however, that pressures in relation to performance may affect the frequency of these continuous pedagogies being employed, and teachers of older classes, and parents, were identified as potential sources of these pressures. Teachers called for further training and support in relation to the transition from FS to Key Stage One.

Translating thinking skills into a play-based curriculum

Thinking, described as the way in which people apply their minds to solving problems and in general to make sense of their learning (Fisher, 2006), is recognised as the process that culminates in an improvement in one's intellectual powers (Venville et al., 2003). The recent and growing interest in 'thinking skills' within curriculum documentation is grounded in the belief that the development of thinking skills supports children's cognitive and intellectual development, draws attention to the process, not the product, of learning, supporting children's efforts to engage with learning, emphasising active rather than passive participation (White, 2013). In addition, according to White (2013), thinking skills support the development of positive learning dispositions and habits of learning that will encourage children to function under conditions of complexity and uncertainty, and equip them with a toolkit for learning required for everyday life.

In the early years of education, a play-based experience is perceived as supporting the development of thinking skills in young children, providing them with opportunities to engage in a variety of creative and open-ended experiences (Taggart et al., 2005; Walsh et al., 2007). So it would seem in terms of fostering thinking skills in young children that the FS curriculum has been moving in the right direction by prioritising a playful learning experience.

However, evidence from the NI classroom paints a somewhat grim picture of teachers' knowledge and understanding about how thinking skills can be effectively infused into a play-based experience. The observations conducted for the purpose of the Early Years Enriched Curriculum evaluation in approximately 110 Year 1 and 2 classes revealed that one key indicator of the Quality Learning Instrument (Walsh & Gardner, 2005) stood out as somewhat different to the rest, i.e. Higher Order Thinking Skills (HOTS), an indicator which addresses more cognitive behaviours such as problem-solving, logical reasoning, creativity and reflection (Walsh et al., 2006; Walsh et al., 2010). In both the Year 1 and Year 2 EC classes, the HOTS mean score was the lowest of all the nine quality indicators. To make matters worse, the HOTS score in the Year 2 classes tended to be lower, in the main, than that of the Year 1 classes, suggesting that even less problem-solving, decision-making and logical reasoning were being promoted in these classes (Walsh et al., 2010).

Such evidence is supported by more recent findings from Hunter and Walsh (2014) in NI FS classes – again the score for HOTS and Multiple Skills Acquisition (an indicator which focuses on a range of skills being addressed to ensure the delivery of a broad and balanced curriculum) in both Year 1 and Year 2 being much lower than all of the other quality indicators, namely: motivation, concentration, confidence, well-being, independence, respect and social interaction.

Unfortunately the expectation that any form of play and more practical activity, irrespective of its quality, will guarantee greater opportunities for children to enhance their overall powers of thinking has not been realised in practice, leading to the assumption that some FS teachers in NI need more help and support in translating policy into practice. Complex and high-level play as a medium to develop children's cognitive powers of thinking and creativity does not appear to be fully understood (Hunter & Walsh, 2014). Such findings are reflective of the challenges and difficulties that EY teachers have in general when attempting to provide a playful learning experience that is rich in opportunities and challenges (Hunter & Walsh, 2014).

REFLECTIVE QUESTIONS: THE FS CURRICULUM IN PRACTICE: CHALLENGES AND TENSIONS

- Ensuring a learning experience that is highly motivating and challenging for young children, but still ensures that children are developing academically, is highly problematic in practice. Reflecting on what you have read in this section of the chapter and beyond, identify what you consider to be the main stumbling blocks for FS teachers.
- In your opinion, discuss how such challenges might be overcome in practice.

- Knowing when to intervene in children's play and when not to poses difficulties for many FS teachers. Discuss the role of observations in supporting effective teacher–child interactions in a play-based environment.
- Identify a range of roles that FS teachers can put into practice in a play-based experience. Do you think there is still a place for a form of 'teaching' on the part of the adult in a playful learning environment?
- Building on children's interests is integral to ensuring a positive learning experience for young children. How, in your opinion, can this be managed in a busy EY classroom, whilst still ensuring that curriculum content is appropriately addressed and understood?
- Drawing on your own experience of EY classrooms in primary schools, debate how you believe positive transitions throughout the school can be effectively nurtured.

Supporting a play-based experience in the FS: some practical suggestions

In this section of the chapter some practical advice, gleaned from research evidence and classroom experience, will be offered to support both practising teachers and students in their delivery of the FS in a NI context. In an effort to make this advice as accessible to the reader as possible, a series of vignettes, drawn directly from FS classes, will be explored and examined, and a reflective commentary and some professional practice tasks will be included.

Place of play in education

CAMEO EVIDENCE

As the children enter the classroom the smell of chocolate is evident and the sounds of 'Willy Wonka and the Chocolate Factory' are playing in the background.

The Year 2 children are all extremely engaged in an array of playful learning experiences. Some are engrossed in the sand tray filled with coco pops searching for 1p and 2p coins using large tweezers in an effort to make up the required sum specified in a selection of 'money pots'. Others are busy using melted milk and white chocolate to paint pictures of their choice. A small group is working with the classroom assistant making chocolate dough, while a boy and girl are working together in an effort to design a chocolate bar wrapper for Mr Wonka using the Paint program on the computer. There is much constructive noise and excitement coming from the corridor where children are using large cardboard boxes, measuring tapes, rulers and masking tape to design a large 3D model of 'Charlie's Chocolate factory'. After a very busy morning some children are found relaxing in 'Wonka's Chocolate Café', where there are chocolate themed menus, chocolate scented candles and a very enthusiastic waiter who is taking orders and collaborating appropriately with the chef who would certainly give Mary Berry a run for her money.

Figure 2.8 Painting with chocolate.

Figure 2.9 Incorporating children's ideas onto the planning board.

REFLECTIVE COMMENTARY

The above displays how learning is effectively being infused into the playful activities, using a theme which is relevant and of interest to the age group of children involved. Several Areas of Learning are being addressed in a relaxed and integrated fashion:

- **PDMU** – Children are working together effectively and they are displaying high levels of motivation, concentration, confidence and well-being.
- **The Arts** – Children are designing and creating pictures using chocolate and models using cardboard. They are also becoming familiar with the Willy Wonka music.
- **Language and Literacy** – Children are engrossed in using their imagination in the café and the Chocolate factory, talking and listening and using their fine

motor skills when painting, using the tweezers and making and moulding the dough. The Charlie and the Chocolate factory story is also being explored and examined.

- **Mathematics and Numeracy** – Children are using the 1p and 2p coins to make up amounts of money, investigating and problem-solving in the factory.
- **The World Around Us** – Children are exploring the properties of chocolate and the origins of the Charlie and the Chocolate, factory story. In their exploration of the theme of chocolate, details about where chocolate comes from and information on Fairtrade could also be explored and examined.
- **ICT** – Children are using the painting tools on the Paint program and in so doing they are also learning how to change the background colour and to develop mouse control when using the computer.

PROFESSIONAL PRACTICE TASKS

Using a theme to plan play is valuable in providing a holistic learning experience, in a fun and connected way. Other themes can be developed based on stories, songs or times of the year:

- 'The Princess and the Pea' offers huge scope around which to develop play activities, including role-play, science investigations, literacy opportunities, mathematical counting and measuring activities.
- 'Twinkle, Twinkle Little Star' affords the teacher the opportunity to introduce Space and the Stars, planning play that allows children to become astronauts, build rockets and use real maps to look at constellations in the sky.
- At Halloween play can include witches potions in the water tray, building haunted houses in the junk art area and writing spells at the literacy table.

Note that the employment of a theme in this way can also connect and extend learning in Key Stage One and Two – what themes can you think of to suit these older age groups?

Pedagogical issues in play

CAMEO EVIDENCE

It's a cold December morning and the children have been told that they will be getting a very special visitor. The teacher enters the classroom dressed as an elf – she is in fact 'SuperElf' and Santa has sent SuperElf to this classroom with an audio message. The message is loaded onto the interactive whiteboard and the children hear Santa explaining that his elves are all very sick and that he needs their help to design and make toys for all the children on Christmas morning. He asks that children follow SuperElf's instructions. The children are hooked. SuperElf now takes to the stage and produces a bag full of elf hats and ears for the children, who now have to become Santa's elves. The children giggle with enthusiasm and chatter excitedly as SuperElf explains their first task. Today the children will be designing and making teddy bears. The children are placed into groups and are given the task of drawing their plans for their teddy bear. The children begin discussing shape, size and features of their teddy and draw their ideas to show to the rest of the class. Next, SuperElf produces brown felt which the children then cut into the shape of their planned teddy, and draw on the planned features. The 'health and safety elf' then takes each group and irons the felt pieces together so children's teddy bears are now 3D. SuperElf gives each group a different material with which to stuff their teddy bear; these include marbles, lego blocks, cotton wool and foam. When the teddy bears have been stuffed and sealed the children then come to the 'workshop' floor to observe each group's teddy. The children then individually feel each teddy bear and vote for the teddy bear they think is the best prototype which Santa can then mass-produce. SuperElf congratulates the children on their hard work, tells the children she will take the information to Santa and the children then remove their elf hats and ears. Upon their return to becoming Year 2 children, the noise levels rise.

Figure 2.10 SuperElf working with Santa's helpers.

Figure 2.11 A child-led planning board.

REFLECTIVE COMMENTARY

The teacher in this scenario became a play participant, as she took on the role of 'SuperElf'. She used 'Santa' to provide the context and in so doing relinquished the power in the classroom to Santa. However, she used Santa effectively to ensure that children still viewed her as an authority figure and emphasised her close relationship with Santa as a mode of behaviour management. The play scenario she developed was real to the children and through the use of dress-up props, children acted 'a head taller' (Vygotsky, 1978). Every person in the classroom had a role to take on – one classroom assistant who was very worried about the iron in the classroom became known as the 'health and safety elf'. This meant that children and adults were totally involved in the classroom (which became known as the workshop). As children removed their hats and ears it was noted that behaviour management was not as easy, and noise levels rose. Children, through their participation in the playful scenario, were doing science and technology, and art and design, and were using thinking skills to plan, predict, explore, design, create, make decisions and engage in fair testing. SuperElf returned to the classroom once per week with a new fair testing activity, with children also producing spinners and wind-powered boats. In these sessions children made their prototypes individually and did so when SuperElf called them to do their 'shift'. When it was not their shift the children were engaged in other play activities such as the role-play corner which was where broken toys were fixed, the computer corner where they made Christmas cards and the writing table where they compiled the naughty and nice lists, read children's wish lists and composed order sheets for what toys needed to be made.

PROFESSIONAL PRACTICE TASKS

Consider the value in developing a role-play scenario to act as the foundation to your play sessions.

- What roles can the children take on? How does the teacher adopting the role of player impact on the learning experience?
- How would you ensure that the teacher maintains control despite being a player with the children?
- What is the learning content and how does the role-play deliver this content?

Transitions

CAMEO EVIDENCE

In Mrs J.'s 'family' there are children from preschool, children from Year 1 and children from Year 2. Mrs J. has welcomed the children to their 'family time' and reads a story, and actively engages the children in some songs and rhymes. She explains to the children the play activities that are available today, and reminds children to play with everyone and ensure that no-one is left out. The children have free choice in deciding where and with whom to play. Around the room the older and younger children play together – in the book corner a Year 2 child is reading a story to two preschool girls. In the sand tray a Year 1 child is crying due to someone flicking the sand – a Year 2 child is cleaning her nose and soothing her cries, whilst also verbally disciplining the child who flicked the sand. The adults move around the room engaging in play activities as players and children interact as they wish. At the end of the play session Mrs J. brings the children back to the carpet and highlights examples of good play, identifying specific examples of mixed-age play. Three other mixed-age families are in different rooms in the school, offering similar activities based on the common theme.

REFLECTIVE COMMENTARY

Through the creation of mixed-age families, children aged 3–6 years participate in play scenarios with a wider range of ages and developmental stages than usual. Play activities are open to progression and children play at their developmental stage. Broader age groups suit children who have capabilities atypical of average children at their developmental stage, as well as the 'average child'. There are models of children's future development present in their environment. As such, children are aware of what a preschool child, what a Year 1 child and what a Year 2 child 'looks like'. Mixed-age play provides opportunities for children to experience smoother transitions between classes. It allows staff to better prepare for transition periods as they interact with children from various age groups and form relationships with them prior to their actual teaching of them. Mixed-age play reduces the length of time children require to become accustomed to new classroom environments and new class teachers during transition periods. Children experience interactions with a wider staff and with a wider circle of peers from different classes. This encourages their social interaction and consequently reduces the fear of moving from one class to another. The use of the term 'family' also encourages social cohesion as children (as evidenced) cared and nurtured one another whilst exhibiting behaviours that were perhaps reflective of caring for a younger brother or sister.

PROFESSIONAL PRACTICE TASKS

Changing the play environment, for example through making it mixed-age, can aid in transition issues as children become more aware of subsequent classes, teachers and routines.

- How could you modify your play environment to support transition?
- What specific features encourage a smoother transition?

Infusing thinking skills into a playful learning experience

CAMEO EVIDENCE

On returning from the lunch break the FS teacher enters the classroom, in the role of what appears to be a princess. She immediately discloses to the children that she is My Fair Lady and that she and Humpty Dumpty have been organising a party to take place next to London Bridge for her birthday. She explains that she is in very bad form because Humpty contacted her over the lunch break to advise that the party would have to be cancelled as London Bridge had fallen down. She explains to the children how she immediately thought of her helpful friends at her local primary school and that is why she is here this afternoon because she knows they can help her out. After assigning the children to different groups, the teacher (i.e. My Fair Lady) explains that she needs each group to work together to create a plan of action as to how London Bridge can be quickly and safely built up again and when they have these different ideas in place she will invite Humpty in and they can share their ideas with him. They then will all work together to test out whose plans might work best. My Fair Lady then leaves the classroom and the teacher immediately reenters no longer in the role of My Fair Lady to support the children throughout the activity, interacting with the children and offering suggestions when appropriate. The children are ecstatic and immediately set to task, working as a team and engaging in a process of problem-solving and logical reasoning to determine a possible outcome from an array of random resources that are available to them. Ideas include building the bridge up again with sand and water in the sand tray; recreating the bridge using straws and plasticine; another group suggests using construction materials such as lego; baking materials such as marshmallows, spaghetti and dough are also recommended; and levelling the bridge and recreating a tunnel using tubing is also offered as an idea. Creating a ladder from string and rope is also put forward as an idea as well as calling upon the help of Spiderman to create a web and get them across. Humpty (the school caretaker) and My Fair Lady (the teacher back in role) are delighted with all of the suggestions but after much deliberation and testing of the ideas in practice there is a general consensus of opinion that the latter suggestion is the most creative and perhaps the most realistic.

REFLECTIVE COMMENTARY

Through adopting the role of another character (i.e. My Fair Lady) and creating an open-ended and collaborative task, the teacher in this cameo immediately develops an ethos which is friendly, relaxed, motivating and encouraging and by seeking the help of the children from the outset, the power dynamics of the classroom context are immediately changed. By involving the children in this open-ended and imaginative task, the children are encouraged to express their ideas freely, make suggestions, ask questions of each other, solve problems, be creative, use their imagination, make connections, provide options and reasons, make decisions and build on each other's ideas and suggestions. In this way an amalgam of thinking skills are being nurtured in young children in a natural and playful context.

PROFESSIONAL PRACTICE TASKS

Think about the importance of injecting a degree of ambiguity into the play experience and consider the impact it might have on the development of children's overall thinking:

- Children are role-playing planning for a party outside and you tell them that a storm has broken out. Encourage the children to talk about possible ways to deal with this.
- Remove any painting utensils from the painting area and urge the children to think of how they might paint a picture.
- The children are playing in a café and you tell them that the electricity has just been switched off. How will they cater for their customers?

Future directions for the FS curriculum in NI

Since 2007, and the introduction of the FS, different perspectives and ways of implementing this curriculum have emerged. This chapter has explored the challenges and issues associated with its implementation, and has provided examples of best practice where these challenges have been eased. As the FS continues to be translated into practice, there have been some recent changes in the NI context, which might impact on its future direction. The following three areas describe the changes, and indicate some potential directions for the future of the FS:

- The 'Learning to Learn Framework' (DENI, 2012) – In 2010 the 'Early Years Draft Strategy' (DENI, 2010) was published to present a more 'joined up' image of EY provision (0–6 years) in NI. In 2012 this document was modified following responses by the EY community and was published as the 'Learning to Learn Framework'. An interesting development in relation to the FS explains that the preschool year will now also be included in the FS. In this way the FS will now embrace EY education for children aged 3–6 years, a new EY context for NI.
- Support for FS teachers – The Chief Inspector's Report (2010–2012) has clearly articulated that the FS phase is an area which requires some attention, noting that: 'Planning and teaching in the FS must take greater cognisance of each child's ability and stage of development' (ETI, 2012:48). In addition the overarching aim of the 'Learning to Learn Framework' (DENI, 2012) is to ensure that all children have opportunities to achieve their potential through high quality EY education and learning experiences. A key objective of this endeavour is to support personal, social and emotional development, promote positive learning dispositions and enhance language, cognitive and physical development in young children, through providing a positive and nurturing early learning experience, as well as a foundation for improved educational attainment and life-long learning. Supporting FS teachers in their effort to provide such a high quality learning experience though appropriate continuing professional development courses provided in Learning Clusters is key to the 'Learning to Learn Framework', where a cross-phase and cross-sector approach is being encouraged and better links fostered to ensure that experiences in primary school build more effectively on the children's previous education and learning. This political recognition to support teachers in their efforts to deliver play as pedagogy marks a positive step forward for EY education in a NI context.
- A 'family pedagogy' in the EY – A research project completed in an NI school where play practices were developed and enhanced following the translation of Vygotsky's theory into practice identified a new theoretical construct for EY education; a 'family pedagogy' (Doherty, 2013). Working with children aged 3–6 years in a primary school with a preschool onsite, the study involved teachers, parents, the children and the researcher collaboratively developing an Integrated Play Programme (IPP), in which play was integrated across age groups and across learning contexts. Children were arranged in mixed-age 'families' and parents employed play practices at home, so that the concept of 'family' was extended to include the school as well as the home. From the implementation and development of this IPP, the value of the 'family' concept in the early years proved extremely valuable. The family pedagogy linked preschool, the FS and the home, and teachers became more like parents, and parents more like teachers. The family pedagogy resulted in the social development of individuals, in enhanced social cohesion, and in the promotion of play as developmental for young children. The family pedagogy is in line with the 'Learning to Learn Framework' (DENI, 2012) in terms of the inclusion of a preschool year. In the research, school transitions became seamless and smooth, and children were excited about the prospect of their 'family' play in school. The family pedagogy provides a potential new direction for EY provision in NI.

References

Alexander, R. (2009) *Children, Their World, Their Education: Final Report and Recommendations of the Cambridge Primary Review*. London: Routledge.

Bennett, J. (2005) Curriculum Issues in National Policy-Making. *European Early Childhood Education Research Journal*, 13(2): 5–23.

Bird, W. (2007) *Natural Thinking: Investigating the Links Between the Natural Environment, Biodiversity, and Mental Health*. Sandy, Bedfordshire: RSPB.

Bodrova, E. & Leong, D. (2007) Playing for Academic Skills. *Children in Europe: Exploring Issues, Celebrating Diversity*, Vygotsky Issue: 10–11.

Bodrova, E. & Leong, D. (2012) Assessing and Scaffolding Make-Believe Play. *Young Children*, January: 28–34.

Bruner, J. (1978) The Role of Dialogue in Language Acquisition. In: Sinclair, A., Jarvelle, J. & Levelt, W.J.M. (eds.) *The Child's Concept of Language*. New York: Springer-Verlag: 241–255.

CCEA (Council for the Curriculum Examinations and Assessment) (2006) *Understanding the Foundation Stage*. Belfast: CCEA.

CCEA (Council for the Curriculum Examinations and Assessment) (2007) *The Northern Ireland Curriculum: Primary*. Belfast: CCEA.

CCEA (Council for the Curriculum Examinations and Assessment) (2009) *Assessment for Learning: A Practical Guide*. Belfast: CCEA.

CCEA (Council for the Curriculum Examinations and Assessment) (2012) *Foundation Stage: Non-Statutory Assessment Guidance*. Belfast: CCEA.

Chaiklin, S. (2003) The Zone of Proximal Development in Vygotsky's Analysis of Learning and Instruction. In: Kozulin, A., Gindis, B., Ageyev, V. & Miller, S. (eds.) *Vygotsky's Educational Theory and Practice in Cultural Context*. Cambridge: Cambridge University Press: 33–64.

Connolly, P. (2009) Developing Programmes to Promote Ethnic Diversity in Early Childhood: Lessons from Northern Ireland. *Working Paper No. 52*, Bernard van Leer Foundation, The Hague, The Netherlands.

DENI (Department of Education in Northern Ireland) (2010) *Early Years (0–6) Strategy*. Northern Ireland: DENI.

DENI (Department of Education in Northern Ireland) (2012) *Learning to Learn: A Framework for Early Education and Learning*. Northern Ireland: DENI.

DfE (Department for Education in UK) (2011) *Early Years Evidence Pack*. London: DfE.

DfE (Department for Education in UK) (2012) *Statutory Framework for the Early Years Foundation Stage*. London: DfE.

Dillon, J., Morris, M., O'Donnell, L., Reid, A., Rickinson, M. & Scott, W. (2005) *Engaging and Learning With the Outdoors. Report of the Outdoor Classroom in a Rural Context Action Research Project*. Slough: NFER.

Doherty, A. (2013) Vygotsky and Play: A Critical Exploration of Theory into Practice. Unpublished thesis, Queen's University Belfast.

Edwards, S. (2011) Lessons From 'A Really Useful Engine'™: Using Thomas the Tank Engine™ to Examine the Relationship Between Play as a Leading Activity, Imagination and Reality in Children's Contemporary Play Worlds. *Cambridge Journal of Education*, 41(2): 195–210.

ETI (Education and Training Inspectorate) (2010) *Chief Inspector's Report 2008–2010*. Belfast: ETI [online]. Available: www.etini.gov.uk/index/support-material/support-material-general-documents-non-phase-related/the-chief-inspectors-report/chief-inspectors-report-2008-2010.pdf [accessed June 2014].

ETI (Education and Training Inspectorate) (2012) *Chief Inspector's Report 2010–2012*. Belfast: ETI [online]. Available: www.etini.gov.uk/index/what-we-do/support-material/support-material-general-documents-non-phase-related/the-chief-inspectors-report/ci-report-2012.pdf [accessed June 2014].

Fabian, H. & Dunlop, A-W. A. (2005) The Importance of Play in the Transition to School. In: Moyles, J.R. (ed.) *The Excellence of Play*. (2nd Ed.). Maidenhead, Berkshire: Open University Press/McGraw-Hill: 228–241.

Fisher, R. (2006) Thinking Skills. In: Arthur, J., Grainger, T. & Wray, D. (eds.) *Learning to Teach in the Primary School*. London: Routledge: 226–238.

Fromberg, D.P. (2002) *Play and Meaning in Early Childhood Education*. Boston: Allyn & Bacon.

Hunter, T. & Walsh, G. (2014) From Policy to Practice? The Reality of Play in Primary School Classes in Northern Ireland. *International Journal of Early Years Education*, *22*(1): 19–36.

Johansson, E. & Pramling Samuelsson, I. (2006) Play and Learning – Inseparable Dimensions in Preschool Practice. *Early Child Development and Care*, *176*(1): 47–65.

Kamen, M. & Murphy, C. (2011) Science Education at the Golden Key Schools—Learning Science in Vygotskian-Based Elementary Schools in Russia. In: Berlin, D.F. & White, A.L. (eds.) *Science and Mathematics Education: International Innovations, Research and Practices*. The Ohio State University, Columbus. OH: International Consortium for Research in Science and Mathematics Education: 3–17.

Kravtsov, G. & Kravtsova, E. (2010) Play in L.S. Vygotsky's Non-classical Psychology. *Journal of Russian and East European Psychology*, *48*(4): 25–41.

Learning and Teaching Scotland (2010) *Curriculum for Excellence* [online]. Available: www.ltscotland.org. uk/curriculumforexcellence/ondez.asp [accessed June 2014].

Leont'ev, A. (1981) *Problems of the Development of the Mind*. (4th Ed.). Moscow: Progress.

McGuinness, C., Sproule, L., Trew, K. & Walsh, G. (2009) *The Early Years Enriched Curriculum Evaluation Project (EYECEP)*, Report produced for Northern Ireland Council for Curriculum Assessment and Examinations (CCEA), September 2009.

Margetts, K. (2000) Indicators of Children's Adjustment to the First Year of Schooling. *Journal for Australian Research in Early Childhood Education*, 7(1): 20–30.

Moss, S. (2012) *Natural Childhood*. National Trust [online]. Available: www.nationaltrust.org.uk/document-1355766991839/ [accessed June 2014].

Murphy, C. (2012) Vygotsky and Primary Science. In: Fraser, B.J., Tobin, K.G. & McRobbie, C.J. (eds.) *Second International Handbook of Science Education*. London: Springer: 177–187.

Murray, R. & O'Brien, E. (2005) *Such Enthusiasm – A Joy to See: An Evaluation of Forest School in England. Report to the Forestry Commission* [online]. Available: www.forestresearch.gov.uk/website/forestre-search.nsf/ByUnique/INFD-6HKEMHS [accessed May 2014].

NCCA (National Council for Curriculum and Assessment) (2009) *Aistear: The Early Childhood Curriculum Framework*. Dublin: NCCA.

Nicol, R. Higgins, P., Ross, H. & Mannion, G. (2007) *Outdoor Education in Scotland: A Summary of Recent Research*. Perth: Scottish National Heritage.

OECD (Organisation for Economic Co-operation and Development) (2006) *Starting Strong II: Early Childhood Education and Care*. Paris: OECD.

Piaget, J. (1962) *Play, Dreams and Imitation in Childhood*. New York: Norton.

RSPB (Royal Society for the Protection of Birds) (2010) *Every Child Outdoors – Children Need Nature: Nature Needs Children*. Sandy, Bedfordshire: RSPB [online]. Available: www.rspb.org.uk/Images/everychildoutdoors_tcm9-259689.pdf [accessed May 2014].

Sproule, L., Rafferty, H., Trew, K., Walsh, G., McGuinness, C., Sheehy, N. & O'Neill, B. (2006) *The Early Years Enriched Curriculum Evaluation Project: Final Report End-of-Phase 1*. Belfast: CCEA.

Stephen, C. (2012) Learning in Early Childhood. In: Jarvis, P. & Watts, M. (eds.) *The Routledge International Handbook of Learning*. London: Routledge: 103–111.

Taggart, G., Ridley, K., Rudd, P. & Benefield, P. (2005) *Thinking Skills in the Early Years: A Literature Review*. Slough: NFER.

Van Oers, B. (1996) Are you Sure? Stimulating Mathematical Thinking During Young Children's Play. *European Early Childhood Education Research Journal*, *4*(1): 71–87.

Venville, G., Adey, P., Larkin, S. & Robertson, A. (2003) Fostering Thinking Through Science in the Early Years of Schooling. *International Journal of Science Education*, *25*(11): 1313–1332.

Verenikina, I. (2005) The Socio-Cultural View. In: Vialle, W., Lysaght, P. & Verenikina, I. (eds.) *Psychology for Educators*. Melbourne, Australia: Thomson Learning: 45–74.

Vygotsky, L. (1933) Play and Its Role in the Mental Development of the Child. *Soviet Psychology* [online]. Available: www.marxists.org/archive/vygotsky/works/1933/play.htm [accessed August 2014].

Vygotsky, L.S. (1978) *Mind in Society*. Cambridge, MA: Harvard University Press.

Vygotsky, L.S. (1986) *Thought and Language* (A. Kozulin, transl.). Cambridge, MA: MIT Press.

Walsh, G. (2000) The Play versus Formal Debate: A Study of Early Years Provision in Northern Ireland and Denmark. Unpublished thesis, Queen's University Belfast.

Walsh, G. & Gardner, J. (2005) Assessing the Quality of Early Years Learning Environments. *Early Childhood Research and Practice*, 7(1) [online]. Available: http://ecrp.uiuc.edu/v7n1/walsh.html [accessed August 2014].

Walsh, G. & Gardner, J. (2006) Teachers' Readiness to Embrace Change in the Early Years of Schooling. *European Early Childhood Education Research Journal*, 14(2): 127–140.

Walsh, G., Sproule, L., McGuinness, C., Trew, K., Rafferty, H. & Sheehy, N. (2006) An Appropriate Curriculum for 4–5-year-old Children in Northern Ireland: Comparing Play-Based and Formal Approaches. *Early Years*, 26(2): 201–221.

Walsh, G., Murphy, P. & Dunbar, C. (2007) *Thinking Skills in Early Years Classrooms: A Practical Guide for Teachers*. Belfast: CCEA.

Walsh, G., Taylor, D., Sproule, L. & McGuinness, C. (2008) *Debating the Transition from Play-Based to Formal Practice: Implications for Early Years Teachers and Policy-Makers*. Report produced for Northern Ireland Council for Curriculum Assessment and Examinations (CCEA), June 2008.

Walsh, G., McGuinness, C., Sproule, L. & Trew, K. (2010) Implementing a Play-Based and Developmentally Appropriate Curriculum in Northern Ireland Primary Schools: What Lessons Have We Learned? *Early Years*, 30(1): 53–66.

Walsh, G., Sproule, L., McGuinness, C. & Trew, K. (2011) *Playful Structure: Six Pillars of Developmentally Appropriate Practice*. Belfast: CCEA.

Welsh Assembly Government (2008) *Framework for Children's Learning for 3–7 Year Olds in Wales*. Cardiff: Welsh Assembly Government.

White, J. (2013) The Nature of the Pedagogical Approach to Thinking Skills and Play in Senior Infant Classes. Unpublished Master of Arts dissertation, Stranmillis University College, Belfast.

Wood, E. (2004) A New Paradigm War? The Impact of National Curriculum Policies on Early Childhood Teachers' Thinking and Classroom Practice. *Teaching and Teacher Education*, 20: 361–374.

Wylie, C. & Hodgen, E. (2007) *The Continuing Contribution of Early Childhood Education to Young People's Competency Levels*. Wellington: NZCER.

Further reading

Early Years Interboard Panel (2005) *Learning Outdoors in the Early Years: A Resource Book*. Belfast: CCEA.

Early Years Interboard Panel (2005) *Learning Through Play in the Early Years: A Resource Book*. Belfast: CCEA.

Websites

Sesame tree: www.bbc.co.uk/northernireland/schools/sesame/

CCEA: www.rewardinglearning.org.uk

Media Initiative: www.early-years.org/mifc/

Playful Science Hub at Stranmillis University College: www.pstt.org.uk www.stran.ac.uk

3 A Scottish perspective

Development of a value based curriculum

Claire Warden and Lynn McNair

The Scottish Government has devolved powers for education and child and family policy (The Scottish Parliament, 1998) that sets it apart from England, Wales and Northern Ireland. The Scottish education system has its own distinct characteristics and has enjoyed an excellent reputation abroad (Knox, n.d.). Concern about an achievement gap identified by the Organization for Economic Cooperation and Development (OECD) initiated the case for change (OECD, 2007); and an aspiration to make Scotland the best place in the world to grow up has driven the cross party consensus in government to radically transform Scottish education. The process began with a Scotland wide consultation, the 'National Debate on Education' (Education Scotland, 2002). The people were asked, 'what do you *want* from our education system?' At the end of the consultation, people *wanted* children who were successful learners, confident individuals, responsible citizens and effective contributors (The Scottish Government, 2004). They wanted a system that reflected the values that parliament itself was founded on: wisdom, justice, integrity and compassion (The Scottish Parliament, 1998).

There followed a period of reflection on how this would be delivered through the architecture of the curriculum design (Education Scotland, 2010). Early in this process the effectiveness of learning in the early years was recognised and a paper on Active Learning was published (The Scottish Government, 2007). This praised the engagement and activity found in the early years and sought to extend this throughout the curriculum across the sectors. Seven design features were developed: personalisation and choice, challenge and enjoyment, breadth, depth, progression, relevance and coherence (Scottish Executive, 2004). Alongside these were entitlements for all children and young people to personal support, additional support for learning and a broad general education (The Education (Additional Support for Learning) (Scotland) Act 2009). The curriculum architecture was explained in a series of publications called 'Building the Curriculum' (Education Scotland, 2010). Alongside this was a published document called 'A Curriculum for Excellence through Outdoor Learning', a daily feature of learning in the early years that was promoted for all children and young people (Learning and Teaching Scotland, 2010).

Using this design, curricular areas were developed, eight in total (The Scottish Government, 2006). These created combinations of subjects that were traditionally separate in primary and secondary schools and were a radical shift in thinking for the early years who were accustomed to five areas based on child development. The progression in the curriculum was to be achieved through experiences and outcomes at the early, first, second, third and senior phase.

The early level would encompass nursery to the end of primary one (children aged 3–6). Building the Curriculum 4 focused on the development of skills, for learning, life and work (The Scottish Government, 2009). Building the Curriculum 5 focused on assessment

(The Scottish Government, 2010). This built on previous work on assessment for learning, engaging the child and parent in learning discussions as well as progress through the outcomes and levels and national qualifications in secondary school. Further, a recent childcare review (Siraj and Kingston, 2015) highlighted the need for greater post-qualification professional development. The report recommended the University of Edinburgh's Froebel in Childhood Practice course as the kind of post development training required. This is due to Froebel trained practitioners having a greater understanding of early years pedagogy (Bruce, 2012).

There has been a strong Froebelian influence in Scotland in the early years (Bruce, 2012), and significantly, many references are made to Froebel within the Curriculum for Excellence (CfE) (MacLaren, 2012: xii). Until 1972, Froebel certificates were offered in many teacher training colleges as an extra qualification. Many of the leading practitioners who have Froebelian Childhood Practice qualifications are at the peak of their careers in Inspection, local authority and government bodies, such as Education Scotland/Foghlam Alba, and are strong advocates for play- and child-centred education, which is in harmony with the CfE. In the City of Edinburgh, Education Convenor of Edinburgh Councillor Marilyne MacLaren (2012) offered her direct support and value of Froebelian practice: '[w]e have a great tradition of Early Years education and development in Scotland and I am proud to say that Froebel underpins Edinburgh's Early Years Strategy and Action Plan' (MacLaren, 2012: xiii).

The Early Years Framework (EYFS) gave a mandate for change (The Scottish Government, 2008). Recent early years policy has been informed by strong advocates for change from the chief medical officer, violence reduction, social enterprise and neuroscience (The Child's Curriculum, 2010). The case for investment in the early years has been made and is becoming statutory through the process of the Children and Young People (Scotland) Act 2014 (The Children and Young People (Scotland) Act, 2014). Within the Act are articulated the rights of the child to play, described in the Play Strategy (The Scottish Government, 2013). There can be no more Froebelian principle than the significance of play (Bruce, 2001, 2010, 2011, 2012; Bruce et al., 1995; Lascarides and Hinitz, 2000; Liebschner, 1992).

The government allocated a budget to change the fund for transformational change to prioritise the needs of young children and their families and early intervention (The Scottish Government, 2011). The Collaborative is a Scottish Government initiative that enables and tasks agencies to work together using a scientific model of change to improve outcomes for children and families (The Scottish Government, 2012). A further attempt at inspiring transforming change for children can be found in the Growing Up in Scotland report (GUS, 2003). Appointed in 2003 by the then Scottish Executive Education Department (SEED), Growing Up in Scotland (GUS) is a large-scale longitudinal research study intended to follow the lives of numerous cohorts of Scottish children (and their families) from the early years through to childhood and beyond. The main aim of the study is to offer information to support policy-making in Scotland. This information will also be available for academics, state, private and voluntary sector organisations and other interested groups. The overall aspiration from GUS is that Scotland's children will have the very best start in life (GUS, 2003).

The Curriculum for Excellence (The Scottish Government, 2006) aims to achieve a transformation in education in Scotland by providing a coherent, more flexible and enriched curriculum for 3–18-year-olds. The curriculum includes the totality of experiences which are planned for children and young people through their education, wherever they are being educated:

- ethos and life of the school as a community;
- curriculum areas and subjects;
- interdisciplinary learning; and
- opportunities for personal achievement.

The entitlement of children and young people is clearly stated by the Scottish Government. The entitlements are:

- a coherent curriculum for 3–18-year-olds;
- a broad general education, including well planned experiences and outcomes across all curriculum areas – this should include the understanding of the world and Scotland's place within it and understanding of the environment;
- a senior phase which provides opportunities for study for qualifications and other planned opportunities for developing the four capacities;
- opportunities for developing skills for learning, skills for life and skills for work;
- opportunities to achieve to the highest levels they can through appropriate personal support and challenge; and
- opportunities to move into positive and sustained destinations beyond school.

HOW DO YOU VIEW THE CHILD?

Skills

Children come to learning with a back pack of skills that have developed through their young lives. The *way* that we deliver the curriculum is detailed in the curriculum document. One of the words used in the CfE is 'relevant'. Many of the pioneers of education such as Froebel and Montessori understood the need to connect to the children to make opportunities relevant.

How do you consider relevancy in your programming?

Challenge

Children who are in an environment that celebrates challenge, understand that it flows across physical, intellectual and emotional boundaries. Challenging experiences and outcomes are created by children and supported by the practitioner. In the Scottish curriculum children are entitled to be challenged, rather than engaged with at a lower level.

How could you increase the connection between the child and the challenges they wish to engage with across physical, emotional and intellectual domains?

Tensions and challenges

Challenge

A tension exists between the view of the child and the opportunities they are offered. Children are not always viewed as capable by practitioners and therefore planned programmes can offer understimulation or indeed overstimulation through a lack of vision. Noticing the moment of relaxed alertness is a skill.

How can practitioners be supported to be mindful to notice so that challenges are seen as opportunities?

Breadth

The breadth of learning presented in the curriculum has been criticised for being shallow, rather than providing depth. In response to this the Scottish Government provide self-evaluation materials that encourage centres to ensure depth. In settings many practitioners have found that the broad curriculum does in fact allow them to drill down into an area of fascination for the children as they are able to easily evidence the learning.

Assessment

In order to do this effectively and consistently there need to be arrangements made for assessment of learning but also of the whole journey and the effectiveness of the structured framework it sits within (see Miller and Pound, 2011).

The assessment practice will follow and reinforce the curriculum and be appropriate to high quality learning and teaching approaches, rather than detached assessment moments.

Assessment of children's and young people's progress and achievement during their broad general education will be based on practitioner assessment of their knowledge and understanding, skills, attributes and capabilities, as described in the experiences and outcomes across the curriculum. The National Assessment Resource Bank supports the individuality and innovation of settings to create assessment and documentation profiles that meet the needs of the child and family.

The standards and expectations that form our aspirations for all learners from 3 to 18 are set out for the whole curriculum in the experiences and outcomes of CfE. They are also reflected in their equivalent in the specifications for qualifications and awards. Reflecting the principles of CfE, progress is defined in terms of 'how well' and 'how much', as well as learners' rates of progress.

This approach will promote greater breadth and depth of learning, including a greater focus on the secure development of skills and knowledge. Assessing progress across a breadth of learning will also help teachers to plan, track progress, summarise achievements in a rounded way and better prepare children and young people for the next stage in learning. This can also be seen when applying learning in different and unfamiliar contexts.

Reporting to parents

Parents will get regular information about their children's strengths, progress and achievements in both a verbal and written form. This will include brief descriptions of progress across the curriculum areas and through the curriculum levels as well as progress towards qualifications in the senior phase.

In addition to written individual reports created on an annual basis, to share the progress of the child or young person, they will receive information on:

- how well all learners and particular groups of learners are achieving;
- the performance of children and young people in the school in relation to expected levels at particular stages in key areas such as literacy and numeracy; and
- how the school is applying national standards and expectations.

ASSESSMENT THROUGH FLOORBOOKS AND FAMILY BOOKS: AUCHLONE NATURE KINDERGARTEN, SCOTLAND

Auchlone Nature Kindergarten sits within eight acres of forest space, comprising of indoor and outdoor spaces for children aged 2–5 years, staff and parents to enjoy over 49 weeks during a calendar year. During the time that the project was being carried out, Auchlone enjoyed the company of 40 children and families, with six staff attending the setting.

The process of action research with its constant reflection and consultation with parents has lead the team at Auchlone Nature Kindergarten to review the style of profiling that has developed over many years. Pedagogical review of the work is an integral part of our way of being, as it ensures that innovation and change are seen as positive attributes and not a thing to be feared.

The centre was asked to share this work in order to:

- demonstrate how we evaluate our approach to profiling and consider the views of all stakeholders in creating a profiling process and profile that met the needs of our learners and their families;
- show how we use assessment such as observation and questioning to gather moments for the profile including identifying 'children's theories'; and
- demonstrate how the Floorbook approach to planning is firmly embedded in the work that we do in the centre, noting that the holistic interdisciplinary records we use for group learning were not reflected in the individual profiles used for reporting to parents.

There were a number of lines of enquiry the team followed throughout the years:

- children's connection to their individual profiles;
- family and carer engagement with their child's learning journeys; and
- staff engagement and perception of relevance.

Methodology of developing 'the profile'

To ascertain the makeup of the profiles, children, families and staff were involved in the consultation process. The children were involved through the use of appropriate questioning: what did they like about their existing profiles and what could be done to improve them? Parents were each mailed a questionnaire and the information was then evaluated and analysed with the staff team. The staff team were consulted further, discussing their thoughts in regards to what would help improve the profile process. The profiles were then developed with stakeholders' suggestions taken into account. Staff with their key worker groups then set out to develop each child's profile. Children decorated the front covers of their profile and bound blank pages of A4 paper, creating a book ready for the documentation of learning.

Developing 'the profiling process'

The staff team of Auchlone have developed over the years an interdisciplinary approach to the CfE through the use of Talking and Thinking Floorbook methodology (Warden, 1994). It was important for us that this child-centred methodology transferred into the profiling of the children's learning journey and that the Floorbook and profiling were part of our coherent approach to learning, teaching and assessment. The Floorbook planning process identifies with learners the significant aspects to be focused on during staff observations of the children's significant learning moments, which are then captured for the profile. It is the belief at Auchlone that we do not need to record every learning moment that occurs, as the staff time would then be consumed with documentation of learning and admin, where less time is spent on further development of learning and engagement with children.

- There is on-going reflection with the Floorbooks.
- It was decided that in order to capture significant learning as it occurred, practitioners would use photography, the scribing of children's words and adult observation of learning recorded in small notebooks to take outside in the hip pouches.
- Each key worker group had an electronic file set up on the laptop, where a basic template was created.
- The transfer of photographs and words would occur (with or without the child) and then an analysis of the child's dialogue was performed to ascertain the theories that they developed during this learning moment.
- Possible Lines of Development (PLODs) were created through adult analysis and through consultation with the child, with the aim to give breadth and depth to their learning journey.
- Once completed, the learning story would be saved and printed off into the child's profile (Family book).
- Children are given opportunities to share their profiles and learning stories with other learners.
- Parents were encouraged to evidence learning moments whilst at home, documenting the moments through hand written notes, electronic means, photography or drawn evidence. Parents were encouraged to follow existing PLODs and record these findings in whatever way best suited their circumstance.

In order to demonstrate this process we will follow Child 1 and their family.

Child 1 and family

Aged 3, having recently arrived in Auchlone after a move from South Africa, Child 1 settled in quickly to his routine. However it was observed that Child 1 demonstrated low emotional intelligence but a high academic level of intelligence. He engaged very well with all children and staff through vocabulary but Child 1 was unwilling to socialise or interact with his peers. His language was vast but became limited due to frustration for the child, as his peers were not able to fully understand and comprehend his meaning as his language was superior to their own, leading to times where the child would stop verbally communicating with friends, opting to engage in solo play only.

After consultation with the children, in regards to each child having a new profile, Child 1 successfully created a front cover for his file, thus creating a sense of ownership and promoting a sense of individuality. Over a period of a day or two (after observations of learning moments), Auchlone staff and children began to gather evidence for the profiles. Child 1 enjoyed selecting photographs from the laptop to his profile: "this is a good one, I like this!" (Child 1), ascertaining what was meant by a 'good one' the child replied, "it shows me doing things and has some of my friends that helped me climb". Once the photographs had been selected, Child 1's key worker would then input the dialogue and observations that had been noted. Printing the profile and filing the new story, the file was ready for Child 1 and family to reflect on. Over a period of the first two weeks where the profiles were being developed, Child 1 requested on a number of occasions: "can we look at my lovely photographs, I love them!" Child 1 became motivated to share his profile with other children, first selecting those children with whom he had shared a particular learning moment with, "look Boy (aged 4), that was you helping me to climb down the tree when I got stuck there", to then sharing it out with those whom he had not. Recently, Child 1 requested that his profile return home over the weekends, "Mummy and Daddy and my little baby (Child 1, younger sibling) read and looked at my photographs! We did some climbing PLODS (P.L.O.D's)" (Child 1).

The profiling process was used to encourage at home learning for the child and family. The profile was encouraged to be taken home and for parents to promote a reflective account through reading with the child on the child's learning journey whilst at Auchlone, to increase confidence and allow communication to flourish. This link provided achievable success for the child to observe and increase an empowerment on their learning journey.

Family of Child 1: "'Child 1' is growing in confidence, social skills and knowledge within the supportive, nurturing and unique environment of Auchlone. He loves coming to Auchlone, thank you!"

Impact on children and families

The children are positively and actively engaging with their learning journeys, sharing with family, friends and staff. Making a connection with the learning and becoming aware that their learning goes beyond the time restraints of the kindergarten, children have become aware that learning can take place anywhere, at any time and with anyone.

The confidence, vocabulary and further learning opportunities are visible to see and easy to document. The language and the children's confidence in their own learning journey has been recorded through capturing their dialogue, with statements being used whilst engaging with friends such as: "me learning it", "oh, I remember that, I really liked doing that" and "this is what me, mummy and daddy did after we learnt about that" demonstrating that the children understood that they were involved in their learning journey.

The children's confidence grew as they were receiving instant feedback from their peers. For example, when Child 1 shared their learning journey with a small group of the children the responses were, "I like seeing you doing that there, can I do it with you maybe?", "That looks like fun", "wow, you do a lot of awesome things!" Child 1, instantly replied, "thank you, yes you can all play with me". This was a huge change from the insecure child that we had known previously.

The children and families took greater interest in their profiles, whereas in the past the families were only interested at parents' evenings or at the end of the academic year. There is a stronger sense of ownership and partnership in the learning journey of each child and that of the setting as a whole. Parents' comments were recorded in the profiles.

Impact on staff

The most common thread during staff feedback was that 'the process was far easier than previous methods' (staff). Upon evaluating this statement further, it was found that the learning story approach provided a more obvious holistic approach to the style of recording, which reflected the teaching style of the setting; it was now felt that 'the teaching and recording went hand in hand' (staff). This approach provided staff with more flow from teaching, evaluating and taking the learning forward through reflective planning.

Using the technology to transfer photographs onto a template and type observations directly on the learning story made the process less time consuming which in turn allowed staff to increase their interaction time with the children.

Educational communication with parents was found to be increased and staff commented that this 'was now an enriched way to communicate the children's learning journey, as this encouraged participation from all adults involved'. Parents that may have not been actively involved in the past were now becoming more engaged with the daily life of Auchlone Nature Kindergarten:

> The process makes tracking so much easier as you can quickly see the progression of learning and quickly establish other areas for development, then the parent can quickly observe this also. I am very much looking forward to sharing these with parents during our next Parents evening.
>
> (staff)

Documenting, evaluating, assessing and planning for children's learning portfolios has become engrained into the daily routine of staff and children, with staff advising that the portfolios are now being valued by children as enjoyable and the child's favourite resource; a child was quoted to say 'I really like looking at my photos of me playing' (feedback from staff).

Leadership and sustainability

The project continues to be manageable; all key workers are recording the profiles of all children. This option for evidencing is occurring with children during sessions or without them during staff non-contact time or during times when no children are present on site. The profiles are evidenced during the working day and not taken home, proving that the profiles were manageable and achievable within the working time frame of a busy Auchlone. The project promotes the whole child and remains to champion the child who is at the centre of their profile.

Teamwork was at the heart of this project. All stakeholders, children and staff were consulted and continually communicated with during the development of the profiles. The project quickly became autonomous with all involved, the success of this being put down to the open and honest approach. Understanding, listening and working with the parent group is key to the success of any project that is carried out with Auchlone.

Positive interaction occurred with parents/children and staff. Positive dialogue created between parents and children encouraged a deeper learning for parents in connecting with their child's learning journey and promoted the understanding of the education delivered by Auchlone staff.

Reflection

Successes

- Children became actively engaged with the documentation of their own learning, expressing a new found enthusiasm to carry out possible lines of development both at Auchlone and at home. Children and families felt positive about furthering their own learning experiences.
- Educational communication between parents and staff increased, which has seen a rise in a general interest in support in the daily, weekly and annual operations of Auchlone.
- Parents became engaged in the learning journey of their child and that of the setting.
- Staff found the process to be less time consuming and found that this style matched the style and delivery of teaching, creating a more meaningful flow between teaching and documenting learning.
- Children, families and staff were involved through creating a working dialogue in the creation of the new individual learning portfolios.
- Support from all staff has been crucial for this project to be a success; support from the managing director, head of early years team, coordinator of Auchlone and all practitioners allowed a smooth delivery and development of the individual learning portfolios.

Challenges

- The transition from written to electronic documentation was a challenge for staff; once they had coaching and a couple of practice attempts, then began to record the documentation electronically, they felt that their I.T. skills had improved and confidence was growing which in turn helped to speed the process of documenting the learning.
- Progress with parents and families took time to develop; however, once they realised the value of the process they became highly engaged with their child's learning journey.
- The staff worked hard to encourage parents to contribute to their child's profile.

Possible lines of development

The debate continues as to the balance between a blend of digital/hard copy books and purely digital formats that allow rapid transfer of the information.

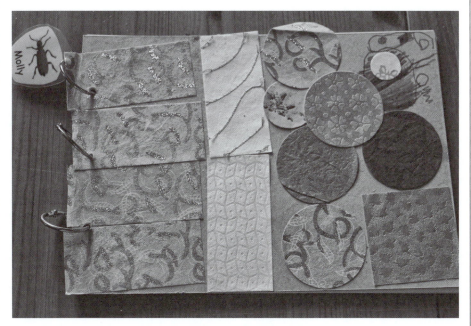

Figure 3.1 Front covers created with the family at home.

Making fairy cakes

Molly: "My mum lets me crack eggs when we bake together."

Lindi: "Ok, we need to add milk now."

Molly: "It's all sticky!" The mixer had stuck to the large wooden spoon. Lindi gave Fi a little spoon to get it off. Then she poured some milk in very carefully.

Once everyone had a taken it in turn to have a go at mixing, Lindi got out the electric whisk and told the boys and girls that it is a very powerful tool.

Lindi: "Why shouldn't we put our fingers in when it moves?" (demonstrating the whisk move).

Molly: "Our fingers will get cut off."

Ffion: "Oh," looking a little shocked.

Lindi: "Ok, so we must be very careful when using the whisk."

Molly had a shot of the whisk. She loved it. As the whisk powered around in the bowl, Molly was laughing and giggling with a huge grin from ear to ear.

Ffion: "It's loud." ☺

Molly: "Wow, it's really fast."

Everyone had a turn and then also took it in turn to spoon the mix into the paper cases. The cakes were then put into the oven to bake.

In the afternoon, Molly helped make red icing that was her choice and Struan picked blue icing. She mixed the icing in with water and Gail put a little red dye in ☺.

Molly: "It's really red," after a few minutes, "It looks yummy."

The boys and girls had their cakes at reflection time, Molly shared her favourite thing with the boys and girls and it was eating the cake. ☺

Figure 3.2 Adult documentation of the talking and thinking with links to the CfE (3–18 years) or Birth–3 documents.

Melting the snow

Children's theories

- Understands that snow melts
- Can play with and alongside her friends

Possible lines of development

- Do some ice art with Maia to explore it a bit more. Once she understands that snow turns into water, show how water freezes and melts.
- See weather floor book for more learning on the weather, rain, wind, etc…

February

Figure 3.3 Children's theories and possible lines of development.
Source: Warden (1994)

Molly and I enjoyed reading stories about her today. She had difficulty remembering some of the details but remembered the events. I think this is a fairly tidied up version – where's all of the stuff about covering herself in charcoal the day I had to take her swimming?!

Figure 3.4 Parent and carer comments and experiences at home.

Self-evaluation

Scotland has a strong culture of self-evaluation. All settings that offer care and education for children and youth from Birth to 18 years are included in the inspection process. The regulations apply to any provision that caters for children and youth for two hours a day and six days or more each year. Education Scotland/Foghlam Alba and the Social Care and Social Work Improvement Scotland (SCSWIS) consult children, parents and staff as part of the inspection. They are regulated under the Regulation of Care (Scotland 2001). The annual care inspection is unannounced but Her Majesty's Inspectorate for Education from Education Scotland/Foghlam Alba give two weeks' notice of arrival. The inspection report is discussed with the setting and then made public with a rating for the quality of care and education.

There are a number of documents that detail quality indicators that are used as the core tool for self-evaluation. The principles that underpin them reflect the UN Convention on the Rights of the Child (The Convention). Each sector of education has a framework of quality indicators: The Child at the Centre (second edition); How Good is Our School? (third edition); External Quality Arrangements for Scotland Colleges; How Good is Our Community Learning and Development; and Quality Management in Education. The online Journey to Excellence shares evaluation and the examples of Journeys of Improvement.

There are nine sections under the five areas of vision and values; centre impact on those it serves; education provision; management; leadership; and improvement plans. These are rated against a six-point scale from excellent and sector leading to unsatisfactory. It is important that Scotland has a system for reporting against standards to provide information for children and families, settings, schools, the education authority and national level. The roles and responsibilities of individuals, groups and organisations are clearly laid out in documents such as Curriculum for Excellence Building the Curriculum 5: A Framework for Assessment (The Scottish Government, 2010):

- Self-evaluation and accountability.
- As detailed under assessment there is a large focus on the process of self-evaluation by settings and the accountability is to the children and families that we work with. The inspection process is rigorous to monitor the quality of provision in education and care and therefore provides a series of benchmarks for quality provision in Scotland. There are increasing opportunities to collaborate on the final report so that the Journey to Excellence continues rather than moves between isolated inspections.
- Professional Development and Qualifications.

This section briefly explores the critical aspect of the Professional Development of practitioners. It is important to say at this point that practitioners are known by a number of different designations, including nursery nurses, nursery officers, early education and childcare workers, practitioners and senior practitioners and so on. We will simply use one term 'practitioner' to encompass all of these designations.

Notably, practitioners may also work in a number of different settings: local authority or independent nursery schools or classes; early years centres; under-fives centres; voluntary centres; private day nurseries; community nurseries; playgroups; mother and toddler groups and Gaelic medium nurseries.

To be considered for this particular early education and childcare role, the practitioners need to hold specific qualifications.

Qualifications

There are many routes to gaining an introductory to advanced early years qualifications (refer to Chapter 5, Table 5.1). However, the most widely recognised early years qualifications are the Scottish Vocational Qualifications (SVQs) level 3 in Early Years Care and Education *or* the Higher National Certificate (HNC) in Childcare and Education.

- SVQs take place in the workplace. The trainee practitioner works while achieving her/ his qualification. Most of the assessing takes place in the workplace, however it is likely that the trainee practitioner will attend a Further Education (FE) college to learn about the various theories that underpin early years practice. It will generally take between 18 months and two years to gain a SVQ level 3. However, the time it takes to complete is often negotiable with the trainee practitioner, SVQ assessor, the FE college and the workplace.
- The HNC in Childcare and Education can be taken on either a full- or a part-time basis at a FE college. The course includes a considerable amount of time spent on a work placement in a care and education setting. Assessment is done at several points throughout the course and includes assessment of practice in the work placement. The mandatory units of the HNC in Childcare and Education are:

  1. Working in an Early Education and Childcare Setting
  2. Children and Young People's Rights: Provision, Protection and Participation
  3. Theoretical Approaches to Development and Learning
  4. Curriculum and Assessment in an Early Education and Childcare Setting or facilitating Playwork opportunities.

Students complete a graded unit around a workplace project to place the research into practice in an authentic way.

Creating a degree-led profession

Worthy of mention here is that all managers/leaders in Scottish day care settings need to either have a degree (BA in Childhood Practice, BACP) or a Professional Development Award (PDA) level 9 or be working towards their degree.

The PDA in Childhood Practice at Scottish Credit and Qualifications Framework (SCQF) level 9: 'develops the skills and knowledge required to manage services for children and young people. It is aimed at those who wish to progress into management within the Childcare and Playwork sectors without having to complete a full-time university programme.' It has been designed to meet the Standard for Childhood Practice (Scottish Social Services Council, 2007) similar to the BACP (Scottish Qualifications Authority, 2014).

The BACP part-time degree programme is available at several Scottish universities. The length of the degree varies from three years to five years depending on the university delivering the degree.

To some degree the programmes also vary, however typically students can expect to study:

- education studies (e.g. curriculum development, social justice and equity in education);
- child and family health education (e.g. health care, child development, health and illness and play);
- child/family development and social policy (e.g. nurturing, play development, supporting parents and children, child and family legislation, child protections and child and family rights);
- management and organisational behaviour (e.g. professions and professionalism, organisational structures and cultures, and managing change and conflict within organisations);
- childhood studies (e.g. child psychology, disability studies, ethnicity studies, gender studies and the sociology of childhood). Should children have the same rights as adults? How do you talk to a seven-year-old? How do you protect children? How effective are services for children and their families? Are children's rights just a Western luxury?

(The University of Edinburgh, 2014)

Students who successfully achieve the BACP are eligible to apply for registration as a manager/leader with the Scottish Social Services Council (SSSC).

Scottish Social Services Council

The education and training of practitioners in the day care of children's service in Scotland are regulated by the Scottish Social Services Council (SSSC).

The Scottish Social Services Council (SSSC) is responsible for registering people who work in social services and regulating their education and training ... Our role is to raise standards of practice, strengthen and support the workforce ... Our vision is a confident workforce, capable of delivering high quality services that has the confidence of the public, those who use services and their carers:

What we do:

- set up registers of key groups of social service staff
- publish Codes of Practice for all social service workers and their employers
- regulate the training and education of the workforce
- promote education and training
- undertake the functions of the sector skills council; Skills for Care and Development, this includes workforce planning and development.

(Scottish Social Services Council, 2014)

As mentioned earlier, to register with the SSSC and work as a practitioner in the early years, practitioners need to have (or be working towards) an early years qualification SVQ level 3 or HNC in Childcare and Education. And as all day care settings in Scotland are run by degree-led professionals, managers need to hold (or be working towards) their BACP degree or a PDA level 9.

Post registration requirements

Following registration, all practitioners in the day care of children's services are required to do post registration training and learning in order to ensure their on-going suitability for registration. Registered practitioners are required to do a minimum of ten days or 60 hours post registration training/continued professional development.

Continued Professional Development (CPD) is a developmental buffet and is defined as any type of learning that increases the registered practitioner's knowledge and understanding. For example, a practitioner may take part in:

*   work-based learning (e.g. job-shadowing, coaching, peer mentoring and/or supervising a student);
*   reflective (and reflexive) thinking on deliberate and spontaneous experiences;
*   completing a professional qualification;
*   experiential learning;
*   presentations (e.g. the practitioner may deliver her/his knowledge to other interested parties).

A record is then maintained by the registered practitioner that illustrates their ongoing professional development. What emerges from this is a crazy quilt of skills and knowledge that practitioners can draw on to respond to individual children and their families.

HOW DO YOU VIEW THE CHILD?

Professional development

Professional development takes time for the practitioner to grow in their understanding within the wider journey of growth in the setting.

How do you make the professional learning of the individual impact on the quality of provision in the setting?

Ownership and autonomy

The great strength of the CfE is that it encourages innovation in learning and discretion for practitioners. The CfE does not assess students at Key Stages and instead outlines outcomes and experiences that are clearly influenced by pedagogy detailed in the principles and practices.

How do you implement a reflective/reflexive approach to your practice?

Tensions and challenges

The Scottish Government is seeking to create a degree-led profession. Scotland has a large rural population that means it has small settings in remote communities. This has led to a tension when the practitioners in these areas do not want to study for further qualifications.

To what extent should the profession be required to hold qualifications up to degree level?

Pedagogical foundations

The definition of the underpinning approach to learning and teaching gives practitioners a clear indication of *how* to deliver the curriculum. Approaches to learning are identified in the support materials provided by Education Scotland/Foghlam Alba, Active Learning, Collaborative and Co-operative Learning, Outdoor Learning and Creativity. Within each of these there is a general acceptance as a Scottish profession that the points below are essential in any teaching and learning situation:

- Engaging and active. The debate on physicality of learning goes on through the early stages of education. 'Building the Curriculum 2 – active learning in the early years' (The Scottish Government, 2007) provides an overview of active learning in practice. Early years environments in primary schools are developing to provide activity for children to the age of eight. The outdoor learning agenda is high in Scotland and many primary schools have taken this aspect to cover active learning.
- Collaborative. The role of talk in settings has radically changed from the days of silent obedience.
- Setting challenging goals.
- Sharing expectations and standards. The use of learning journals and the discursive nature of teaching and learning is evident in primary schools. The interaction in early years is developing to encourage practitioners to consult children from a very young age.
- Providing learners with timely, accurate feedback.
- Connecting the learning intentions, success criteria and personal learning planning.
- Reflecting the ways that different learners progress.

The Scottish Government launched the national Practice Guidance on Early Learning and Childcare to detail the context for high quality early learning and childcare as set out in the Children and Young People (Scotland) Act 2014. The gradual change in society which views children as trustworthy, capable, able learners connects strongly with the CfE. The CfE aims to accomplish transformation in education by providing a continuous curriculum that includes children from the age of 3 to 18 years. The flexibility of the CfE enables practitioners to implement a creative approach to this holistic document, for example experiences are child-led (not to be confused with the term child-run); children are involved in the planning of their everyday experiences (The Children and Young People (Scotland) Act, 2014). This is in stark contrast to the traditional view where children were viewed as passive recipients of knowledge (Whittaker, 2014). The four capacities of the CfE are: confident individuals, successful learners, responsible citizens and effective contributors (The Scottish Government, 2004). These capacities are clearly visible in early years environments as children become intrinsically motivated to learn through play. However, young children's lives at school are much more circumscribed. The school day can be highly structured, with curriculum input, especially in the areas of literacy and mathematics, from the moment they arrive until they go home.

Tensions and challenges

Pedagogical tensions are visible as (passionate) primary school teachers are affected by the tensions between practice and the challenge of implementation of practice guidance.

How do practitioners balance innovation of practice with slow pace change that arises from embedded knowledge?

How can practitioners support transitional moments for children and families?

The individual learner has the right to personal support through their time in education through the following:

- a review of learning and planning of next steps;
- access to learning activities which will meet their needs;
- planned opportunities for personal achievement;
- preparation and support for changes and choices;
- pre-school centres and schools working with partners.

This foundation of beliefs and values has to be clearly understood as they lie at the heart of the general methodologies of learning and teaching. At this point we can start to explore the principles of the curriculum so that we can place the knowledge, skills and attitudes within a cohesive framework and not be tempted to pull them out as individual targets.

The principles that underpin the design of the curriculum are:

- **Challenge and enjoyment**. The joy of childhood sits at the centre of the CfE. Children need to be challenged emotionally, physically and intellectually in an effective environment.
- **Breadth**. The experiences and outcomes are a base line to ensure a breadth of experience, they do not represent the totality of learning, nor are they intended to be used in separate areas.
- **Progression**. Practitioners are aware of the need to acknowledge prior learning in skills.
- **Depth**. The curriculum does not denote a severe pace of learning; this is often imposed through adult need and self-driven pressure. There is a need to allow children to explore fascinations in depth over long blocks of time, rather than many issues at a shallow level.
- **Personalisation and choice**. Mindfulness in order to notice the individual child must sit at the root of early education. Children learn in different ways and have a right to be heard.
- **Coherence**. The links across and within curriculum areas enable the child to think and play in a holistic way. The application of a skill-based programme across multiple contexts allows a deeper level understanding of the connectivity of the world.
- **Relevance**. The connection for children encourages a greater link to home, community and the setting.

The creation of curricular documents varies in the content and styles of presentation. In the CfE there is a set principles for design. The seven principles of curriculum design give us a framework to consider our practice and they are the key influences on the pedagogy of the practitioners when they consider 'how' to teach/scaffold experiences that will explore the curriculum content or 'what' to teach.

Take each one and consider the place of this principle in your current practice. What effect does the principle have upon the day-to-day experiences of the child?

Tensions and challenges

The emphasis in some settings is to focus on 'what' to teach and not the 'how' or 'why'.

How do practitioners create a balance in their professional roles of understanding and applying pedagogy to the delivery of experiences and outcomes?

Curriculum areas

The Scottish CfE (The Scottish Government, 2006) has eight curriculum areas:

- expressive arts
- health and wellbeing
- languages
- mathematics
- religious and moral education
- sciences
- social studies and
- technologies.

Each of which makes its own distinctive contribution to developing the four capacities, previously mentioned as:

- confident individuals
- successful learners
- responsible citizens and
- effective learners.

The main purposes and principles of the curriculum areas are examined below.

Expressive arts

> The inspiration and power of the arts play a vital role in enabling our children and young people to enhance their creative talent and develop their artistic skills. By engaging in experiences within the expressive arts, children and young people will recognise and represent feelings and emotions, both their own and those of others. The expressive arts also play an

important role in supporting children and young people to recognise and value the variety and vitality of culture locally, nationally and globally.

Learning in, through and about the expressive arts enables children and young people to:

- be creative and express themselves in different ways;
- experience enjoyment and contribute to other people's enjoyment through creative and expressive performance and presentation;
- develop important skills, both those specific to the expressive arts and those which are transferable;
- develop an appreciation of aesthetic and cultural values, identities and ideas; and, for some,
- prepare for advanced learning and future careers by building foundations for excellence in the expressive arts.

(Scottish Executive, 2006: 5)

The role of the arts in defining a society is unparalleled and symptomatic of cultural wellbeing. Individual creativity and adaptability is of course crucial to their successes as is the ability to creatively communicate and identify one's own inner thoughts; an advanced skillset which finds usage and analogy in nearly every professional capacity. Scotland demarcates itself amongst other developed countries with a long and impressive cultural legacy not just in the spheres of invention, engineering, philosophy – it is internationally renowned as an artistic, architectural and creative hub which belies its small size. The pedagogical approach that the CfE has taken in trying to cross-pollinate areas of study makes sense for it is hard to think of a single subject that does not benefit from the inclusion of artistic ability in modern society and indeed throughout history. Even those most polar areas of study such as physics need diagrammatic assistance in communicating ideas. Moreover, the ability to confidently communicate ideas visually, to experiment, to play with abstract ideas as the artist does, are all fundamental skills for successful learning and growth.

Most importantly, however, the negation to prioritise the pursuit of aesthetic quality, beauty and art in any society always has negative repercussions for those living in it – and the CfE's approach should ensure that beauty finds its way into every young mind and many a burgeoning career.

HOLISTIC LEARNING – 'FISH': AUCHLONE NATURE KINDERGARTEN, SCOTLAND

Auchlone Nature Kindergarten is on the edge of a large wooded area that is bounded by a stream and a loch. The children spend 80–100 per cent of their time outside in the garden or out in the wilder spaces. The pedagogy of nature that has developed over 20 years relies on the materials that we harvest sustainably from nature. There are a few materials that we use to extend learning in the garden area and a Tool wrap that we transport to the forest. The documentation of learning is through collaborative working documents called Floorbooks (Warden, 1994) with individual moments shared in a learning story format in the Family Books.

Figure 3.5 Grinding charcoal and applying to white tiles to explore line and pattern.

The children were exploring the transformation of the charcoal when combined with water; they identified it as paint and decided to make further pots of paint to use. They collected more charcoal from the fire pit and a pestle and mortar to crush the charcoal to make a beautiful black natural paint. Discussions focused on the texture, density, 'floating bits' and the changing effect of wood ash to the ground charcoal.

There is an area set up in the outdoor garden that supports transient art. The children were working in the fire area which is adjacent to the transient art area. The children moved to work with the white tiles in the area. The movement of the shades with their fingers encouraged the comparison between shades of grey, the intensity of white and the black.

The flowing movements lead to talk of water and then into a conversation about fish. This was supported by the adult providing black and white images and line drawings of fish intentionally removing colour to focus more on line and form.

Whilst charcoal painting, the practitioner used the opportunity to explain how the same idea can be used to create a print to keep, unlike the charcoal which would be washed away by the rain. So the children decided that the temporary fish painting on the tile should be the 'art piece', not the printed copy, and proper printing paint was needed for 'keeping fish'.

The children found some Styrofoam and the focus on line continued as they enjoyed drawing on the foam. The children decided the fish were to be ' fierce Piranhas' and two of the Piranhas were to go in the tree as flying Piranha fish to scare someone climbing very high.

The children decided the rest of the foam fish should go swimming in a foamy sea. A foam sea was created, with essential sea colours. The focus moved from line to the texture of slipperiness as the children moved the smooth Styrofoam around the 'sea'.

Figure 3.6 Investigating fish.

Children who live in this area are familiar with hunting and fishing as part of life. When the staff brought in real fish the children explored the movement of the fish and the feel of the gills, scales, tail and mouth. After a good investigation of the fish the life drawing of the fish with charcoal and charcoal paint was revisited with new vigour.

The next step was to prepare the fish for cooking on the fire in the forest. The day flows at a nature kindergarten and one moment flows and affects the next. Foraging for materials on the walk up to the fire hut in the forest allowed the children to gather natural materials to add texture to the children's printing plate, representing the scales and hard fins the children felt when investigating the real fish.

The children were in charge of lighting the fire, stoking the fire and making sure the fish was evenly cooked and not burning. Cooking their own snack and respecting the fish as a source of nourishment is important as it encourages children to acknowledge a fascination with nature, but not disrespect.

The printing plates were made using some natural materials that were collected on the forest walks. Sticking materials on was a problem solving task that encouraged real perseverance. We spoke about the colours on the print plates not being the final colours and that a print is like a mirror image.

The Nature Kindergarten has an ancient printing press, with felt sheets and high quality cartridge paper. The children had to squirt the printing paint out, roll it on to the printing plates, place the pre-soaked paper on themselves (which they did in preparation). The gravitas of the machine itself gave the process a sense of ceremony; a lot of concentration was used to peel off the paper to reveal their work. Unexpectedly the stickiness of the paint enthralled the children as much as the rolling.

The children then decided that fishing in a self-build loch was just the thing to do while the printing ink was drying. The sticks were whittled to make them 'clean' and string and wire used for lines and hooks.

Figure 3.7 Representations of the 'wild fish' in black and white charcoal paint, made by the children.

Figure 3.8 Talkaround time (Warden, 1994) to share thinking of individuals with a wider audience to invite engagement.

Figure 3.9 Exploring the Talking Tub (Warden, 1994) to provocate thinking and deepen exploration.

Figure 3.10 Developing a sense of gravitas through the use of ancient equipment.

While adding colour to some of the printed work we spoke about using light colours and ones that contrasted to blue; the children used water colour blocks all the time so they added colour along the sides, some at the base and others carefully added in between the blue print. The finished prints were framed and put into an exhibition for parents in the forest alongside the Loch.

The holistic nature of learning is clearly shown through a child's family experience entering the world of the kindergarten and then extending through the interactions and experiences put in place by the staff. The experiences and outcomes of this opportunity can be pulled out by the adults, but the team would not split up the outcomes and experiences and design an activity to meet them, unless they felt that there were gaps in experience.

Figure 3.11 Application of a secondary colour to the fish pictures.

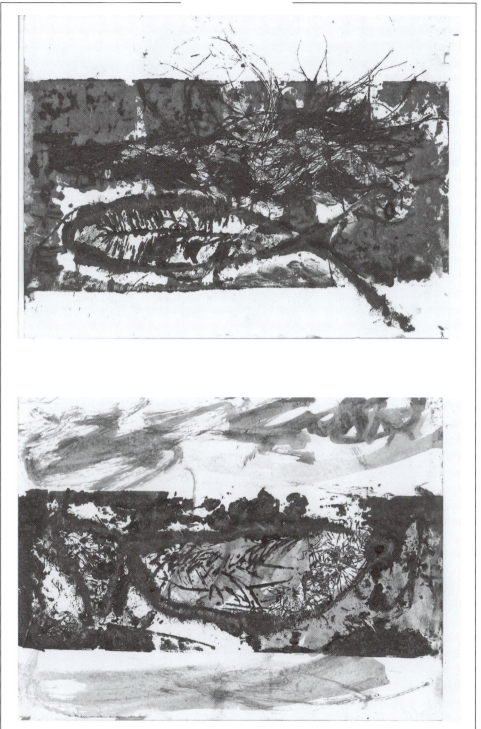

Figures 3.12 and 3.13 A selection of the print blocks, created after a long block of investigation, skill development and heightened understanding.

Figures 3.14 and 3.15 A selection of the print blocks, created after a long block of investigation, skill development and heightened understanding.

Health and wellbeing

> Learning through health and wellbeing promotes confidence, independent thinking and positive attitudes and dispositions. Because of this, it is the responsibility of every [practitioner] to contribute to learning and development in this area.
>
> (Scottish Executive, 2006: 8)

Learning in health and wellbeing ensures that children (and young people) develop the knowledge and understanding, skills, capabilities and attributes which they need for mental, emotional, social and physical wellbeing now and in the future. Learning through health and wellbeing enables children and young people to:

- make informed decisions in order to improve their mental, emotional, social and physical wellbeing;
- experience challenge and enjoyment;
- experience positive aspects of healthy living and activity for themselves;
- apply their mental, emotional, social and physical skills to pursue a healthy lifestyle;
- make a successful move to the next stage of education or work;
- establish a pattern of health and wellbeing which will be sustained into adult life, and which will help to promote the health and wellbeing of the next generation of Scottish children.

The detriment to the uninformed person facing life-changing decisions cannot be overstated. Of course for Scotland, a move to greater and more comprehensive health and wellbeing teaching must be made. Modern societies are plagued by the illnesses of contemporary living, whether it's acute back pain, obesity or just general unfitness. To move towards a healthier, happier and more efficient Scotland, it is the generation still in compulsory education that will shift the paradigm back to health and moderation.

In terms of emotional wellbeing, it is clear that a more conscientious, caring and emotionally intelligent society is a better one. An awareness of the thoughts of others, understanding one's own emotions, and dealing with novel and adverse situations effectively are pivotal skills needed to develop an even safer, kinder and happier Scotland.

Surely there is no more important a goal for the educational system than to equip young people with the tools that will help them sustain emotional, physical and social wellbeing as much as possible throughout their lives and the CfE caters for that goal.

'ARMS UP THERE'S JAGGYS': COWGATE NURSERY EDINBURGH

Cowgate Under Fives is a City of Edinburgh provision situated within the heart of Edinburgh's Old Town, underpinned by Froebelian principles. Our garden creates daily opportunities for our children to freely choose to play within a natural space. A responsive pedagogical approach to our children's request 'to play in the woods' inspired our Nature Kindergarden, named by our children as Stickland. We have daily access to a 26-acre mixed woodland site nestled in the foothills of the Pentlands. We have spent long uninterrupted time together with our children at Stickland Nature Kindergarden, mapping, risk assessing, playing, exploring the uniqueness of nature. 'The pioneers' developed a responsive approach to 'sharing' Stickland; we work

Figure 3.16 Stickland May 2014 'Arms up There's Jaggys'.

together as a community; all children, families and staff have the opportunity to visit Stickland. The children start and end their day in the centre where they help to create the 'list', choosing when and with whom they wish to share time in the wild space. At Stickland we have the time, space and opportunity for our adventures.

B explores the grassy space beneath BD's thinking tree. As she gathers her finds she calls to her friends: "look, look at the difference in these leaves, look this one is pointy, this one is dark green and this one is smooth and shiny."

B carefully places the leaves upon the fence,

I ask: "What have you found?"

B: "I found these different leaves, this one is so smooth and shiny." B strokes the surface of the leaf and places it back upon the fence. B lifts the leaf by the stem, "this one is dark green". B feels the tip of the next leaf, "this one is pointy it has a point look".

I respond: "your leaves are so different, I think we have picked the dark leaf before."

Figure 3.17 B's photo of her 'Clump of nettles'.

B: "yes, when we got stung by the nettle . . . It's a dock leaf." B recalls the healing properties of the dock leaf as she identifies its shape, colour, texture and name. B shares her knowledge of nettles through her mapping of Stickland and connections with a memory from home. B: "I picked nettles with mama on the canal path, I wore my gloves."

As B moves through her secret path she alerts her friends to potential 'stings', identifying the Jaggys. Our children have created a peer history through travelling the site exploring its affordance the pioneers gifted their knowledge "Arms up There's Jaggys". B perpetuates this knowledge, adding the element of foraging (wearing gloves).

A and C's response to B's shared knowledge is to gather dock leaves before our adventure, filling their pockets 'just in case'. The friends have traced the pathways where the nettles thrive and the dock leaves are scarce. Threading their way through the 'jaggys' the children approach Big Stickland in search of 'ripe' berries. R alerts the friends: "there's a shark", he peers into a hole in the pathway, the small aperture reveals a flow of water. R continues: "If you put your finger near he'll bite your toe!" R reassures RA: "It's ok he's friendly really he won't bite you."

R forges on ahead in search of the berries. He travels with BS who informs him: "the dinosaurs are here they live here but they live under the ground." R adds "yeah and the dragon lives here up at the top of the hill." R and BS search the prickly bushes scouring amongst the jaggy, thorny bushes. B is rewarded, with "*a real life berry, a raspberry*".

The friends forage for the berries. They move deftly into precariously prickly spaces, delicately fine tuning their pincer grip. A balances her body as she picks the

Figure 3.18 "Arms up There's Jaggys."

Figure 3.19 "He won't bite you!"

Figure 3.20 "A real life berry."

Figure 3.21 "This is a raspberry, they are red, the blackberry has to be black, the red ones are not ripe yet . . . we need to leave some for the birds."

fruit; she coordinates her movement mirroring her actions. A negotiates the steep gradient, tickly grass and spiky stems to gather her ripe raspberry. The fruit is harvested, some sampled straight from the stem: 'plenty left for the creatures.' R tastes the blackberry, recalls a previous harvest: "I'm collecting some for Angela." The berries are gathered into buckets and pots and carried carefully back to our yurt. T recalls a problem he encountered last Autumn when their friend, AS, could not reach the elderberries. T searches for a stick, he finds a long forked stick which he and A use to reach for the berries. T manoeuvres the stick into position, bending and lowering the branches and holding them in position whilst A nimbly removes the heads of the elderberries.

The children help to transport the fruit back to Cowgate with Angela (a staff member) and help while the fruit is washed, boiled and transformed into Stickland Jam to share with family and friends.

Our Stickland adventures celebrate a holistic approach, nurturing the whole child through 'real life' sensory exploration. Our adventures are shared, yet are unique to each child as they master skills through repetition, enthusiasm, encouragement and growing confidence.

Figure 3.22 A spots a 'ripe' berry.

Figure 3.23 Testing the ripeness of the berries.

Languages

Language and literacy are of personal, social and economic importance. Our ability to use language lies at the centre of the development and expression of our emotions, our thinking, our learning and our sense of personal identity. Language is itself a key aspect of our culture. Through language, children and young people can gain access to the literary heritage. Children and young people encounter, enjoy and learn from the diversity of language used in their homes, their communities, by the media and by their peers.

Literacy is fundamental to all areas of learning, as it unlocks access to the wider curriculum. Being literate increases opportunities for the individual in all aspects of life, lays the foundations for lifelong learning and work, and contributes strongly to the development of all four capacities of Curriculum for Excellence. Competence and confidence in literacy, including competence in grammar, spelling and the spoken word are essential for progress in all areas of the curriculum. Because of this, all [practitioners] have responsibility for promoting language and literacy development. Every [practitioner] in each area of the curriculum needs to find opportunities to encourage young people to explain their thinking, debate their ideas and read and write at a level which will help them to develop their language skills further.

(Scottish Executive, 2006: 18)

If the CfE sets out to promote lifelong learning in the young person, then it is the acquisition of literacy and the development of it that most facilitates this need. The written word, in all its forms, and the additional use of electronic media has the power to communicate the idea remotely. Especially in modern times with the web of information available to everyone, knowledge is so readily accessible that teaching an individual good literacy and linguistic skills, even if just in their mother tongue, gives them almost unlimited knowledge at their fingertips.

The goal of lifelong learning is one achieved both through culture and pedagogy and also through the provision of the basic tools to access information quickly and efficiently.

Knowledge of a foreign language is at the heart of the balanced and open mind. The ability to think as others do and the cultural doors that are unlocked with the acquisition of a second or tertiary language are invaluable. It is of note that as many European citizens and people of the world learn English as a matter of course, it is the onus of those native English-speaking countries to extend their own understanding and adaptability by learning another language. Similarly, the cross-pollinating pedagogy of the CfE opens up manifold possibilities to the intrepid, bilingual child or young person.

'THIS DEN WAS MADE BY COWGATE'

'As the play materials become less tangible so there is a greater advance in creative expression' Froebel (Lilley 1967:113).

'O' invited his mum and brother to share our Stickland spring adventure. We gathered our resources, shared our song 'bag and boots' and travelled by Stevie's mini bus to our Nature Kindergarden 'Stickland'.

OB helps to transport our resources up the hill to our yurt. En route OB surveys the site, the lashed fence enclosing the Teepee Village, the scattered timbers and loose materials. We share our snack and once replenished OB begins to explore the site.

OB gathers lengths of timber. Using the fence support as the main beam, he starts to construct. OB assesses the length of the timber. Starting at the base of the den he begins to carefully place the timber loosely against the post to form an A frame 'skeleton' of 'the den'. OB continues to enclose the space following the height and angle of the support beam.

As he moves the timber, O, A, OD, C and M watch him work. The friends follow OB. They discover a 'really long' plank. The friends find their own space along the length of the plank. They coordinate their movement, lift and begin to carry the

Figure 3.24 O's den.

Figure 3.25 The long plank.

Figure 3.26 Walking the plank.

plank. As they move up the gentle slope, OB offers gentle support by holding the front of the plank. He smiles at the forward-stepping friends and gently guides them moving slowly backwards.

'A' (mum) comments: "you are working so well together, people will think you have staged this!"

OD secures his arms and looks to OB who edges backwards steering the friends to the den. A is central in her position upon the plank. She takes a secure cradling hold upon the plank. She looks intently at OB. Fixing her gaze she supports the forward movement of the 'builders'. M steers from the rear. M giggles and mirrors the expression of OB and is pulled by the moving friends.

OD looks to OB for direction, he gently guides: "Let's put it here." The friends in unison 'drop' the plank away from their bodies. A and O return to the wood pile. O, M and C flatten the plank, smoothing it with their feet. They feel the 'crack in the plank'.

O, A and O lift the plank and feel the twist in the 'broken' end. O steers from the front. A pinches the middle and O cradles the end. The friends move together to deliver the plank to the front of the den.

M gathers a piece of timber approximately the same height as herself. She shifts the timber, fits it snugly under her arm, balances the wood and moves steadily forward up the hill to the den: "I'll see if it fits."

O, C and A return to the wood pile and manoeuvre between their bodies the broken, 'heavy' scaffolding plank. O and CF walk alongside on opposite sides of the plank, the timber rests in their outstretched arms. AF steers the plank from behind. OB approaches and assists by taking the weight of the plank. He walks backwards and they synchronise their movement. OB then lifts the timber into position.

Figure 3.27 The twist in the plank.

O, C, M and OB roll one of the large timbers.

"I can pull it!" says OB.

As M, A and C push it, OB lifts the end of the log and drags it to the den creating an enclosed perimeter around the den. OB says: "this can be the seating for the wee ones."

O returns to the log site. He huffs and puffs. A joins him, their bodies and movements are synchronised. They kneel and push, extending their arms to create a full stretch. OB lifts and drags the log, balancing and trotting over to the den site. O and A attempt to move the larger branch. They leave it in situ as they join OB to gather loose materials to cover the den.

OB: "If you lift this piece you can go in. It's the door."

M lifts the shorter piece and stoops to enter the den.

OB gathers twigs, leaves, bushy branches. He carefully places the materials and steps back to survey the den.

OB then climbs onto the fence post adjoining the den space and observes how the wee ones use the carefully positioned seating logs, how they access the den and how the children peep out of the den.

O and A adjust the entrance so that they too can access the space.

"Lets go on our adventure" says OD.

We head over the long field and follow the sand tracks. H, C and C play hide and seek in the bushes as OB scales the holly tree. O and G explore the properties of the mud, stomping, splashing and sliding. The tree-lined pathway opens into the 'field river'. OB runs into the open space. He is followed by our friends. H exclaims this is where the fox lives as they head over towards the log pile. M tests the wobbliness of herself and the logs.

OB balances nimbly across the logs, leaps onto the grass and runs at speed across the grassy meadow. O mirrors the movement of the den building log rolling. He uses his own body to roll towards his brother.

OB discovers the remains of a spent fire. He selects a piece of the charcoal and scribes his name onto the post. Inspired by this, H, C, M and N select their own pieces and make their own marks. We rest and replenish in the open space.

The friends make their way down through the long grass to the river.

OB: "I'll see what it says on the sign."

We wait for our friends to join us then move through the 'swishy' grass to the river bank.

"I can hear the river."

We gather on the shallow bank, tracing the flow of the 'deep' river. O and OB sit on the edge of the river and place their feet into the river to feel its movement. As O sits back a welly comes adrift and is carried away by the force of the river. It swirls and dips into the deep. We try to retrieve it. OB gathers some string to try to fish it out. Mum steps into the icy waters, but no joy. We problem solve looking for strong long sticks as we know through measuring with our bodies that the river is "deep here".

OB: "Look, look over there some frog spawn" floating gently in the water, which we explore before heading back up the hill to dry out.

Figure 3.28 Feeling the force of the river.

Figure 3.29 Frog spawn.

C, H and A avoid the Jaggys as they wind their way barefoot up through the long grass. C makes staccato movements and declares: "it hurts my feet." We stop to place our wellies back on.

When OB returns to the den he creates a declaration; lifting and cupping the sand from the trench OB creates letters with his hands. He crafts out the words: 'This den was made by Cowgate.' He then invites each of the children to join him to form their hand prints and OB crafts their names. He offers to G and M: "you could make a bottom print instead of a hand print if you like."

As we create our fire OB helps the children to embellish and celebrate their den.

"There that's every one."

Figure 3.30 This den.

Figure 3.31 Embellishing.

Figure 3.32 Handprints and footprints.

CfE celebrates:

- active experiential learning;
- a holistic approach to learning;
- learning through play;
- interdisciplinary learning;
- the ethos and life of the setting as a community.

The ethos of our community is underpinned by Froebelian principles. Froebelian principles support long uninterrupted time spent in nature, exploring, playing and simply being.

We celebrate the uniqueness of each child, their creativity, their resilience and their play. We celebrate the connection our children feel with their special place, through all of their senses, their whole body, their sense of self, their relationship with each other and place. As Cobb (cited in Ornstein and Sobel, 1990) suggests, our children learn about the world in ways that help them to discover a sense of self.

In this one wee adventure we explore all of the areas of the curriculum.

We encounter intrinsic motivation, curiosity, affordance of nature, the richness of the moment and the opportunity of found treasures. The den build is both a personal and a shared experience in which the inner and outer concepts are truly explored. The self-awareness of shared space, where communication is felt throughout the whole body, the rhythm and flow of creativity, is reflected within our natural environment. 'In any environment, both the degree of inventiveness and creativity, and the possibility of discovery, are directly proportional to the number and kind of variables in it' (Nicholson, 1971:30).

Figure 3.33 M's signature.

Mathematics

> Mathematics is important in our everyday life, allowing us to make sense of the world around us and to manage our lives. Using mathematics enables us to model real-life situations and make connections and informed predictions. It equips us with the skills we need to interpret and analyse information, simplify and solve problems, assess risk and make informed decisions. Mathematics plays an important role in areas such as science or technologies, and is vital to research and development in fields such as engineering, computing science, medicine and finance. Learning mathematics gives children and young people access to the wider curriculum and the opportunity to pursue further studies and interests.
>
> Because mathematics is rich and stimulating, it engages and fascinates learners of all ages, interests and abilities. Learning mathematics develops logical reasoning, analysis, problem-solving skills, creativity and the ability to think in abstract ways. It uses a universal language of numbers and symbols which allows us to communicate ideas in a concise, unambiguous and rigorous way. To face the challenges of the 21st century, each young person needs to have confidence in using mathematical skills, and Scotland needs both specialist mathematicians and a highly numerate population.
>
> (Scottish Executive, 2006: 18)

Mathematics equips us with many of the skills required for life, learning and work. Mathematics plays an integral part in lifelong learning and should be appreciated for the richness it brings.

Numeracy in Scotland is highly renowned. For many decades the Scottish school-leaver has been way ahead of their UK counterparts. Today, numeracy remains one of the fundamental skills in the capable adult in all spheres of life, from financial and budgetary competence to business sense. Economically, little explanation needs to be made for the importance of the numerate society, and good understanding of basic to advanced maths is a criterion for university students and those in careers.

In an increasingly interconnected world, the importance of maths, the universal language, is greater than ever. Many jobs require fast and efficient mathematical ability and many of the highest-paid jobs from those in the financial sector to computer programming rely heavily on mathematical competence, and it is absolutely essential that Scottish pupils and students remain highly valued and adaptable international citizens.

'SPECIAL CLAY'

The autumn time in Scotland gives us lovely mud. The site we work at Auchlone Nature Kindergarten is clay based and has an area of natural clay near the Loch. This is the story of a little boy's special clay.

Findlay was working in the outdoor kinderkitchen. He wanted to make his special clay. Mona (adult) offered to help to record the recipe.

M: "What do you need Findlay for your clay?"
F: "I just need salt."
M: "How much salt do you think you might need?"
F: "That much (points at bucket). That is just how much I need."

Figure 3.34 Creating the recipe.

M: "Ok, what next Findlay?"
F: "I need paint."
M: "Will it be more or less than the salt?"
F: "Less."

Next Findlay wanted hot water. Findlay pointed to the number that was at the place where he wanted his water to go to.

Figure 3.35 Exploring quantity.

F: "2+5+0."
G *(a child):* "Now that makes a very big number it is 250!!!"

Findlay told Mona to 'stop' when the water had reached 250ml. Findlay turned the hot water around in the bucket until it had cooled down.

F: "The hot water is important to make the clay work."

Findlay then wanted to measure his sand. Mona and Findlay thought that it was not a good idea to use kitchen equipment for that job. They remembered the scales in the mud kitchen!

M: "I wonder how these work, can you show me Findlay?"

Figure 3.36 Linking learning to outdoor provision.

F: "Yes, you put something in there. It goes down, you have to put something in there. I need it to balance." (He adds more until it does.)
M: "Well done Findlay that's amazing, thank you!"

Findlay keeps stepping back to get a better look until he is sure they are the same. Findlay then crushes up some charcoal from the fire pit and adds that. Then it is time for building and to see if his special clay works. It does! The clay was given the name 'Cosmis'.

M: "Well done Findlay you did an amazing job and also for helping me understand scales and for helping H to make your recipe too, Thank you! From Mona."
F: "This is the girl alarm made with the clay . . . it senses when a girl is at the door so they know to answer."

Figure 3.37 Creating the girl alarm.

Findlay's theories:

- I can make my own recipes and if I write them down I can make them again exactly the same.
- I can measure using different tools so that it is exact.
- I like to help my friends when they need my help.

Possible lines of development:

- Continue to encourage Findlay to measure using different technologies so that his knowledge of these and bigger numbers increases. For instance, using the kitchen scales when baking, measuring larger pieces of wood.
- Encourage Findlay to investigate the different uses of clay and experiment with the effectiveness of different types, e.g. clay on site, stoneware, etc. Activities for uses could involve making sculptures, bowls, etc. This will help with the development of his problem-solving skills and bringing his imaginative ideas to life.
- CfE: HWB 9,11,19,23 EA 2,5,6 SOC 15,17,18 TEC 1,11,12,14,15 RME 2,5 N&M 1,2a,7,11,17,20c L&T 4,7,9a WRI 26 SCI 7,15.
- GIRFEC: Achieving, Responsible.

Religious and moral education

> Scotland is a nation whose people hold a wide range of beliefs from the many branches of the Christian faith represented throughout the land to the world's other major religions and to beliefs which lie outwith religious traditions. Such diversity enriches the Scottish nation and serves as an inspiring and thought-provoking background for our children and young people to develop their own beliefs and values.
>
> Religious and moral education enables children and young people to explore the world's major religions and views which are independent of religious belief and to consider the challenges posed by these beliefs and values. It supports them in developing and reflecting upon their values and their capacity for moral judgement. Through developing awareness and appreciation of the value of each individual in a diverse society, religious and moral education engenders responsible attitudes to other people. This awareness and appreciation will assist in counteracting prejudice and intolerance as children and young people consider issues such as sectarianism and discrimination more broadly. Religious and moral education is a process where children and young people engage in a search for meaning, value and purpose in life. This involves both the exploration of beliefs and values and the study of how such beliefs and values are expressed.
>
> (Scottish Executive, 2006: 22)

Children and young people must become aware that beliefs and values are fundamental to families and to the fabric of society in communities, local and global. There is an intrinsic value in learning about religion as well as learning from religion, as children and young people develop their understanding of diversity in our society and their own roles in it. Scotland has a strong cultural identity that is a lived culture. It does have tokenistic representations as with any culture and yet for many diverse groups this definition makes no attempt to dominate others but merely wishes to be acknowledged as something and somewhere in its own right. The skills of reflection and critical thinking and an enhanced understanding of the beliefs and values of others are all crucial in assisting this process. Learning through religious and moral education enables children and young people to:

- recognise religion as an important part of human experience;
- learn about and from the beliefs, values, practices and traditions of Christianity and the world religions selected for study, other traditions, and viewpoints independent of religious belief;
- explore and develop knowledge and understanding of religions, recognising the place of Christianity in the Scottish context;
- investigate and understand the responses which religious and non-religious views can offer to question about the nature and meaning of life;
- recognise and understand religious diversity and the importance of religion in society;
- develop respect for others and an understanding of beliefs and practices which are different from their own;
- explore and establish values such as wisdom, justice, compassion and integrity and engage in the development of and reflection upon their own moral values;
- develop their beliefs, attitudes, values and practice through reflection, discovery and critical evaluation;
- develop the skills of reflection, discernment, critical thinking and deciding how to act when making moral decisions;
- make a positive difference to the world by putting their beliefs and values into action; and
- establish a firm foundation for lifelong learning, further learning and adult life.

Religious and moral education is therefore an essential part of every child or young person's educational experience.

The idea that schools should provide the child and young person with moral education is a relatively new one – but it makes sense. The more sources from which the individual is gleaning moral and philosophical ideas and approaches, the more they are enabled to make informed moral decisions.

The awareness of religious diversity is a prerequisite to the possession of religious tolerance, which is a facility that western and middle-eastern society would do well to exercise. Scotland itself is a highly multicultural society with immigrants from an astonishing variety of countries gracing our shores and enriching our society as they do. The CfE, then, aims to reinforce and maintain the intercultural bonds which tie our society together with peace and tolerance, starting with children and young people.

'TREE NECKLACE'

Learning Story (Carr and Lee, 2012) presented in the Family books for children to re-visit:

I saw you with your friends in the forest. You spent a long time carefully tying and threading the ribbons round and through the branch. You tied the ribbon on tight. You said "its happy for the tree, but we can't make it too tight."

The next day Anine and some of the children had made a special tree for us to paint and decorate in our garden. You were keen to join some of the children who were decorating the tree with beads.

Figure 3.38 Developing a sense of ceremony.

Figure 3.39 Making empathetic choices *for* the tree.

We quickly found that it was tricky to thread the beads onto the wool so we tried wire instead. You really concentrated on threading each bead onto the end of your wire and showed your friends how you did it. "It's coming through." You enjoyed choosing which bead to put on next, making a pattern with your beads. You added more beads and bent your wire round to stop the beads sliding off.

"These are like necklaces. I hope this is going to be good."

We talked about tying the ends so that the beads didn't slide off. You showed us how to do it.

"You put your finger through there and the wire through here. It's looking good."

Finally you tied up your tree bead necklace and showed your friends.

"Look, I made it all myself."

You chose a branch to hang it on. You made a fantastic bead necklace and its bright colours looked lovely on our special tree. Well done F!

Figure 3.40 Persevering with the task.

Children's theories:

- I can be creative with ribbon, wire and beads.
- Bending the wire up and tying the ends stops the beads falling off.
- I can show my friends how to do things.

Possible lines of development:

- Make our own necklaces, making patterns with the beads and practising threading and tying natural materials to make our own decorations.

Figure 3.41 Creating objects to 'dress the tree'.

Sciences

> Science is an important part of our heritage and we use its applications every day in our lives at work, at leisure and in the home. Science and the application of science are central to our economic future and to our health and wellbeing as individuals and as a society. Scotland has a long tradition of scientific discovery, of innovation in the application of scientific discovery, and of the application of science in the protection and enhancement of the natural and built environment. Children and young people are fascinated by new discoveries and technologies and become increasingly aware of, and passionate about, the impact of science on their own health and wellbeing, the health of society and the health of the environment. Through learning in the sciences, children and young people develop their interest in, and understanding of, the living, material and physical world.... They engage in a wide range of collaborative investigative tasks, which allows them to develop important skills to become creative, inventive and enterprising adults in a world where the skills and knowledge of the sciences are needed across all sectors of the economy.
>
> (Scottish Executive, 2006: 30)

What are the main purposes of learning in the sciences?

Children and young people participating in the experiences and outcomes in the sciences will:

- develop a curiosity and understanding of their environment and their place in the living, material and physical world;
- demonstrate a secure knowledge and understanding of the big ideas and concepts of the sciences;
- develop skills for learning, life and work;
- develop skills of scientific inquiry and investigation using practical techniques;
- develop skills in the accurate use of scientific language, formulae and equations;
- recognise the role of creativity and inventiveness in the development of the sciences;
- apply safety measures and take necessary actions to control risk and hazards;
- recognise the impact the sciences make on their lives, the lives of others, the environment and on society;
- develop an understanding of the Earth's resources and the need for responsible use of them;
- express opinions and make decisions on social, moral, ethical, economic and environmental issues based upon sound understanding;
- develop as scientifically literate citizens with a lifelong interest in the sciences; and
- establish the foundation for more advanced learning and, for some, future careers in the sciences and the technologies.

The aforementioned Scottish propensity for invention and our status as harbinger of The Enlightenment should demonstrate a long and healthy tradition of science. Scottish universities are internationally renowned in the areas of medicine and scientific research. In young people, an understanding of scientific processes and ways in which we pursue truth in the world will benefit them and help them to think and look as a scientist does – with an open but critical mind. It is inarguable that critical thought and an ability to be spoon fed information is what great thinkers possess. If the new curriculum encourages more children and young people to be interested in scientific and engineering disciplines then the results will be more jobs, a stronger economy and, most importantly, a more advanced society.

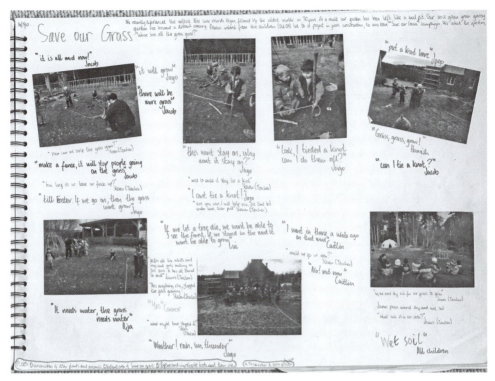

Figure 3.42 Floorbook (Warden, 1994) 'Save our Grass?'

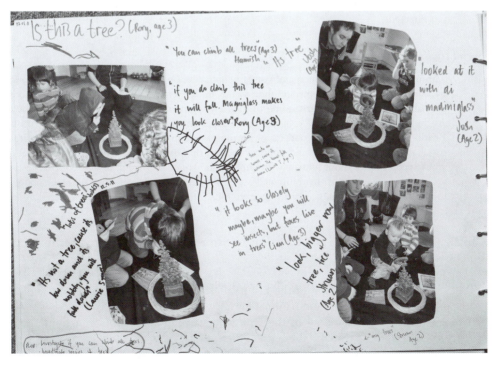

Figure 3.43 Scientific questioning and exploration . . . 'What is a tree?'

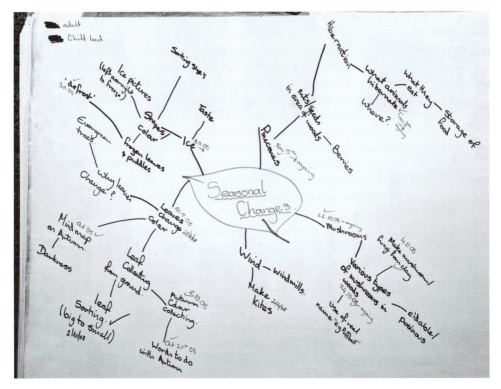

Figure 3.44 Concept mapping through a 2D mind map built up with children rather than adult directed.

Social studies

> Through social studies, children and young people develop their understanding of the world by learning about other people and their values, in different times, places and circumstances; they also develop their understanding of their environment and of how it has been shaped. As they mature, children and young people's experiences will be broadened using Scottish, British, European and wider contexts for learning, while maintaining a focus on the historical, social, geographic, economic and political changes that have shaped Scotland. Children and young people learn about human achievements and about how to make sense of changes in society, of conflicts and of environmental issues. With greater understanding comes the opportunity and ability to influence events by exercising informed and responsible citizenship.
>
> (Scottish Executive, 2006: 34)

Children and young people, as they participate in experiences and outcomes in social studies, will:

- develop their understanding of the history, heritage and culture of Scotland, and an appreciation of their local and national heritage within the world;
- broaden their understanding of the world by learning about human activities and achievements in the past and present;
- develop their understanding of their own values, beliefs and cultures and those of others;

- develop an understanding of the principles of democracy and citizenship through experience of critical and independent thinking;
- explore and evaluate different types of sources and evidence;
- learn how to locate, explore and link periods, people and events in time and place;
- learn how to locate, explore and link features and places locally and further afield;
- engage in activities which encourage enterprising attitudes;
- develop an understanding of concepts that encourage enterprise and influence business; and
- establish firm foundations for lifelong learning and for further specialised study and careers.

Is it possible that it is through the lens of history that the decisions in the present can be made for the future? The repetition of past failures is avoidable if the past is clearly communicated to children and young people. The people, events and stories of history are able to give children and young people ideas of how the world they find themselves in came to be and gives them a cultural grounding. This book was written at a time when we were undergoing a referendum on the independence of Scotland. The closeness of the vote demonstrated the depth of feeling within Scotland. There are clear differences in the way that the framework and structure of Scottish education is presented as demonstrated through this book.

Understanding geographical and meteorological phenomena opens the young person's mind and allows them to look at the awe-inspiring history and processes of Earth. For Scottish children and for all young people, a good level of knowledge about other countries, societies and peoples of the world will foster a strong worldview and temper ignorance.

WHAT IS SCOTTISH?

These are children's thoughts on Scotland recorded when exploring a Talking Tub to explore 'What is Scottish?' (Warden, 1994).

D (4): "I am wearing this hoodie, it's got Clyde the thistle man on it because it's from Glasgow in the summer time."

Adult: "What was happening in Glasgow in the summer?"

D: "Umm, I'm not sure . . . (thinking) . . . Oh yes, people played some games, it was on the television."

G (4): "I've been to Glasgow, it's in Scotland you know."

C (4): "I live in Scotland too. The Scotland flag is blue and white. I've seen a black bit on it too."

We looked at an image of the Scotland flag.

C: "That's the Scotland flag 'cause it's got blue bits on it. There is a yellow one too."

We looked at other images, tartan and bagpipes . . .

D: (excitedly) "I've worn a kilt!!"

G: "I had a kilt when I was a tiny baby, maybe someone's wedding then."

Figure 3.45 Authentic cultural experiences.

Technologies

Technology – the application of knowledge and skills to extend human capabilities and to help satisfy human needs and wants – has had profound effects on society. Scotland has a strong tradition of excellence and innovation in technological research. This is especially true in areas such as engineering, electronics, optoelectronics, biomedical research, genomics and cell engineering. Scotland's people need to be skilled in technologies and to be aware of the impact of technologies on society and the environment, now and in the future. Learning in the technologies provides a strong foundation for the development of skills and knowledge which are, and will continue to be, essential in maintaining Scotland's economic prosperity.

Within CfE, the technologies curriculum area relates particularly to contexts that provide scope for developing technological skills, knowledge, understanding and attributes through creative, practical and work-related activities. For this reason, the framework provides experiences and outcomes which can be applied in business, computing science, food, textiles, craft, design, engineering, graphics and applied technologies. These experiences and outcomes offer a rich context for the development of all of the four capacities and for developing the life skills that are recognised as being important for success in the world of work. They also offer an excellent platform for a range of technology-related careers. The technologies framework offers challenging activities which involve research, problem-solving, exploration of new and unfamiliar concepts, skills and materials, and the rewarding learning which often results from creating products which have real applications. It provides progression in cognitive skills. Children and young people will develop their creativity and entrepreneurial skills and be encouraged to become innovative and critical designers of the future. These attributes are essential if, in the future, our children and young people are to play a major part in the global economy and embrace technological developments in the twenty-first century.

'THE CLOCK'

One day Mona (adult) and Charlie decided to take apart an 'old-fashioned' clock to see how it worked and to see if they could fix it as it had stopped working a long time ago! They had to use a thin straight-edged screwdriver to take it apart and pliers for the stiff bolts as they had no spanner small enough. Charlie worked slowly and carefully, collecting all the screws and nuts so that they didn't get lost. They were very excited to get the clock open finally to see what was inside ...

It was amazing, there were lots of cogs and a giant spring!

C: "I'll tell you things about this clock. The thing is it's very old and sometimes the cogs don't work."

M: "Thank you Charlie that would be amazing! This clock is fantastic!"

C: "All the cogs I can see some of them are not moving."

M: "I wonder if we attached this to wind it up again they might move then, what do you think Charlie?"

C: "Yes but look at all the cogs, it's very dirty inside!"

M: "Maybe we should give it a clean first with a soft paintbrush. That way we won't damage anything and can get in all the parts."

Charlie carefully cleaned all the parts of the clock, he did a very thorough job. Mona and Charlie tried winding up the clock but it still didn't work! Mona wanted to know how it worked as then they might be able to find the problem.

M: "Charlie can you show me how it works?"

C: "Yes, in the nights the windie bits wind up the cogs inside then the spring winds up. When it slowly winds that moves the hands but not this clock because it is very old!"

Figure 3.46 Deconstructing the clock.

Figure 3.47 Exploring real mechanisms.

Mona and Charlie then attached back the mechanism to wind up the clock to see if they could see where the problem was.

Mona and Charlie wound and wound and noticed that the spring was getting smaller and smaller!

C: "That bit moving with the tick tock is the spring."

Then all of a sudden the clock started making a noise like it was an alarm going off. The most amazing part was that the spring was now getting bigger and bigger! They soon realised that this was the alarm so they wound up the spring again and moved the hands on the front until it went off again and again! They then discussed that each cog would move the next and the next.

They needed to put the clock back together again! At the beginning of term they decided that they would do this, it was also R's first day and he was a little nervous. Charlie soon put him at ease by inviting him to join them. Sitting at the table with the clock in parts, Charlie shared his knowledge of clocks with R. R really enjoyed this and he and Charlie sat together looking at the clock's cogs and then put it back together again perfectly. Charlie and R also sat looking through the books on clocks that Charlie and Mona had brought in for each other to look at. They showed diagrams of what was inside different items.

Charlie, you are an amazing friend, you really helped R to feel at home here and now he has made a friend!

Children's theories:

*   Working methodically is important when fixing items.
*   When things are old they sometimes don't work!
*   I can share my knowledge with others to work together to solve problems.

Possible lines of development:

*   Continue to encourage Charlie to share his knowledge of things important to him, thus building his confidence to deconstruct objects to gain understanding, i.e., machines, clocks.
*   Investigate other technologies and how they work and help us, i.e., books, taking things apart to see their workings. This will further his knowledge of forces and their effects.
*   Extend the exploration into digital clocks, wrist watches, etc.

Learning in the technologies enables children and young people to be informed, skilled, thoughtful, adaptable and enterprising citizens, and to:

*   develop understanding of the role and impact of technologies in changing and influencing societies;
*   contribute to building a better world by taking responsible ethical actions to improve their lives, the lives of others and the environment;

- gain the skills and confidence to embrace and use technologies now and in the future, at home, at work and in the wider community;
- become informed consumers and producers who have an appreciation of the merits and impacts of products and services;
- be capable of making reasoned choices relating to the environment, to sustainable development and to ethical, economic and cultural issues;
- broaden their understanding of the role that information and communications technology (ICT) has in Scotland and in the global community;
- broaden their understanding of the applications and concepts behind technological thinking, including the nature of engineering and the links between the technologies and the sciences; and
- experience work-related learning, establish firm foundations for lifelong learning and, for some, for specialised study and a diverse range of careers.

Technology, by its very definition, is always at the fore of societal development. The CfE has acknowledged the criticality of an understanding of technology for children and young people in Scottish society. The axiom that the ten highest-paid jobs did not exist ten years ago highlights the rapid development of technology and the desirability for employers to find young, creative and technologically proficient young people. In fact it is hard to think of any profession which has not been revolutionised for the current generation of young people with computers, and it seems a proficiency in these realms is crucial. Many areas of Scotland are rurally isolated and the interaction with technology has given links and social connections for both education and industry.

A tension does, however, exist around the overuse of technology in the early years that has resulted from government funding in the area. Whether such proficiency pertains to information technology, a particular computer program or just computing literacy, the job of our educational system should be to give children and young people the mental and physical tools to continue to advance as fast as the technology that is ubiquitous around them.

HOLISTIC LEARNING

How do you view the child?

Practitioners are to be able to view the child through a holistic lens. The child's learning grows through their parents, family members and other people connected to the child so that a curriculum should be meaningful to many groups.

Consider how the methodology section of the Scottish curriculum sets out an expectation that the practitioners make links in learning whilst ensuring that children are enabled to be agents of their own learning?

Tensions and challenges

There is a tension for some practitioners between the way that the subjects are divided and then presented in the curriculum areas and the methodology section which describes holistic thinking.

Consider how you would address this issue.

Crosscurricular and intercurricular dimensions

The curriculum levels describe progression and development rather than set outcomes put forward as targets. Evidence of Bruner's work (1996) can be explored through the text of the curriculum as it is expected to spiral so that aspects can be revisited over time and in different ways to aid deeper level retention. In order to reflect this there are three aspects that are highlighted as being the responsibility of all:

- health and wellbeing across learning;
- literacy across learning;
- numeracy across learning.

In order to reflect the holistic nature of the learning process, the CfE supports learning across the curriculum, interdisciplinary working and themes across learning such as global citizenship.

The newest reviews in 2013/2014 have been to explore the place of sustainable practices in education so that the political forums cannot easily affect the learning for children. There are many cross party forums in the Scottish Government that have now supported outdoor learning, global citizenship and health and wellbeing within the overarching area of sustainable development education.

The vision for outdoor learning in Scotland is that:

- all children and young people are participating in a range of progressive and creative outdoor learning experiences which are clearly part of the curriculum;
- schools and centres are providing regular, frequent, enjoyable and challenging opportunities for all children and young people to learn outdoors throughout their school career and beyond;
- teachers and educators embed outdoor learning in the curriculum so that learning in the outdoor environment becomes a reality for all children and young people.

The core values of the CfE resonate with long-standing key concepts of outdoor learning. Challenge, enjoyment, relevance, depth, development of the whole person and an adventurous approach to learning are at the core of outdoor pedagogy. The outdoor environment encourages staff and students to see each other in a different light, building positive relationships and improving self-awareness and understanding of others.

All settings are expected to deliver outdoor experiences for children. In some settings that were licensed before the CfE was in place, the outdoor experiences have to be shown to be taking place through excursions. The small areas physically provided for outdoor play and the challenges of access in older style buildings have created a range of provision.

In order to support this vision, working groups have built up options for indoor and outdoor learning across many of the Experiences and Outcomes presented within the CfE. These are presented through the Education Scotland website so that the message is consistent across all materials for children and families.

It is very significant that policy, practice and professional standards have all come together with the same messages for teachers. At a One Planet Schools Ministerial Working group, the Scottish Government announced in March 2014 that 'all learners should have an entitlement to learning for sustainability'. Rosa Murray stated in May 2014 that 'The "permission" to play and learn outside has always been there, these changes ensure there is an accountability to deliver'. This will have an impact on the quality of provision and the attention given to these aspects of the curriculum.

The Scottish Government's Action Plans for the UN Decade of Education for Sustainable Development (2005–2014) set out actions for all sectors of education. Learning for Sustainability weaves together and builds upon these themes. The Scottish Government has accepted the Learning for Sustainability report's recommendations that:

- all learners should have an entitlement to Learning for Sustainability;
- every practitioner, school and education leader should demonstrate Learning for Sustainability in their practice;
- every school should have a whole school approach to Learning for Sustainability that is robust, demonstrable, evaluated and supported by leadership at all levels;
- school buildings, grounds and policies should support Learning for Sustainability;
- a strategic national approach to supporting Learning for Sustainability should be established.

The professional actions, values, skills and knowledge of Learning for Sustainability are embedded within the Standards for Registration/Career-Long Professional Learning/ Leadership and Management, recognising that all teachers should be confident in their knowledge and understanding of the challenges facing society locally and globally (General Teaching Council Scotland, 2012).

In order to be able to deliver this practice the government has defined a pathway for career-long professional learning from the early phase into developing their pedagogic expertise and leadership. It has been generated from research studies exploring the relationship between professional learning and enhancement of practice, for example:

- Reflection on practice: where through professional learning, practitioners are curious about and critically explore practice.
- Experiential learning: learning through structured activities to question, try out and enhance practice.
- Cognitive development: developing ideas to challenge assumptions and deepen understanding of practice.
- Collaborative learning: learning with and through others to enhance practice.

(Education Scotland, 2014)

This approach to professional learning has influenced the creation of learning communities around the local settings linked to the location of secondary schools, rather than central administered local authority wide provision.

Conclusion

Scotland has a strong sense of itself. Educationally it has defined itself through the creation and implementation of a forward thinking curriculum that is holding on to the real sense of childhood and the image of a child as key to the future of the country. The framework that sits around the Curriculum for Excellence is developing. In this development of quality, the inspection process, the support services for health and care for children and their families have clearly stated that the most important person remains at the centre, the child.

References

Bruce, T. (2001) *Learning through Play: Babies, Toddlers and the Foundation Years.* London: Hodder and Stoughton.

Bruce, T. (ed.) (2010) (2nd edition) *Early Childhood: A Student Guide.* London: Sage Publications.

Bruce, T. (2011) (4th edition) *Early Childhood Education.* London: Hodder Arnold.

Bruce, T. (2012) *Early Childhood Practice: Froebel Today.* London: Sage Publications.

Bruce, T., Findlay, A., Read, J. and Scarborough, M. (eds) (1995) *Recurring Themes in Education.* London: Paul Chapman Publishing.

Bruner, J.S. (1996) *The Culture of Education.* Cambridge, MA: Harvard University Press.

Carr, M. and Lee, W. (2012) *Learning Stories: Constructing Learner Identities in Early Education.* London: Sage Publications.

Education Scotland/Foghlam Alba (2002) *National Debate on Education* [online] www.educationscotland.gov.uk/thecurriculum/whatiscurriculumforexcellence/howwasthecurriculumdeveloped/processofchange/timeline.asp (accessed 21 February 2014).

Education Scotland/Foghlam Alba (2010) *The Building the Curriculum Series* [online] www.educationscotland.gov.uk/thecurriculum/howdoyoubuildyourcurriculum/curriculumplanning/whatisbuildingyourcurriculum/btc/ (accessed 21 February 2014).

Education Scotland/Foghlam Alba (2014) *Transforming Lives through Learning* [online] www.educationscotland.gov.uk/thecurriculum/howisthecurriculumorganised/curriculumareas/index.asp (accessed 26 August 2014).

General Teaching Council Scotland (2012) [online] www.gtcs.org.uk/about-gtcs/about-gtcs.aspx (accessed 11 May 2015).

GUS (Growing Up in Scotland) (2003) Background [online] http://growingupinscotland.org.uk/about-gus/background/ (accessed 20 August 2014).

Knox, W.W. (n.d.) A History of The Scottish People. The Scottish Educational System 1840–1940 [online] www.scran.ac.uk/Scotland/pdf/SP2_1Education.pdf (accessed 21 February 2014).

Lascarides, V.C. and Hinitz, B.F. (2000) *History of Early Childhood Education.* New York: Falmer Press.

Learning and Teaching Scotland (2010) *Curriculum for Excellence through Outdoor Learning* [online] www.LTScotland.org.uk/Images/cfeoutdoorlearningfinal_tcm4-596061.pdf (accessed 21 February 2014).

Liebschner, J. (1992) *A Child's Work. Freedom and Guidance in Froebel's Educational Theory and Practice.* Cambridge: The Lutterworth Press.

Lilley, I.M. (1967) *Freidrich Froebel. A Selection From His Writings.* London: Cambridge University Press.

MacLaren, M. (2012) Preface: Froebel. In Bruce, T. (ed.), *Early Childhood Practice: Froebel Today.* London: Sage Publications, p. xii.

Miller, L. and Pound, L. (2011) *Theories and Approaches to Learning in the Early Years.* London: Sage Publications.

Murray, R. (2014) Speech. Outdoor Learning Conference May 2014. West Lothian Forest Education Initiative.

Nicholson, S. (1971) How Not to Cheat Children: The Theory of Loose Parts. *Landscape Architecture,* 62, pp. 30–34.

OECD (Organization for Economic Cooperation and Development) (2007) *Quality and Equity of Schooling in Scotland* [online] www.oecd.org/edu/school/reviewofnationalpoliciesforeducation-qualityand equityofschoolinginscotland.htm#3 (accessed 21 February 2014).

Ornstein, R. and Sobel, D. (1990) *Health Pleasures: Discover the Proven Medical Benefits of Pleasure and Live a Longer, Healthier Life.* New York: Perseus Books.

Scottish Executive (2004) *Curriculum for Excellence* [online] www.LTScotland.org.uk/curriculumforexcellence/index.asp (accessed 21 February 2014).

Scottish Executive (2006) *The Curriculum for Excellence: Building the Curriculum 1: The Contribution of Curriculum Areas* [online] www.educationscotland.gov.uk/Images/building_curriculum1_tcm4-383389.pdf (accessed 17 December 2014).

Scottish Qualifications Authority (2014) [online] www.sqa.org.uk/sqa/47050.html (accessed 24 August 2014).

Scottish Social Services Council (2007) [online] www.sssc.uk.com/about-the-sssc/multimedia-library/publications/70-education-and-training/193-childhood-practice/244-the-standard-for-childhood-practice (accessed June 2015).

Scottish Social Services Council (2014) [online] www.tellmescotland.gov.uk/organisations/scottish-social-services-council/ (accessed 24 August 2014).

Siraj, I. and Kingston, D. (2015) *An Independent Review of the Scottish Early Learning and Childcare (ELC) Workforce and Out of School Care (OSC) Workforce* [online] www.gov.scot/Resource/0047/00477419.pdf (accessed 21 October 2014).

The Children and Young People (Scotland) Act (2014) [online] www.legislation.gov.uk/asp/2014/8/contents/enacted (accessed 20 August 2014).

The Child's Curriculum (2010) Conference at Edinburgh [online] www.childscurriculum.org.uk (accessed 21 February 2014).

The Education (Additional Support for Learning) (Scotland) Act (2009) [online] www.opsi.gov/legislation/scotland/acts2009/pdf/asp_20090007_en.pdf (accessed 21 February 2014).

The Scottish Government (2004) *A Curriculum for Excellence: The Curriculum Review Group* [online] www.gov.scot/Publications/2004/11/20178/45862 (accessed 23 January 2015).

The Scottish Government (2006) *Curriculum for Excellence Building the Curriculum 1: The Contribution of Curriculum Areas* [online] www.educationscotland.gov.uk/thecurriculum/howdoyoubuildyourcurriculum/curriculumplanning/whatisbuildingyourcurriculum/btc/btc1.asp (accessed 21 February 2014).

The Scottish Government (2007) *Curriculum for Excellence Building the Curriculum 2: Active Learning in the Early Years* [online] www.educationscotland.gov.uk/publications/b/publication_tcm4533529.asp (accessed 21 February 2014).

The Scottish Government (2008) *The Early Years Framework.* Edinburgh: Scottish Government [online] www.scotland.gov.uk/resource/doc/257007/0076309.pdf (accessed 21 February 2014).

The Scottish Government (2009) *Curriculum for Excellence Building the Curriculum 4: Skills for Learning, Skills for Life and Skills for Work* [online] www.scotland.gov.uk (accessed 20 February 2014).

The Scottish Government (2010) *Curriculum for Excellence Building the Curriculum 5: A Framework for Assessment* [online] www.scotland.gov.uk (accessed 20 February 2014).

The Scottish Government (2011) *Early Years Change Fund* [online] www.scotland.gov.uk/resource/003800389841.doc (accessed 21 February 2014).

The Scottish Government (2012) *Early Years Collaborative* [online] www.scotland.gov.uk/Topics/People/Young-People/early-years/early-years-collaborative (accessed 21 February 2014).

The Scottish Government (2013) *Play Strategy for Scotland: Our Vision* [online] www.scotland.gov.uk/Publications/2013/06/5675 (accessed 21 February 2014).

The Scottish Parliament (1998) Scotland Act. [online] www.legislation.gov.uk/ukpga/1998/46/contents (accessed 21 February 2014).

The University of Edinburgh (2014) [online] www.ed.ac.uk/schools-departments/education/undergraduate/degree-programmes/childhood-practice (accessed 24 August 2014).

Warden, C. (1994) Talking and Thinking Floorbooks. Pub Mindstretchers. UK.

Whittaker, T. (2014) (3rd edition) *Dealing with Difficult Teachers.* New York: Routledge.

Further reading

Baker, M. (2012) Family Songs in the Froebelian Tradition. In Bruce, T. (ed.), *Early Childhood Practice: Froebel Today.* London: Sage Publications, pp. 81–94.

Brehony, K.J. (2001) *The Origins of Nursery Education: Friedrich Froebel and the English System, Volume IV, Friedrich Froebel's Education by Development.* London: Routledge.

Bronfenbrenner, U. (1979) *The Ecology of Human Development: Experiments by Nature and Design.* Cambridge, MA: Harvard University Press.

Brown, S. (2012) The Changing of the Seasons in the Child Garden. In Bruce, T. (ed.), *Early Childhood Practice: Froebel Today.* London: Sage Publications, pp. 29–42.

Cross, B. (2012) *Building Bridges, Forming Friendships A Report on the Evaluation of Craigmillar Books for Babies Early Literacy Project*. info@craigmillarbooksforbabies.org.uk.

Education Scotland (n.d.) *The Journey to Excellence* [online] www.journeytoexcellencescotland.gov.uk (accessed 11 May 2015).

Education Scotland (n.d.) *What is Curriculum Excellence* [online] www.curriculumforexcellencescotland. gov.uk (accessed 11 May 2015).

Eke, R., Butcher, H. and Lee, M. (2009) *Whose Childhood Is It? The Roles of Children, Adults and Policy Makers*. London: Continuum International Publishing Group.

Higgins, P. et al. (2014) New Innovations . . . Education for Sustainability. Report for the Scottish Government.

McNair, L. (2012) Offering Children First Hand Experiences through Forest Schools: Relating to and Learning About Nature. In Bruce, T. (ed.), *Early Childhood Practice: Froebel Today*. London: Sage Publications, pp. 57–68.

Ouvry, M. (2012) Froebel's Mother Songs Today. In Bruce, T. (ed.), *Early Childhood Practice: Froebel Today*. London: Sage Publications, pp. 107–120.

Prout, A. (2003) Participation, Policy and the Changing Conditions of Childhood. In Hallett, C. and Prout, A. (eds). *Hearing the Voices of Children: Social Policy for a New Century*. London: Falmer Press, pp. 11–25.

Read, J. (2012) The Time-Honoured Froebelian Tradition of Learning Out of Doors. In Bruce, T. (ed.), *Early Childhood Practice: Froebel Today*. London: Sage Publications, pp. 69–80.

Scottish Social Services Council (2007) [online] www.sssc.uk.com/doc_view/625-delivering-the-standard-for-childhood-practice (accessed 24 August 2014).

The Scottish Government (2002) *Working with Children* [online] www.scotland.gov.uk/ Publications/2002/04/14534/2764 (accessed 24 August 2014).

The Scottish Government (2013) *Play Strategy for Scotland: Action Plan* [online] www.scotland.gov.uk/ Publications/2013/10/9424 (accessed 21 February 2014).

The Scottish Government (2014) Building the Amition-National Practice Guidance on Early Learning and Childcare-Children and Young People (Scotland) Act 2014.

United Nations (1989) United Nations Convention on the Rights of the Child (UNCRC) [online] www. unicef.org/crc/Rights_overview.pdf (accessed 21 February 2014).

Whinnett, J. (2012) Gifts and Occupations: Froebel's Gifts (wooden blockplay) and Occupations (construction and workshop experiences) Today. In Bruce, T. (ed.), *Early Childhood Practice: Froebel Today*. London: Sage Publications, pp. 121–136.

4   The Welsh Foundation Phase

Alison Prowle, Linda Davidge-Smith and Diane Boyd

Introduction

The Foundation Phase is the statutory curriculum for all three- to seven-year-old children in Wales in both maintained and non-maintained settings. Described as a radical approach to children's early learning (Siencyn, 2015), this play-based curriculum places a strong emphasis on experiential learning and the development of thinking skills in order to produce a strong foundation for children's future educational, social, emotional and economic success. It is designed to support the United Nations Convention on the Rights of the Child (UNCRC) Article 31 which emphasises the importance of every child's right to play.

This chapter begins by setting the Foundation Phase in a wider context, considering the impact of devolution on education in Wales, and examining a range of social, political and economic factors which impact on the delivery of the Foundation Phase and which in turn, the Foundation Phase seeks to influence in the longer term. The history of the Foundation Phase is then critically examined, along with its pedagogy and the principles and values that underpin it. The seven areas of learning are considered from a range of perspectives, with an emphasis on the key role of the practitioner in making the Foundation Phase work for children. The chapter concludes with a consideration of the challenges currently facing the Foundation Phase and an exploration of possible future directions. Throughout the chapter practice examples, case studies and practitioner perspectives are woven in order to allow the reader a deeper insight into the Foundation Phase as experienced by practitioners and children in Wales.

The Welsh context

Wales is a small country, with a population of approximately 3.1 million people and is situated on the Western side of the UK. It has its own language and many distinctive cultural aspects. The last few decades have seen increasing devolved powers to the National Assembly of Wales (now referred to as Welsh Government), and the development of many distinctive policy agendas. Many of these policies related to children, families and education issues.

In this section we discuss some Welsh contextual factors which impinge on the Welsh Foundation Phase. These are considered under different headings: political and socio-economic. It is important to consider these factors in order to understand some of the particular challenges which the Welsh education system faces, and which, in turn, the Foundation Phase is attempting to address.

Political

Until 1965, all public services in Wales were the responsibility of the relevant Minister and government department based in London. Thus, for example, the Department of Education in London was responsible for Welsh schools. The post of Secretary of State for Wales came into existence in 1965 and from this point in time, responsibility for education and training, health, trade and industry, environment, transport and agriculture within Wales became the responsibility of that Secretary of State and the government department known as the Welsh Office. The Welsh Secretary was still a member of the UK Government (and may not even have represented a Welsh parliamentary constituency) but it became inevitable that from this point in time there would be some divergences in policy between London and Cardiff on matters such as education and health.

In 1989, Wales (along with Scotland and Northern Ireland) achieved a significant devolution of political power with the creation of the National Assembly for Wales and the Welsh Government. Responsibility for services of education, health, etc. transferred from the Welsh Office (which was still part of the UK Government) to the directly elected assembly for Wales. From this point onwards, there was a further divergence in public policies, regarding health and education, between the Welsh Government in Cardiff and the UK Government in London, even though the two governments were of the same political hue.

In 2010, a Conservative led coalition government was elected in London while a Labour controlled government was responsible for public services in Cardiff. These differences in political outlook led to yet further differences in policy between Cardiff and London on education matters including well known controversies concerning matters such as GCSE reform, student fees, etc.

The Welsh Foundation Phase had its genesis in 2004 and started a process of policy differentiation with England in relation to early years. Such differentiation has continued, leading to distinctive approaches between Wales and England.

Socio-economic

There are a number of socio-economic factors impacting on the Welsh Foundation Phase and these are explored below.

Demographic factors

The science of demography is concerned with the size and structure of a country's population and the trends taking place. Projections made by the Welsh Government suggest that between 2011 and 2026, the total population of Wales will increase by between 0.9 per cent and 1.4 per cent depending on assumptions made about factors such as fertility rates, life expectancy and migration.

The population of 0–4-year-olds in Wales has been rising for some years and is expected to peak in 2016 before starting to gradually decline for the remainder of the projection period up to 2030. This trend is seen across all local authorities in Wales, except Monmouthshire which expects to see increases in the population of 0–4-year-olds from 2007 to around 2013, after which the population of 0–4-year-olds will start to decline as in most local authorities.

Wales has experienced an estimated net inflow of migrants in every year from mid-1998 to 2011, with an average net inflow of just over 9,000 people per year. A significant proportion of these migrants will be represented by children whose first language is neither English nor Welsh. This presents a challenge for the Foundation Phase, particularly, perhaps in relation to the delivery of bilingual (English/Welsh) provision.

Economic factors

The overall economic situation of Wales is not good when compared to most other parts of the UK. At the outset, there are a number of key points to be noted:

- The Welsh economy is the least productive in the UK. In terms of gross value added per head of population, Wales is at the bottom of the UK league table (ONS, 2013).
- Unemployment rates in Wales are traditionally amongst the highest in the UK (ONS, 2012). Within Wales, unemployment rates vary enormously with the highest rates being found in the South Wales valleys.
- Within the UK, Wales has one of the highest rates of benefit claimants as a proportion of the total population, with particularly high rates of incapacity benefit claimants (Welsh Government, 2014b).
- Average gross weekly earnings in Wales are lower than any other part of the UK except for the North East and Northern Ireland (Welsh Government, 2013).

Not surprisingly, the combination of these factors leads to high levels of poverty in Wales. Using the most widely accepted measure of poverty (defining poverty as the percentage of the population in households with income below 60 per cent of median before housing costs) places Wales as equal first on the UK poverty index. This, in turn, feeds through into child poverty. In 2014, Save the Children stated that Wales has the highest level of poverty in the UK (Save the Children, 2014). This means that one-third of Welsh children are affected by poverty, going without essentials or living in homes which are cold or damp. Nearly 15 per cent live in severe poverty – the highest proportion of any UK nation. In the valleys and other parts of Wales where industry and manufacturing have declined significantly, poverty is deep, longstanding and often intergenerational. The consequences of this are that, statistically, poorer children can expect fewer qualifications, lower-paid jobs and shorter lives than their richer classmates. This presents a real challenge to Foundation Phase practitioners working in areas of high deprivation, and often attempting to mitigate the impact of poverty on the children with whom they are working.

Geographic factors

Although a small country, Wales has significant variations in natural and social geography. In addition to large urban conurbations based around Cardiff, Swansea and Newport, parts of Wales, such as Powys, are among the most sparsely populated rural areas in the UK. Such variations in geography have significant implications for public services such as schools and health services in terms of such factors as location, access and the range of services provided.

Cultural factors

One of the distinctive factors affecting Wales is that it is a nation with two official languages, Welsh and English. Government support for the language increased significantly in the last

50 years. The Welsh Language Act 1993 and the Government of Wales Act 1998 provide that the Welsh and English languages be treated equally in the public sector, as far as is reasonable and practicable. Since 2000, the teaching of Welsh has been compulsory in all schools in Wales up to age 16, and that has had a major effect in stabilising, and to some extent reversing the decline in, the language. Whilst all children in Wales study Welsh as part of their curriculum, the past few decades have also seen a rise in Welsh medium education, which is available to all age groups from nursery (meithrin) through to schools and higher education. In some areas of Wales children accessing Welsh medium education very often come from non-Welsh speaking homes so are taught through a process of second language immersion with a strong emphasis in early years on speaking and listening skills.

There are significant regional variations in relation to Welsh speaking with Welsh speaking heartlands in the North and South West of Wales. Census figures released by the Office for National Statistics (ONS) in 2011 showed that 19 per cent of the population in Wales speak Welsh. This figure represented a decrease of 2 per cent on previous statistics with much of the decline taking place within traditional heartlands of Welsh speaking such as Carmarthenshire and Ceredigion. However, in steep contrast to this is the rise in the percentage of children accessing Welsh medium education provision – in 2011/2012, 23.2 per cent of primary pupils were in Welsh medium schools (a figure which has risen steadily from 18.81 per cent in 2000/2001). The percentage of children in Welsh medium secondary schools is slightly less than in primary schools (at 20.84 per cent), but is also growing. Much of this growth is in areas such as Gwent with traditionally low levels of Welsh speaking.

The Government identifies children's early years as an important opportunity for Welsh language development.

Educational outcomes

Wales faces a number of challenges in relation to the education system, many of which are related to the factors described above. In particular, the following factors should be noted (Prowle, 2012a, 2012b):

- The PISA statistics produced by OECD showed that in 2010 the UK school system as a whole slipped several places down the international league table. Within the UK, Wales was bottom of the pile, a situation the then Welsh Education Minister admitted was unacceptable. Subsequently, the 2014 PISA statistics indicated that Wales had made no progress at all in this area.
- The Welsh regulatory body for Education (Estyn (HM Education and Training in Wales)) ranks local authority education services on a four-point scale from 'unsatisfactory' to 'excellent'. In recent years there have been no 'excellent' services, a high number of 'adequate' ones and a few 'unsatisfactory' ones.
- The Welsh Government's own schools banding system shows that only 13 per cent of Welsh secondary schools are performing in the top band and more than a quarter of Welsh Local Authority areas have no schools in the top band.
- When we consider the percentage of children who obtain grades A–C in their GCSE examinations what we see is a picture of increasing pass rates in both Wales and the rest of the UK over a period of years in the first decade of the twenty-first century. However, there was a sharp reversal in pass rates in 2012 with Wales showing a drop of 1.1 per cent compared to a drop of 0.4 per cent in the rest of the UK. The net effect

of all this is that the pass rates in Wales still remain a full 4 per cent below the rest of the UK and the gap has widened.

It is against this challenging background that the Foundation Phase is working to improve outcomes for young children. The importance of early years education for improving children's life chances cannot be overestimated. Studies such as the EPPE Project (Sylva et al., 2004) highlight the potential for high quality early years services, delivered by committed and qualified staff to improve outcomes for children. Other reports, such as *Early Intervention: The Next Steps* (Allen, 2011), highlight the unique window of opportunity for working with children and parents in early years in order to improve outcomes. The Welsh Government emphasises the importance of early years initiatives such as the Foundation Phase and Flying Start for improving children's educational outcomes and life chances.

Health status

Generally speaking the Welsh appear to be more likely than the English to report themselves having ill health and disabilities (Prowle and Potter, 2012). Some of this is a genuine carry over from the days when many older people had been employed in mining, steel making, etc. Some is the consequence of their living environment and lifestyle choices. Some seems to be a higher willingness to report as sick.

In terms of objective measures of sickness and death we can look at league tables and compare to the past and with other countries. There is much variation in health status across the different areas of Wales. Healthier areas of Wales are broadly similar to healthier areas in the rest of UK, and poorer areas share similarities with poorer areas elsewhere. What does cause concern is that we have areas with good health (Monmouth, the Vale of Glamorgan, parts of Powys) bordering directly onto areas with life expectancies perhaps a decade shorter (Blaenau Gwent, Merthyr, urban areas in Powys).

Turning to the factors which determine health status, Dahlgren and Whitehead (1991) suggest that the determinants of health are many but can be classified as shown below in Figure 4.1.

Leaving aside the age, sex and hereditary factors which are uncontrollable, we see a range of other important factors including lifestyle, housing, education, poverty, etc. In relation to Wales, we see the following (Welsh Government, 2014c):

- one in four adults reported that they currently smoked;
- one in five adult non-smokers reported being regularly exposed to other people's tobacco smoke indoors;
- almost half of adults reported drinking above the guidelines on at least one day in the past week. One in four adults reported drinking more than twice the daily guidelines (sometimes termed binge drinking);
- almost 60 per cent of adults were classified as overweight or obese, including 23 per cent obese;
- among children, 34 per cent were classified as overweight or obese, including 19 per cent who were deemed obese – these factors are strongly linked to the increasing prevalence of Type 2 diabetes in children;
- while there has been a slight decrease in smoking rates and a slight increase in levels of obesity over the nine years of the survey, there has been little change in physical activity during this time;

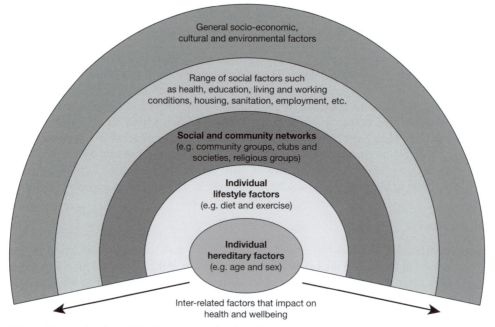

Figure 4.1 An adaption of Dahlgren and Whitehead (1991).

- compared with guidelines there has been a small decline in levels of drinking and in fruit and vegetable consumption since 2008 (when the current questions were introduced);
- the 2011/2012 dental survey of five-year-olds shows the proportion of children with experience of dental decay in Wales was 41.4 per cent (representing a 6 per cent decrease on 2008/2009 figures).

The above data gives the situation for the whole of Wales but there are strong regional variations. Overall these factors put Wales among the worst in the UK. Again, in relation to health promotion activities, the early years is seen as an important area for improving health behaviours, and the Foundation Phase provides an opportunity for working with children and parents to 'turn the curve' in relation to tackling Wales' poor health.

The Welsh early years Foundation Phase

History and policy background

The concept of a new early years curriculum for Wales was launched by the Welsh Assembly Government in 2001 with *The Learning Country: A Paving Document* (WAG, 2001). The purpose of this document was to develop 'A Comprehensive Education and Lifelong Learning Programme' for Wales, within which early years was seen to play a vital role, providing strong foundations for lifelong learning and achievement. It set out proposals for a 'statutory foundation Phase with a curriculum extending from age 3 to 7' (WAG, 2001:20). The policy intention for the Foundation Phase was further

Table 4.1 Timeline for development of the Foundation Phase

2000	Expert advisor produced recommendations
2001	Development work involving civil servants, practitioners, Special Interest Groups, academics
2002	Consultation period
2004	Pilot in 41 schools across all 22 Welsh local authorities
2005	Guidance for practitioners published
2009	Roll out to nursery and reception children
2011	Roll out to all 3–7-year-olds

articulated within *The Learning Country: Foundation Phase 3–7* (WAG, 2003a). Its stated aims were to:

- raise children's standards of achievement;
- enhance their positive attitudes to learning;
- address their developing needs;
- enable them to benefit from educational opportunities later in their lives; and
- help them become active citizens within their communities.

The Foundation Phase was piloted in September 2004 with 3–5-year-olds in 41 settings across the 22 local authorities in Wales. The evaluation of the pilot identified a number of key strengths, including the ethos and vision of the Foundation Phase, the broad and balanced curriculum with a skills and disposition bias and the emphasis on active learning experiences. The report also highlighted a number of areas where more needed to be done in order to realise the ambitious vision for the Foundation Phase, particularly in relation to staff qualifications and training.

Values and ethos

Tackling inequality

The Foundation Phase is part of a raft of initiatives developed to help deliver the Welsh Government's vision for young people set out in *Children and Young People: Rights to Action* (WAG, 2004):

> We want to make sure that children and future generations enjoy better prospects in life, and are not landed with a legacy of problems bequeathed by us. The children and young people who make up almost one quarter of the population of Wales are our future. We aim to support all children and young people to achieve their potential. We are committed to assisting children and young people who are disadvantaged, for example through disability, poverty, family and community circumstances, illness, neglect or abuse. They need particular help if we are to improve opportunities for them.

Table 4.2 highlights some of the other initiatives designed to deliver the Welsh Government's vision for children and young people. Some of these initiatives, such as the

Table 4.2 Summary of key Welsh Government initiatives for children and young people

Initiative	Key elements	Target age range
Flying Start initiative	A geographically targeted early years programme that aims to tackle child poverty and improve children's outcomes. The core elements of the programme are: • free quality, part-time childcare for 2–3-year-olds; • an enhanced Health Visiting service; • access to parenting programmes; and • early language development.	Children 0–4 and their parents
Families First initiative	A family intervention programme designed to improve outcomes for children, young people and families offering bespoke, intensive, multi-agency packages of support and intervention.	Children 0–16 and their parents
14–19 Learning Pathways	14–19 Learning Pathways is an initiative designed to encourage young people to achieve their potential so they are increasingly better equipped for the world of work and to become better informed and more active citizens. It aims to improve qualifications, improve the proportion of 16-year-olds progressing to further learning in education and training, widen choice and promote equality of opportunity. The six key elements are: • individual Learning Pathways to meet the needs of each learner; • wider choice and flexibility of programmes and ways of learning; • a Learning Core which runs from 14 through to 19 wherever young people are learning; • Learning Coach support; • access to personal support; and • impartial careers advice and guidance.	Young people 14–19
Welsh Baccalaureate (WBQ)	WBQ is an officially accredited and established qualification delivered by schools, colleges and training providers across Wales. It aims to provide broader experiences than traditional learning programmes, developing transferable skills useful for higher education and employment. The qualification is offered at the Foundation, Intermediate and Advanced levels and is studied alongside a range of traditional academic and vocational qualifications.	Young people 14–19

Foundation Phase and 14–19 Learning Pathways, represent part of a universal entitlement, in line with the Welsh Government's rights-based approach. Others, such as Families First and Flying Start, represent a targeted approach which aims to reach children who may be considered 'disadvantaged' with a view to 'narrowing the gap' in outcomes between these children and their peers.

A rights-based approach

The Welsh Assembly Government's priorities for children and young people are based on the UNCRC. These have been translated into seven core aims to ensure that all children and young people:

1. have a flying start in life;
2. have a comprehensive range of education and learning opportunities;
3. enjoy the best possible health and are free from abuse, victimisation and exploitation;
4. have access to play, leisure, sporting and cultural activities;
5. are listened to, treated with respect, and have their race and cultural identity recognised;
6. have a safe home and a community which supports physical and emotional well-being;
7. are not disadvantaged by poverty.

The Foundation Phase is viewed as part of a child's universal entitlement to a range of educational and learning opportunities (core aim 2) with children viewed as active participants in their own learning. Woodhead (2005) considers the challenges and implications of recognising children as social actors in their own learning, with their own perspective on child development issues, while at the same time ensuring they are adequately guided and protected by adults who are tuned in and sensitive to their needs. This emphasis on children's rights has led some Welsh local authorities, notably Swansea and Blaenau Gwent, to promote the Unicef Rights Respecting Schools Award across all phases, including the Foundation Phase. Abertillery Primary School, for example, was awarded the UNICEF Level 2 award for rights respecting schools, in recognition of its work to place the rights of the child at the heart of the school's policy, ethos, planning and practice. The school's Estyn report described the emphasis on children's rights as sector leading and stated that:

> A very strong emphasis on children's rights permeates the school. This has had a very positive impact on pupils' wellbeing and their understanding of their right to be listened to and their opinions valued. The innovative "rights respecting group" promotes awareness and identifies a specific right of the child to endorse each month. This excellent practice is not limited to within the school but extends to its work with other schools and the wider community.
>
> (Estyn, 2013a:4)

The embedding of a rights-based agenda communicated meaningfully to even the youngest children represents a belief in the 'social agency' of children; that is the idea that children are competent and capable (e.g. James et al., 1998; McDowall Clarke, 2013) and therefore can make informed decisions and choices about things which affect their lives and indeed their learning. This positive view of the child's ability to be an active participant echoes Malaguzzi's concept of the 'rich' child who is 'rich in potential, strong, powerful and competent' (Malaguzzi, 1993:10). The emphasis on the child's agency and ability to actively determine their learning demands that practitioners find ways to tune in to the voice of the child and actively listen to what Malaguzzi described as 'the hundred languages of children'.

STUDENT REFLECTION

1. How does the Foundation Phase help deliver the Welsh Government's seven core aims?
2. Is there a tension between targeted approaches designed to 'narrow the gap' for the most disadvantaged children and the universal rights-based approach which is the bedrock of the Welsh Government's policy agenda for children and young people?

A play-based pedagogy

The Foundation Phase advocates a play-based curriculum that aims to 'help children learn how to learn; develop thinking skills; and acquire positive attitudes to lifelong learning' (WAG, 2003a:12). It is based on a child-centred approach which views children as interested in the world around them. Hence, the Welsh Government defines the Foundation Phase as a curriculum approach that starts with children and allows them to make meaningful connections whilst supporting and encouraging their disposition to learn (WAG, 2008c). It recognises the ways in which children learn from sensory experiences, from active, experiential play and from social interaction.

Andrews (2012) argues that whilst the common parlance of play suggests something frivolous, and indeed the opposite to work, children's play is actually very purposeful and inextricably linked to their exploration of the world around them. Janet Moyles similarly describes play as 'a series of processes, which in turn include a range of motivations, opportunities, practices, skills and understandings' (Moyles, 1994:5). This builds upon the ideas of the early childhood pioneer, Susan Isaacs, who believed that children's play was an important form of self-expression that enabled children to release their real feelings safely and to rehearse ways of dealing with a range of often difficult emotions. Play was the vehicle for the child's development, the 'breath of life to the child, since it is through play activities that he finds mental ease, and can work upon his wishes, fears and fantasies so as to integrate them into a living personality' (Isaacs, 1951:210).

This view of the importance of children's play is enshrined within the Foundation Phase:

> Play is an essential ingredient in the curriculum which should be fun and stimulating. Well-planned play helps children to think and make sense of the world around them. It develops and extends their linguistic and communication skills, enables them to be creative, to investigate and explore different materials, and provides them with opportunities to experiment and predict outcomes.
>
> (WAG, 2008d:5)

Play within the Foundation Phase enables holistic learning whereby children follow their own interests, make links across areas of learning and engage in learning opportunities which are deep and meaningful. The practitioner's role is to plan an enabling environment, to be aware of when to intervene in order to extend or challenge, and to scaffold children's learning when they are struggling with an activity.

The Foundation Phase places a strong emphasis on children's dispositions. Lillian Katz defines a disposition as 'a pattern of behaviour exhibited frequently ... in the absence of coercion ... constituting a habit of mind under some conscious and voluntary control ... intentional and oriented to broad goals' (Katz, 1993:16). Bertram and Pascal (2002) argue that to be effective, teachers need to pay more attention to nurturing children's dispositions. Conversely, practices that undermine the development of positive dispositions jeopardise the likelihood that children will become lifelong learners.

Building on children's interests

Within the Foundation Phase, children are viewed as unique, and able to make choices that support their own learning. Children's learning is seen as holistic in nature and there is recognition that during a single activity a child may be acquiring skills, knowledge and understanding in more than one area of learning. The Foundation Phase aims to start with the child's interest and build upon prior experiences and learning in order to make learning meaningful and encourage a disposition to learn. Activities should provide sufficient stimulus and challenge to engage children's interest and deep involvement (Laevers, 1993).

Within the Foundation Phase, the practitioner is viewed as a facilitator of learning, responding to the needs of individuals, willing to learn alongside the children, using appropriate methods to manage the process of learning and continually reflecting on and improving practice in the light of research (WAG, 2008c).

Indoor/outdoor learning

The importance of outdoor learning is well recognised within early childhood theory. Many of the early childhood pioneers emphasised the importance of the outdoors, with both Jean-Jacques Rousseau (1712–1778) and Johann Pestalozzi (1746–1827) viewing the natural environment as having a positive role within children's learning. Friedrich Froebel (1782–1852), inspired by Pestalozzi, founded the kindergarten movement with its strong focus on outdoor play learning from the natural environment.

Within the UK policy context, there is a growing recognition that the number of societal factors (such as increased fear amongst adults in relation to children's safety and techno-logical advances such as television and computer games) have reduced the access and use of outdoors for many young children. This has resulted in a renewed emphasis on the importance of outdoor learning for children's wellbeing and learning.

There is a widespread recognition that outdoor learning supports the development of healthy and active lifestyles by offering opportunities for physical play, freedom and move-ment. It allows children to benefit from interaction with the natural world and provides unique opportunities to learn about their environment. Outdoor play can also support children's problem-solving skills and nurture their social skills through interactions with others, enhance creativity, and allow opportunities for risk taking within a safe envi-ronment. White (2014) argues that one of the benefits of outdoor learning is that it can take place on a large scale and free from restrictions of noise. Hence, it allows freedom of movement that can facilitate play narratives that continue over many days.

The Foundation Phase places great importance on children using the outdoors to experiment, explore and take risks.

In their report of 2011 on Outdoor Learning, Estyn identified that Welsh children were benefiting from their time outdoors. They reported that when outdoors children displayed high levels of engagement and enjoyment, their knowledge and understanding of the world and physical development improved. They also reported that the majority of practitioners say that children's behaviour, physical fitness and stamina improve when presented with opportunities for outdoor play.

CASE STUDY: OUTDOOR LEARNING IN YSGOL BRYN GWALIA SCHOOL

The school context

Ysgol Bryn Gwalia is described in their current Estyn (2010) report as a primary school in the centre of Mold, the county town of Flintshire. Its catchment area is described as serving a socio-economically deprived community. The majority of children attending the school predominantly have English as their first language. There is a small group of children (ten) from mixed ethnic home backgrounds and five from Welsh speaking homes. It is a state school catering for boys and girls from three to 11. In the Estyn report it acknowledges good features of practice and provision including the learning environment, described as good (2010:7): 'Effective use is made of outside areas for the Foundation Phase classes. The school grounds are well-maintained and are used well for a wide range of activities that enrich pupils' learning experiences.' The importance of a school having a shared vision with core goals recognising the importance of the outdoors cannot be stressed enough. In 2004 a wide range of individuals and organisations, of which Estyn and Education and School Inspection Service (ESIS) Wales developed and endorsed the 'Vision and Values for Outdoor Play'. They set out ten clear principles that teachers should follow (see box on p. 179).

This case study will consider some of these 'activities that enrich' through effective and inspiring use of the outside space.

Educating children about eco sustainable awareness and development

Research conducted by OFSTED in England over the three-year period 2005–2008 investigated the effectiveness of education for sustainable development (OFSTED, 2003, 2008, 2009). They concentrated upon the overall general ethos of the target schools and also measured children's understanding of what is 'sustainability'. The importance of children understanding global issues that concern their world is crucial for the future. The research has shown that if schools actively engage with eco sustainable issues it promotes positive improvements across the whole curriculum recognising the holistic nature of this approach. The renowned early years pioneer Doctor Maria Montessori (1870–1952) in her London lectures after the Second World War (1946) suggested that society needed both education and the developing child to ensure the disasters of war were not repeated again (Montessori, 2012). These ideas resonate with the famous Reggio Emilia approach pioneered by Loris Malaguzzi. The same cry Montessori stressed then about education being 'the hope of the future of the world' (2012:1) is applicable today when considering global sustainable issues. The *Out of Classroom Learning* document (WAG, 2007:3) reiterates the same important message stating: 'This generation is likely to face the toughest environmental challenges yet to be experienced by mankind, in terms of climate change and the ever-increasing pressure on natural resources.' Therefore the Welsh Assembly advocated that schools must play their part in reconnecting children with nature whilst also recognising the tensions teachers may feel, 'hampered' by curriculum pressures, health and safety, finances and even their own lack of confidence in utilising the outdoor spaces.

To support this implementation, a document was published for new teachers called *Education for Sustainable Development and Global Citizenship – A Strategy for Action Updates* (WAG, 2008a), suggesting ways of implementing sustainable education within their schools. It was considered as a 'cross cutting theme' emphasising it was not subject based, but a holistic approach that schools need to embrace through their ethos. It allowed schools to utilise their own community and culture with a 'bottom up' approach. They suggested the strategies shown in Figure 4.2 to help schools deliver this.

Within *The Skills Framework* (WAG, 2008e:15) there is also an emphasis on the importance of teaching strategies. It stresses that teachers should not just transfer facts but promote 'collaborative learning, active and interactive learning, including questioning, planning, problem solving, creativity and reflection'. Additionally, in their findings research, the National Foundation for Educational Research (NFER) and

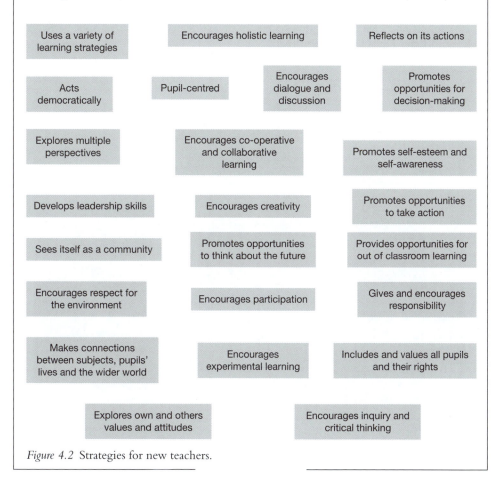

Figure 4.2 Strategies for new teachers.

King's College London (2004) also concluded that first hand experiences have the greatest impact on learning. Rickinson et al. (2004:53) suggested that: 'The use of school grounds to stimulate interest in learning outdoors and in appreciating the environment is something that might usefully be considered.' The school in this case study has embraced this very ethos. In September 2013, Estyn published *Supplementary Guidance: Education for Sustainable Development and Global Citizenship*, with its aim being 'To provide guidance to inspectors for evaluating education for sustainable development and global citizenship in Wales when it is a line of enquiry' (Estyn, 2013b:3). All of these directives and policy documents demonstrate the Welsh Assembly's commitment to sustainable education.

Ysgol Bryn Gwalia was recently in the news regarding 'greener issues'. They reportedly have the oldest tree in North Wales known famously as the Bryn Gwalia Oak, which the school uses for its logo. Jill Griffiths, the forest school practitioner, uses this Oak tree in her forest school activities, so it is very much part of the school and community. Additionally, the Oak tree is fondly remembered by parents and grandparents: 'Many of the parents and grandparents of today's children also came to this school and remember the tree', says Mrs Griffiths, 'So this strengthens an oral tradition of story-telling.' This also links with the area 'Knowledge and Understanding of the World' through its range of activities, 'adults recalling their own past' (WAG, 2008b:32). The Oak is estimated to be about 770 years old, dating back to King Edward I and Llewellyn Ap Gruffydd.

Figure 4.3 The Bryn Gwalia Oak.

The school first applied to the Woodland Trust in November 2013 and received a pack of 30 free trees. Since the autumn the Woodland Trust has supplied over 35,000 free trees to schools and communities to promote greener environments. (Details are at the end of this case study on who to contact for these trees.) During the spring of 2014 the school has planted a further 450 trees. The new trees will develop the designated forest area to provide a wider and extended area for potential learning. These trees at Ysgol Bryn Gwalia will not only develop the forest school area but will promote an awareness of sustainable eco education with the children. Every child has planted their own tree so it will foster not only an awareness of the developing environment, but also a degree of ownership.

The school is already committed to the 'Eco school Wales' initiative. It has an eco-committee that meets once a half term and has two children from year three up to year six on its panel. In practice, however, this can change dependent on issues or if a situation arises. The school believes it is very easy to integrate eco-friendly issues into a holistic curriculum. For example, the eco-committee goes on a 'Learning Walk' to inspect the school and its grounds. They ask the question "What's grot and what's not?" It is a very proactive committee both reflectively and actively. Thea, a year four member, believes, "Our role as Eco-Committee is to make sure that everybody in our class gets a Healthy Snack. We make sure that people are not dropping litter, we plant flowers and vegetables in our Eco-Garden and we help to keep the school clean." By planting and caring for the environment of vegetables and flowers in this manner, Thea will understand the natural unity of the world as advocated by Froebel and Rudolph Steiner (1861–1925). Liebschner (1992:39) reminds practitioners that Froebel saw each individual organism of life as part of the greater whole or sphere: 'The tree though complete in itself, is part of a larger whole. It takes from the soil and the air and gives back to both.' It will also support the area of Moral and Spiritual development in the Framework: 'practitioners need to provide activities that allow them to begin to understand how they can protect the environment and become more environmentally friendly in their everyday lives.'

Froebel actively encouraged a community spirit within the garden. At Ysgol Bryn Gwalia they too recognise the importance of involving the community. Whilst the children were trying to plant the first saplings they found the ground too hard and rooty to dig. The children knew they needed help. So they contacted 'Grounds Work', a national charity involved in community participation. A working day was organised and the adults were able to prepare the ground to enable the children to then plant their saplings. The children later wrote to them to thank them and invite them back to see the trees in situ.

Another child embarked on a mini project of his own. He wanted to know where the saplings had come from originally and how they had been nurtured. In line with key pioneers from early years, an awareness and understanding of how simple organisms fit into the universe and the shared responsibility of them is crucial in today's society. The child used the internet and sourced the original farm, Alba Trees, in Scotland. The children were incredibly interested to know about the journey from West Lothian to Wales. Jill Griffiths, the class teacher, said: "Children need to understand Alba Trees were responsible for them originally, but that responsibility has passed over to them now." At Ysgol Bryn Gwalia the children, within their continuous provision time, regularly check the trees and water them.

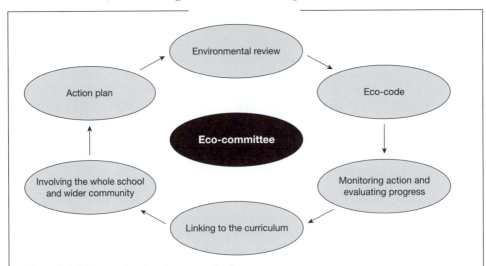

Figure 4.4 A forest school pedagogy and ethos.

The Eco school structure has seven elements which work together to ensure that 'there is continuous momentum towards setting targets and working to achieve them' (Eco-Schools, 2006:7).

In the Welsh Assembly document, *Learning and Teaching Pedagogy* (WAG, 2008c), it recognises the importance of making learning 'meaningful' to young children. Any activity, both indoors and outside, must be in response to observed practice and recognise the needs or interests of the children. This will encourage their intrinsic disposition to learn. Additionally, it will also support their wellbeing and holistic development, another area highlighted in the school's Estyn report (2010) as a strength of the school. According to the Welsh Assembly document *Outdoor Learning Handbook* (2009), Wales leads the way within the four home nations in regard to its development of learning outdoors through the Foundation Phase. This is further highlighted in the Framework for Children's Learning which supports the practitioner implementing the curriculum and outcomes. It advocates that 'indoor and outdoor environments that are fun, exciting, stimulating and safe promote children's development and natural curiosity to explore and learn through first hand experiences' and it should 'promote discovery and independence' (WAG, 2008b:3). It specifies that this should be with a 'greater emphasis on using the outdoor environment.' There is a specific section on forest schools which clearly sets out the Welsh philosophy about it. It sets out three essential elements that 'make a Forest school':

- use of a woodland, or 'wooded area', which they can visit regularly over a prolonged period of time;
- a Level three qualified forest school leader;
- regular visits to the same woodland over an extended period (aiming for a minimum of ten weeks), which allows learners to become familiar with the site and develop a sense of ownership for the environment.

(WAG, 2008b:6)

This emphasis on 'prolonged' and 'extended' reflects the ideas behind Pestalozzi, Froebel and Steiner developing an understanding of the rhythms of the seasons. The prolonged element ensures that the children 'make the most of the daily change, uncertainty, surprise and excitement that weather, seasons and nature provide' (WAG, 2009:7).

What exactly is a 'forest school' approach? During the 1700s, the Romantic view of the child was developing. An early years pioneer, Rousseau, viewed the child as an innocent that needed protecting from the corrupt society and adults. In his book, *Emile*, published in 1762, he describes a boy being raised exclusively in the natural environment with a wise pedagogue to teach him. Pestalozzi took the ideas and writings of Rousseau and developed them into practice, a 'curriculum' involving general methods of instruction. Pestalozzi advocated that children needed hands-on active experiences in the natural world to make sense of their learning. This was the first original 'forest school'. Later theorists (Dewey, Piaget and Montessori) built upon this idea recognising the importance of real life experiences using real tools to construct knowledge. Williams-Siegfredsen (2012:18) emphasises the importance of the 'extended' and 'prolonged' periods in the woods when describing Danish forest school pedagogy:

> By going out each day in the same environment all year round, their children construct their understanding of their world. Together with the pedagogues they try to understand why things are the way they are and begin to understand their place in nature.

The children at Ysgol Bryn Gwalia therefore needed an opportunity to engage over a period of time in the 'woods' on site and use real tools safely. Sigman (2008, cited in Oldfield, 2012:54) reminds practitioners that: 'using tools ... deploys and strengthens a variety of widely distributed, highly interactive networks of brain cells called neurons ... A child's hands are particularly sensitive to perceiving and transmitting exceedingly sophisticated information to their learning brain.' At Ysgol Bryn Gwalia, a decision was made to utilise their school grounds more effectively to meet these requirements of the framework. There is a wide range of research that supports the use of the outside environment. It offers opportunities that are restricted within an indoor space. Children have more freedom to move creatively, investigating and exploring the natural world across the seasons. It provides countless multi-sensory experiences and opportunities of using their whole body. It also provides the space to be boisterous making a range of noises and alternatively to find a quiet spot to study a dandelion or mini beast alone. White (2008:34) states that practitioners must prepare children for their future development by utilising the natural environment. She maintains that growing has a 'strong emotional element, masses of learning in every aspect of the curriculum, lots of moving and doing and the potential of laying down interests and habits for life.'

At Ysgol Bryn Gwalia the parents were actively encouraged to become involved in the development of the forest school area. There is a web site dedicated to it and it is constantly revisited. The families have donated items to support the development. One Granddad arrived with a load of snowdrops for the children to plant and another family donated bird houses. The family receive a letter informing them of the six weeks of forest school activities their child will be involved with. With this level of communication, the children are able to talk openly and happily, sharing their stories from the forest with them. However, there is an issue of funding too. This level of teaching needs two practitioners in the woods and another teacher in the class-room. Therefore both the school and the Welsh Government need to ensure a budget to accommodate this level of interactive learning for all Foundation Phase children in Wales.

Jill Griffiths notes that the effects of working outside must be recognised. The level of engagement and interest is obvious whilst in the woods. The children have time and space to wonder. Sometimes they may flit from one thing to another initially, as there are so many new things to see. Children need to reconnect with nature again, with activities such as scavenger hunts, back pack walks and camp fires. Parents tend to plan out-of-school activities with a strict timetable. Children are ferried around from place to place in the back of a car. These activities provide an awakening of the senses and reinforce the elements within the seasons. A simple game of hide and seek provided an additional learning discussion around camouflage. There are fewer opportunities for 'constant surveillance' outside or interruptions. When the children are in the woods there are no breaks for play, assembly or a teacher coming in for resources, as inside. Outside provides quality sustained time to engage.

Case study

On a forest school visit by Liverpool John Moores University (LJMU) students to Ysgol Bryn Gwalia they were in the woods with a group of children from the Foundation Phase. All of the students and children were sitting quietly on logs when a hedgehog snuffled out of the undergrowth. The hedgehog sat by the logs. Both the children and students were in awe about the closeness of the hedgehog. They gathered around to look and observe its features at close hand. Surprisingly, the students were just as in awe as the young children. They too had never seen a hedgehog this close before. This reiterates the fact that fewer children and students engage in nature.

The hedgehog inspired many possible lines of enquiry with the children afterwards. They made clay hedgehogs, decorated them with straws and painted them. They investigated hedgehogs on the internet and through books in the library, both in school and outside with their families. They became aware of how the hedgehog's home environment is gradually being eroded. Thus it supported their understanding of their world and their responsibility for its care. The children have since built little piles for the hedgehogs to live in (Figure 4.5).

From field to fork

Early years pioneer Froebel believed that young children needed to be immersed in nature to understand it, feel it and study it. Liebschner (1992:39) stated that to Froebel, 'the garden of the kindergarten was not only a symbol; it was an essential means for the physical, intellectual, social and emotional development of the child.' The children in his kindergarten had their own plot of land to care for as well as a garden filled with herbs, flowers, vegetables and fruit trees. For him the idea of his practical life skills (occupations) was 'to learn from the environment around the school . . . yet it was equally important to teach children to care for this environment' (Liebschner, 1992:39). Children today have little understanding of the wider world of nature, and research is constantly highlighting poor nutrition and lack of exercise in the young. With this in mind, Tesco started an initiative called 'The

Figure 4.5 Hedgehog hide.

Tesco Eat Happy project'. It is marketed as a nationwide programme aimed at moti-vating children to have an awareness of the origins of the food they eat. Through their 'Farm to Fork' partners (farms, fisheries and factories) children will learn about how a cow is milked, the process of making butter and how vegetables are grown. This links with the Foundation Phase Outcome 4 for Personal and Social, Well Being and Cultural Diversity: 'they are aware of healthy eating habits' (WAG, 2011). Inspiring as this Tesco programme is, Jill Griffiths, the forest school leader at Ysgol Bryn Gwalia, introduced this idea into her teaching calling it 'From field to fork', showing that she was ahead of the game!

There are official guidelines that practitioners must adhere to when undertaking any off site trips. However, in the Welsh Government's *Educational Guide: A Safety Guide for Learning Outside the Classroom* (WAG, 2010a:5) it states that 'educational visits offer an invaluable opportunity to enrich young peoples' learning, raise their self-esteem, increase their motivation and appetite for learning and raise levels of achievement in many aspects of their life and education.' This builds upon the con-tinual emphasis across all Welsh Government learning and teaching documents of the importance of utilising both indoors and outdoors effectively.

Rhug Estate, near Corwen, were looking for schools interested in visiting and working with them. The practitioner Jill Griffiths was discussing healthy eating at that particular time, theoretically talking about the food chain. She was looking for a farm to support this topic practically through a visit. Unlike in Denmark, the children would not have the opportunity to witness any killings (there is no abattoir on site) but it would provide a practical appreciation rather than just through a discussion in a classroom.

Figures 4.6 and 4.7 Children from Ysgol Bryn Gwalia school visiting the Rhug Estate near Corwen.

The children were able to have a tour of the farm with a safety talk reinforcing health and safety issues such as hand washing. The children saw turkeys in preparation for the Christmas markets as well as bison.

This was a new experience for many children seeing both animal and bird close at hand. It prompted conversations about how different the 'real' turkeys looked in comparison to their Christmas dinner.

They also visited the butchers shop and saw the master butcher at work. This provided further discussions about how meat looked raw and how meat arrived at the butchers! A misconception from the children was that the animals just died naturally in the field and the butcher then carried them off to their shop. They had no understanding that 'lamb' was in fact a baby sheep very much alive!

The children discussed how the meat was prepared and how it is cooked. One little boy minced some meat with a variety of spices and seasonings, and it was made into burgers, which they all enjoyed eating. The whole trip 'enriched' their understanding and learning about healthy eating and the food chain supply. It was developed at school further with writing instructions on how to make burgers and some children made them at home too, so linking the off site trip to their families too.

Useful contacts

- The Tesco Eat Happy project.
  www.eathappyproject.com/farm-to-fork-trails/
- The Rhug Estate, Corwen North Wales.
  www.rhug.co.uk/
- Alba Trees West Lothian Scotland.
  www.albatrees.co.uk/
- Woodland Trust contact details for trees for schools.
  www.woodlandtrust.org.uk/learn/children-and-families/resources-for-teachers/free-trees-for-schools/

The vision and values for outdoor play

The box that follows shows the ten key aspects of the vision and values designed by a core group or early years individuals and organisations across the UK. All settings can embed these key principles into their practice. In a staff meeting/inset training discuss the vision and values considering ways to do this effectively.

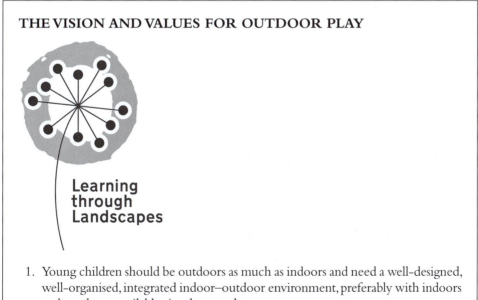

THE VISION AND VALUES FOR OUTDOOR PLAY

Learning through Landscapes

1. Young children should be outdoors as much as indoors and need a well-designed, well-organised, integrated indoor–outdoor environment, preferably with indoors and outdoors available simultaneously.
2. Play is the most important activity for young children outside.

3. Outdoor provision can, and must, offer young children experiences which have a lot of meaning to them and are led by the child.
4. Young children need all the adults around them to understand why outdoor play provision is essential for them, and adults who are committed and able to make its potential available to them.
5. The outdoor space and curriculum must harness the special nature of the outdoors, to offer children what the indoors cannot. This should be the focus for outdoor provision, complementing and extending provision indoors.
6. Outdoors should be a dynamic, flexible and versatile place where children can choose, create, change and be in charge of their play environment.
7. Young children must have a rich outdoor environment full of irresistible stimuli, contexts for play, exploration and talk, plenty of real experiences and contact with the natural world and with the community.
8. Young children should have long periods of time outside. They need to know that they can be outside every day when they want to and that they can develop their ideas for play over time.
9. Young children need challenge and risk within a framework of security and safety. The outdoor environment lends itself to offering challenge, helping children learn how to be safe and to be aware of others.
10. Outdoor provision must support inclusion and meet the needs of individuals, offering a diverse range of play-based experiences. Young children should participate in decisions and actions affecting their outdoor play.

STUDENT REFLECTION

Try (with their permission) to observe children in a variety of play situations. What are the children gaining from these experiences? Do you think learning is taking place and on what evidence do you base this judgement?

Some additional things to think about:

1. What skills, knowledge and understanding does a practitioner need in order to facilitate a play-based curriculum? How can this play-based approach be articulated to other stakeholders, such as other teachers, parents and governors? Is there a role for Head teachers here and if so can they support the play-based agenda?
2. What are the benefits of outdoor learning for children? Are there any challenges and if so, how can these be overcome?
3. How can practitioners use observations of children's play to facilitate planning?

Developing thinking skills and ICT

These are both considered to be skills across the curriculum and therefore should be planned throughout the areas of learning and continuous and enhanced provision.

Importantly, ICT is not an area of learning and should be carefully monitored to ensure that all children are provided with opportunities to develop these skills throughout their everyday experiences. Where practice is deemed to be good, schools track and monitor the progressions of ICT skills following the skills across the curriculum guidelines (WAG, 2008e).

The pedagogical approaches to the Foundation Phase, links to topic based learning and pupil voice all promote thinking skills. Learners are encouraged to follow their own interest in topics through discussions with the practitioners and peers; the practitioner is then able to plan and facilitate these exciting learning opportunities. Often a whole school topic is covered but each class takes a different perspective on the topic as the interests lie with the learners rather than pre planned by the practitioners. By encouraging pupil voice in this way, learners are more likely to remain engaged and thinking skills and metacognition are deeply embedded in practice. Howard (2014) emphasises that by allowing children freedom to exercise choice and control, practitioners are promoting flexible and adaptive thinking skills, which in turn contributes to creating resilience. Citing the work of Anna Craft (2005), she argues that the pattern of thinking, challenging and questioning supports learning throughout the lifecycle. So how can children's thinking skills best be supported? Fisher argues that practitioners can achieve this by focusing on the 'know how' rather than the 'know what'. He further argues that this focus on thinking skills will help children to 'make more sense of their learning and their lives' (Fisher, 2005:209). Cathy Nutbrown emphasises the importance of the practitioner supporting continuity and progression in children's thinking. This, she argues, involves going much further than simply providing materials and assessing learning outcomes. Rather it entails a focus on the processes as well as the outcomes, providing opportunities (both adult led and child initiated) for continuity of thinking through tuning into children's ideas and meaning making (Nutbrown, 2011). However, it is also important to mention the importance of children's interactions with their peers for supporting thinking skills and joint problem solving. Robson (2012) emphasises the value and potential of collaborative and cooperative activity between peers as a means of encouraging children's thinking.

STUDENT REFLECTION

Prensky (2001) describes today's children as 'Digital natives', for whom technology is a natural and integral part of their lives. Practitioners, by contrast, are immigrants to the digital era and may have all sorts of internal (attitudes, values, beliefs) and external (skills, knowledge, access) barriers to engaging proactively with digital learning. Do you agree? What are the tensions generated by this for practitioners working with children to support ICT? How could these be overcome?

It has been argued that thinking involves bringing together the cognitive skills of perception, memory, language, and symbol and concept formation (Fisher, 2005). How would you define the process of thinking? Is children's thinking different to adult's thinking? What is the relationship between thinking and play?

What skills does a practitioner need in order to help support children's thinking processes? How does this relate to theories of cognitive development articulated by theorists such as Piaget, Vygotsky and Bruner?

Bilingualism

In Wales there is a strong government vision for achieving a bilingual Wales (WAG, 2010b). One of the key principles of this vision is that all children in Wales have the right to feel a sense of belonging to Wales and to enjoy experiences in and through the Welsh language. In Wales, parents/carers have the option to choose either English or Welsh medium provision. The early years is seen as an important window of opportunity for second language acquisition (WAG, 2010c). Initial research and influences to support the implementation of bilingualism was based on the Te Whariki Curriculum in New Zealand. Practising Teacher Standards (PTS) 11, 23 and 55 highlight the importance and ensure practitioners are fully committed to raising standards in the bilingual nature of Wales.

Iaith Pawb – A National Action Plan for a Bilingual Wales (WAG, 2003b:39) sets out the following key target: 'The long term goal for our early years provision is to achieve a situation in which very many more under 5s have had sufficient exposure to Welsh to be able to move into either Welsh-medium or effectively bilingual schools.'

During the Foundation Phase, children in English medium settings are given opportunities through play/active learning, as well as structured activities, to acquire familiarity with Welsh language and to encourage further language learning and positive attitudes towards Welsh.

A number of studies highlight the benefits of bilingualism for children's development. Baker (1996) identifies a number of cognitive and social benefits of bilingualism. Speaking specifically about bilingualism in Wales, Sian Wyn Siencyn suggests a number of benefits of providing bilingual opportunities for children, including allowing children:

- earlier awareness of the arbitrariness of language,
- earlier separation of meaning and sound,
- greater adeptness at divergent thinking,
- greater facility at concept formation.

(Siencyn, 2011)

Tabors (1997) identified a four-stage process for additional language learning:

1. Child uses home language (in this case, English).
2. Silent or nonverbal stage.
3. Child beginning to use target language (in this case Welsh).
4. Child uses target language (Welsh) consistently.

Understanding these stages, and providing effective support and appropriate valuing of both languages by the practitioner, can enable children to transition through the stages, and reap the many benefits of bilingualism.

The Welsh Government commitment for early bilingualism is supported by significant research from many disciplines including neuroscience and psycho-linguistics and phonology. Siencyn (2014) cites Kuhl who argues that: 'phonetic development follows the same principles for two languages that it does a single language. Bilingual infants learn through the exaggerated acoustic cues provided by infant-directed speech ... as do monolingual infants' (Kuhl, 2008:232).

This, suggests Siencyn, contributes towards the idea encountered earlier in the chapter of children as strong and capable, with skills that adults are only just beginning to understand and appreciate.

CASE STUDY: SUPPORTING EARLY BILINGUALISM AT YSGOL FEITHRIN PONT-Y-PŴL

Ysgol Feithrin Pont-y-Pŵl is situated in a community hall in the centre of Pontypool. The setting welcomes children from two-and-a-half-years-old until they begin their statutory education in one of the three Welsh medium primary schools in Torfaen. Ysgol Feithrin Pont-y-Pŵl offers Welsh medium education and the majority of children attending the nursery live in the Pontypool area.

The majority of children arrive at the setting with very little or no spoken Welsh. All the children come from English speaking backgrounds apart from one child who has one Welsh speaking parent. The setting has five members of staff who have many years of experience in working with young children in a community setting. The setting was completely refurbished in 2010 and all staff members were involved in the planning of both inside and outside areas. The setting now enjoys a large bright open hall with plenty of space for a wide range of exciting learning areas and an attractive outside play space with areas of hard surfaces, grassy banks, planting areas and shelter. Free flow is encouraged.

Practitioners work very well together as a team and take time to get to know the children well. The staff members use the wide range of children's backgrounds in a natural way to celebrate diversity. Daily staff meetings focus on what children have learned and planning for the next day. All children are encouraged to share and express their opinions as well as their likes and dislikes. Daily routines are well-established and children feel safe and secure. Practitioners have a close relationship with the families of the children based on mutual respect and trust. In combination, these features create an extremely positive, caring ethos where all children are treated fairly and consistently. A parent helper rota enables parents to spend time in the setting and reinforces the parent–practitioner partnership, which staff members see as crucial to enabling the children to meet their potential. Parents and staff recently worked together to create a book of Welsh songs and rhymes to use at home as well as in the setting to aid language acquisition.

As a Welsh medium setting, the main focus is on developing children's Welsh language skills. The setting achieves this by creating an exciting learning environment where there is a very wide range of stimulating opportunities for children to listen to the language and use their developing Welsh skills. There are daily opportunities for the children to explore and experiment in all areas of learning both indoors and outdoors. Staff members encourage children to interact purposefully with their peers through the regular use of such things as board games and puzzles. Staff members constantly listen to the children and review the provision as a result of their findings. Wherever possible, staff members encourage the children to initiate their own learning and provide them with the materials to do this. Resources are plentiful and well matched to children's interests. The nursery makes effective use of the outdoor environment using its natural landscape for imaginative learning opportunities. For example, the sloping grassed area provides excellent opportunities for the children to develop problem-solving skills by experimenting with things they can push, pull and roll. The tarmacked area provides a large space for parachute games and fun number recognition activities, all through the target language of Welsh.

The team of staff ensure that they involve the children in all aspects of the setting resulting in confident and independent learners who are not afraid to try new things, including trying out their developing Welsh skills. The range and breadth of experiences means that children are happy and content in their environment and are keen to experiment, solve problems and be adventurous in their learning.

Case study adapted from Estyn Best Practice profile (Estyn, 2013c).

STUDENT REFLECTION

Whitehead (2010) suggests that language binds us to culture via song, idioms, story and folklore. In turn, a strong sense of cultural identity can have benefits for self-esteem and resilience. How does the Foundation Phase facilitate this via its approach to bilingualism? How could the practitioner support children as they transition through Tabors's stages of second language acquisition?

There is much debate about how effective the Foundation Phase is in enabling children to become truly bilingual. Whilst many schools and communities in North Wales are genuinely bilingual, within the mainly English speaking areas in South and East Wales, schools tend to be either English speaking and teaching some Welsh, or Welsh medium, but comprised largely of children from English speaking homes. In the case of the former, it has been argued, children are acquiring some ability in spoken, read and written Welsh but certainly not enough to be considered bilingual. In the case of the Welsh medium schools, children do attain a high level of spoken, read and written proficiency in both languages, but tend to view their Welsh as the language of school but not of life, with all their interactions outside of school, including online, taking place in English. What is the role of the Foundation Phase in helping to achieve a bilingual Wales? What would need to happen politically, socially and within education settings in order to make the vision of a bilingual Wales a reality?

Foundation Phase: seven areas of learning

The Foundation Phase framework sets out the curriculum and outcomes under seven areas of learning. These are:

- Personal and Social Development, Wellbeing and Cultural Diversity
- Language, Literacy and Communication Skills
- Mathematical Development
- Welsh Language Development
- Knowledge and Understanding of the World
- Physical Development
- Creative Development.

There is a strong recognition within the Foundation Phase that the areas are interrelated and together provide opportunities for children's holistic development: 'All aspects of learning are interlinked for young children; they do not compartmentalise their learning and understanding into curriculum areas. The seven Areas of Learning are complementary' (WAG, 2008c:5).

The areas must complement each other and work together to provide a cross curricular approach to form a practical relevant curriculum. They should not be approached in isolation. Emphasis is placed on developing children's skills across the areas of learning, to provide a suitable and integrated approach for young children's learning. The introduction of the Literacy and Numeracy Framework (2013) also supports the appropriate emphasis on embedding literacy and numeracy skills through contextual approaches where the learner is made fully aware of the skills being used to ensure success in a given task or challenge. Each area of learning contains skills and range that covers developmental needs for three to seven years. Practitioners base their medium and short term planning on the skills they need the children to practice and consolidate and the range provides guidance on how the skills can be introduced and embedded.

The following sections consider each of the areas of learning in detail.

Personal and Social Development, Wellbeing and Cultural Diversity

Personal and Social Development, Wellbeing and Cultural Diversity (PSDWBCD) is at the heart of Foundation Phase pedagogy and practice. The development of the holistic learner is fundamental to ensure that opportunity for developing lifelong skills and an attitude to a positive approach to learning are embedded at the earliest possible opportunities. For this to take place effectively within the classroom environment (both indoors and out) it is essential that all practitioners take account of the stages of child development (WAG, 2008f) and incorporate this effectively in the provision. Learners learn through doing and active involvement; it is through this deeper level of understanding that practitioners can fully support the philosophy of the Foundation Phase through appropriate use of observations and knowledge of the background and the current interests of the learner. With this in mind the practitioner is in a position to provide appropriate learning opportunities and engage in discussions that enhance and support development.

An awareness of self is needed through progressive support and guidance. Learners need to understand that they have an identity and thus develop a true sense of belonging. The supportive environment and characteristics of the adults they are surrounded by have a direct impact on a young learner's impression of the world in which they live. Practitioners need to be mindful of the rate at which a young learner's 'potential' brain is developing and the connections that are made can remain with the learner for a long period of time.

Circle time activities (Mosley, 2014) are often used to explore self-awareness and the awareness of others. The principles of circle time can also be adopted to use in outdoor learning where there is a log circle. Aspects of Healthy Schools initiatives and Curriculum Cymreig are dominant features in the area of learning.

The skills in PSDWBCD are addressed under the headings of:

*   personal development
*   social development
*   moral and spiritual development
*   wellbeing.

Wellbeing is seen as 'at the heart' (WAG, 2008b:15) of the Foundation Phase, and linked to children learning about self and the world, developing respect for others, alongside a sense of self-worth and cultural identity. Practitioners and students often argue that the personal, social and emotional aspects of learning underpin all other learning. Moreover, many practitioners identify the importance of whole school approaches in supporting children's personal, social and emotional learning.

STUDENT REFLECTION

This important area of learning covers a whole range of important aspects. How can the practitioner ensure that they are providing opportunities to support children's learning and development holistically across these aspects?

  Some of the concepts linked to this area of learning are somewhat nebulous and ill defined. How do you conceptualise 'wellbeing' or 'spiritual development' or 'self-esteem'? How do the beliefs and values of practitioners, and the ethos of the setting, impact on the delivery of this area of learning? Is there a role for leadership and if so what form does that take?

Language, Literacy and Communication Skills

As in all areas of learning, practitioners are provided with skills and a range that must support contextual or direct teaching to ensure progression is taking place. Language, Literacy and Communication (LLC) are addressed under the headings of Oracy, Reading and Writing. The skills are not progressive in the framework for children's learning and should not be planned as such. For standards to be continuously raised, the practitioner needs sound knowledge of the stages in Oracy, Reading and Writing in order to select appropriate skills, plan for them at the correct level of understanding and ensure they work in conjunction with stages of child development. The appropriate use of continuous, enhanced and focused task provision can ensure this takes place in the learning environment and is observed and assessed daily to inform future lessons and resource appropriate activities. Practitioners must acknowledge that Oracy underpins LLC and therefore a greater emphasis is often placed on this, in particular in nursery and reception to ensure that learners can access the curriculum and express opinions. Supportive materials and language resources are used in many schools to support individual progress to broaden their vocabulary and develop an awareness of language structure and its use in a range of contexts. Alongside opportunities for 'talk', the continuous and enhanced provision must be used to allow learners opportunities to freely practice their pre reading and pre writing skills in a non-threatening environment. Practitioners need to have good knowledge of the stages in pre reading and pre writing to allow for learning to be challenged to ensure progression takes place; thus linking with the Zone of Proximal Development (Vygotsky). As learners progress, more direct approaches to reading and writing can be adopted; however, in conjunction with the pedagogy practitioners must be mindful that where contextual learning can take place it should be taught in this way. Where standards are good in LLC, schools adopt a whole school systematic approach to Oracy, Reading and Writing, with a particular emphasis on daily short sessions of synthetic phonics leading towards individual reading and guided reading sessions:

> The overall quality of teaching in English and Welsh of most five to seven year olds is good. There is often skilful direct teaching of reading and writing through approaches such as guided reading and shared writing. In the best practice, teachers link oral,

reading and writing work and provide a careful blend of structured and active-learning activities.

(Estyn, 2009:6)

This is very different to a previously taught literacy hour; the sessions are 15–20 minutes and aimed at small groups based on ability, therefore taking account of stages of development. What is taught during these sessions is then transferred into learning opportunities that often link with the topic being covered or available in the continuous provision for learners to consolidate.

Mathematical Development

Mathematical Development (MD) is also a core area of learning and is reported on at the end of the phase. For learners to engage and develop knowledge of MD, this area of learning should be taught purposefully and where possible contextualised. In order for this to be effectively planned, practitioners must take account of the learners' own cognitive development and communication skills (stages of child development) in conjunction with the main skills that will be taught: solving mathematical problems, communicating mathematically and reasoning. The curriculum supports the skills through providing guidance on a range of experiences through: number, measures and money; shape, position and movement; and handling data. Concepts need to be taught through progressive planning and learners must then be provided with opportunities to consolidate and embed this knowledge through well organised and effectively planned enhanced and continuous provision. The outdoor environment provides many opportunities for learners to really experience mathematical problems and allows for meaningful 'hands-on' problem-solving activities. Many schemes are used to support the teaching of number and topic based MD; where practice is effective the practitioner relates activities and concepts to everyday situations that are part of the young learners' immediate experiences. This is further embedded through numeracy where the concept is taught in the MD session and then opportunities are used for this to be reinforced through other areas of learning. For standards to continue to improve, learners need to have daily taught number and mental maths session. These sessions should be short and concise.

The skills for MD are addressed through the headings:

- solve mathematical problems
- communicate mathematically
- reason mathematically.

The suggested range for children to explore these skills comes under the headings:

- number
- measures and money
- shape, position and movement
- handling data.

Welsh Language Development

Welsh Language Development (WLD) is fundamental to reinforcing the bilingual nature of the Welsh curriculum. Schools are encouraged to engage children from a very young age in incidental Welsh that can be used throughout the day. Where practice is good, signs and labels around the classroom and school environment can be viewed and children are encouraged to read them whenever possible. Basic language patterns are taught and built upon as the children move through the phase and into K.S.2. The Practising Teacher Standards (PTS) 11, 13, 23 and 55 reinforce the importance of WLD and Curriculum Cymreig by ensuring particular standards have a direct link to bilingualism and the development of Welsh in the classroom is met. Trainee teachers also have this requirement for the Qualified Teacher Status (QTS) and the use of Welsh by both the practitioner and children is assessed throughout block school experience. In order to support the use of language in trainee teachers, modules are set to engage trainees in developing their own skills and use of the language. Strategies are then provided and support is given as to how this knowledge can be transferred into practice in the classroom.

As with LLC, WLD is also skills based in Oracy, Reading and Writing, although the emphasis is more on Oracy in nursery and reception. The range in the framework supports practitioners with how WLD can be developed. Songs and rhymes are encouraged and Welsh language books are made available to learners in reading areas throughout the school.

Knowledge and Understanding of the World

Knowledge and Understanding of the World (KUW) is an area of learning that feeds into the history, geography and science subjects at K.S.2. The skills cover all aspects of the range and are not divided as they are for these subjects in K.S.2. The range, however, is based around Places and People, Time and People, I and other living things and I and non-living things; a contextual approach to learning is effective when delivering this area. KUW provides many opportunities for exploratory work and outside learning opportunities. Although these can also be developed in other areas of learning, due to the nature of KUW, it is often viewed as the main area to support outdoor learning as the range that it covers promotes experiences outside. Children are invited to explore their local environments and research habitats, plants and animals and make weather comparisons amongst many other things. With such opportunities for learning taking place there are effortless links into Curriculum Cymreig and Education for Sustainable Development and Global Citizenship (ESDGC). It is important, however, that practitioners ensure that these links are made explicit to learners at all stages.

Physical Development

Physical Development (PD) takes account of personal development as well as adventurous and physical play and health, fitness and safety. Practitioners are expected to take account of the physical development of the children from an early age, with an emphasis on both fine and gross motor skills. Investigations of body awareness and movements should be encouraged both indoors and out, and this also links closely to wellbeing and knowledge of how to look after themselves. A 'Play to Learn' programme has been developed to encourage schools and practitioners to link PD to a topic based approach, thus contextualising it through other areas of learning (particularly aspects of PSDWBCD). By linking it in this way, children gain a better understanding of why exercise and caring for their own bodies is important. The outdoor environment needs to be equipped and planned for to encourage gross motor skills that will then have a direct impact on fine motor skills that are often refined through LLC and MD.

Creative Development

Creative Development (CD) links art, craft and design, music and creative movement together. The range specifically requires practitioners to allow for child initiated learning to develop alongside planned activities. Again, learning should be contextualised where possible and children should be encouraged to explore and experience that which celebrates both Wales and other cultures. Using the outdoor environment not only allows for natural space but also for children to make observations of the natural world that can then be interpreted through a range of mediums.

STUDENT REFLECTION

Some practitioners and academics have argued for the scrapping of the areas of learning in favour of a more explicitly postmodern approach to thinking about children and their learning. Siencyn, for example, argues that MD is as much socio-cultural and linguistic as anything else (Siencyn, 2011). Hence, they suggest, Wales should move away from the old framework towards a Te Whariki model based upon strands of learning, such as wellbeing, belonging, contribution, communication and exploration.

What would be the potential merits of such an approach? Are there any risks, and if so, how could these be overcome?

Implementing the Foundation Phase

Until this point in the chapter, we have considered the background and context to the Foundation Phase, the underpinning ethos and pedagogy and its key principles and areas of learning. However, much of the success of any curriculum will depend upon how well the policy intent is communicated from national to local level and also how well it is then implemented at local level. The following sections, therefore, consider a number of important aspects which are critical to the successful implementation of the Foundation Phase. The emphasis here has been to consider what good practice might look like, and to examine some of the tensions which practitioners face when implementing policy at local level. This section draws heavily upon the recent stocktake of the Foundation Phase in Wales (Siraj, 2014), Estyn recommendations and the experiences of practitioners.

The key role of the practitioner

For the Foundation Phase to successfully raise standards and improve the quality and future life chances of all learners in Wales (holistic development) it is vital that all adults (practitioners) fully understand, and more importantly engage, in the philosophy of the Foundation Phase and its pedagogical approaches. A recent review (Siraj, 2014) of the Foundation Phase identified that where practice is most effective there is an emphasis on the Foundation Phase pedagogy, and this practice is taken and built upon through K.S.2. Head teachers and senior leaders within a school need to have knowledge and experience of the stages of child development to ensure that there is a balance between what is taught and how it is delivered; thus preventing a 'top down' approach to learning and teaching and strategies and pedagogy remain driven through a constructivist theory of learning. Strategies for learning are crucial and practitioners need to have sufficient training and support from senior leaders to ensure that correction provision is available and that it is used effectively to raise standards. Tracking and systemic approaches are fundamental; practitioners must plan learning opportunities through observations and knowing the needs of the individual. Understanding the balance of delivery for focused task teaching and the opportunities for setting challenges in the enhanced provision areas are crucial, as the deployment of the practitioners is often closely linked to this level of understanding. It is not effective to deploy adults where they are all working with groups of learners on planned focused tasks with the expectation that when work is completed they can 'play' in the environment. Opportunities to engage in shared sustained thinking and problem solving are missed and key learning that is taking place in the provision is not observed and acted upon. This way of delivery also has a direct impact on levels of independence – learners become over reliant on adults to support them in set tasks. The following headings will address possible challenges and provide examples of how practitioners can ensure standards are raised through effective Foundation Phase pedagogy.

Planning and ensuring progression

Planning in the Foundation Phase is both challenging and complex. Not only do practitioners need to know and understand the curriculum (seven areas of learning) and provide the correct range of contexts to ensure the skills are practised and met, but they also need to have knowledge of the stages of child development, observational skills and techniques and be able to organise and plan for provision that embraces child initiated learning. Systems must be in place and embedded into the practice throughout the Foundation Phase; progression and continuity is essential as the learners move through the phase. Where practice has been recognised as sector leading by Estyn, a whole school topic based approach has been adopted where learning of the areas and subjects is contextualised; this supports the Welsh Government Curriculum 2008 (a skill based curriculum) unlike the previous National Curriculum that was very content driven. Schools ensure that 'skills across the curriculum' (developing ICT and Thinking) and the Literacy and Numeracy framework are clearly identified and tracked through all stages of planning.

Challenges that have arisen for many school and classroom practitioners, whilst planning teaching activities, have been encountered through the broad skills that are provided for each of the areas of learning; the skills are also to be taught throughout the four years of the phase with limited support as to how the skills can be taught at an appropriate stage of development. During the local authority introductory training for schools provided through Welsh Government modules, additional guidance was provided by individual authorities to support the planning process. Many schools used this as a basis and then modified the strategies to suit the needs of their individual schools. As in all effective planning there needs to be planning to suit the long, medium and short term. All are equally as important in the Foundation Phase as it is essential that each year group has a long term overview of the skills that should be covered. The areas of continuous provision need to have long term planning that will support child initiated learning and are linked directly to stages of child development. Many schools and educational providers within the Newport Local Authority in particular have adopted this approach to planning for the continuous provision, allowing learners to engage in worthwhile conversations with adults and peers through activities that support the holistic nature of child development (see Table 4.3).

By ensuring that every area of continuous provision has a long term plan that links to the stages of child development, practitioners are able to engage and provoke discussions encouraging dialogue that is more likely to be in line with what the learner is attempting rather

Table 4.3 Continuous provision. Year 2. Construction

What children do naturally	Key Learning (Linking with the DCELLS Developmental Stages. Not Key Skills)	Resources (Vital: – audit!)
Build	**Cognitive 60–72 months**	K'nex
Connect	Produces drawings with detail	Wooden hollowblocks
Create models	Identifies which is bigger	(Outdoors)
Role play Make	Begins to think in a more coordinated way	Solid wooden blocks
signs and labels	Can hold more than one point of view	Polydrons
Use small world	Can extend the sequence of events in a logical way	Cleversticks
Plan	**Cognitive 72–84 months**	Etc . . .
Design	Enjoys the challenge of experimenting with new	
Record	materials	
Evaluate	Confident enough to tackle new mathematical and	
Make changes	scientific concepts	
Talk	**Physical fine 60–72 months**	
Share ideas	Can build a tower of bricks that is virtually straight	
. . .	**Social Development 60–72 months**	
	Asks permission to use item belonging to others	
	Initiates activities in small groups	
	Social Development 72–84 months	
	Takes responsibility for appropriate care of materials	
	and the environment without reminders	

Source: adapted from the Welsh Assembly Government's training materials (2008)

than asking incorrect or inappropriate questions that often leads to a lack of engagement from both the practitioner and learner. It is clear from the long term developmental stages that there is no content for the learning; this allows for the opportunities for child led and child initiated learning to take place. The practitioner is able to facilitate this learning through knowledge of what is appropriate play for this particular cohort of learners. Once these plans have been put in place by practitioners focusing on the stages of development for their age group (remembering that normal development can range for a year either side of the child's chronological age) they can remain on display in these areas – they do not need to be altered as they are encouraging holistic development. This will also ensure that the activities and range of experiences taking place in a particular area of continuous provision will be progressive from Nursery to Year 2. Practitioners have this planning available to them in each particular area so the interaction between the learner and practitioner becomes much more focused and guides the appropriate outcome of working.

In order to contextualise learning experiences it is important that practitioners link their areas of learning to the topic that will be covered in each medium term. The 'Skills across the Curriculum' and Literacy and Numeracy can be identified and highlighted making them explicit so they are not overlooked in short term/daily planning. Again, tracking of skills is crucial and for the learner to fully engage in the skills being taught the learner needs to identify why the learning experience is relevant to them. Table 4.4 gives an example of a medium term planning frame, based on a model used by Gaer Infant school (Newport) that ensures that all areas of learning each week are linked to the focus headings for each week. The skills from the Framework for Children's Learning (WAG, 2008b) are then selected and identified in the final column; as the topic progresses so do the learning objectives leading to achievement of the identified medium term skill.

Table 4.4 Medium term planner (half termly) topic: Jack and the Beanstalk

Literacy skills:
Numeracy skills:

Skills taken directly from the LNF that link appropriately to the topic will be written here.

Areas of Learning	Week 1 Jack and his family	Week 2 Farm life	Week 3 Cause and effect – weather	Week 4 Planting and growing	Week 5 Helping others	Week 6 Buying and selling	Week 7 Harvest	Skills
LLC	*Suggested activities written here*							*Skills from the framework are selected and copied here.* **Be realistic as to how many skills can be covered.**
MD	*Each AOL activity links to the weekly theme*							
PSDWBCD								
KUW								
PD								
WLD								
CD								
Skills across the curriculum								

The weekly theme will ensure all areas of learning link. The practitioner is able to then plan which areas of learning can be developed, practised and embedded in enhanced provision and plan for the areas of learning that need to be taught in a focus task.

Skills are built upon each week in each area of learning through learning objectives in short term lesson planning

Foundation Phase practitioners undertake daily lesson planning that is based on what is taught that day in a focus task. The South East Wales Centre for Teacher Education and Training (SEWCTET), based at both the University of South Wales and Cardiff Metropolitan University, places great emphasis on effective planning. The BA Primary Undergraduate Degree Programme provides a whole year dedicated to effective learning and teaching throughout the Foundation Phase before the students focus on K.S.2 in their second year of training. Each area of learning is studied and demonstrated by tutors to show how this knowledge can be transferred into classroom practice. Trainee teachers are then able to practise this whilst on block school experience; the planning format for both PGCE students and undergraduate students is used and monitored throughout the placement.

Learning and teaching plan

Date:	Year group/Class:	No. of learners:	Time/Duration:
Context/Topic/Subject/NC Ref:			
In response to previous assessments and evaluations of learning, what actions are you taking?			
Which specific literacy and/or numeracy skills are being consolidated/progressed?			

Learning objectives *By the end of the session, we will be able to:*	Success criteria *We will be successful if we:*	Assessment strategies (including literacy and numeracy)

Differentiation (What specific strategies will you use to ensure access <u>and</u> challenge for the range of ability?)		

Timing	**Activities** (including literacy & numeracy), **key questions, organisation & management**	**Resources**

Learning and Skills across the curriculum (see guidance)
Development of Welsh language/incidental Welsh
Health and safety issues (as applicable)
Homework set (as applicable)
Evaluation/Review of lesson with targets for the next stage of learning

Resourcing

The Foundation Phase can only succeed if resourcing within the school is given high priority; again this is dependent on the Head teachers and governors of the school and the level of importance they place on the philosophy and pedagogy of the Foundation Phase; the most valuable resource being the practitioner. Macblain asserts that for settings to effectively meet the needs of diverse groups of children, it is essential that settings are appropriately resourced and staff receive adequate training (Macblain, 2014). The Welsh Government provides a recommended ratio for best practice 1:8 for 3–5 years and 1:15 for 5–7 years; it is again dependent on the school and funding as to how effective this is in each school. However, as previously discussed, even if the ratio is available it is only effective if deployed correctly within each classroom/setting.

With learners actively engaged in a very practical setting, each area of continuous provision needs to be clearly identified and well-resourced with high quality materials.

Practitioners need to regularly audit each provision to ensure resources are maintained and well looked after. The previous example of planning for continuous provision contained a column for resources. If this is in place at the start of each academic year then it supports practitioners in a half termly audit to ensure everything is where it needs to be. As learners progress in their competency and independence they are also able to take responsibility for ensuring each area is well maintained and meets their needs. Through learner voice they are able to discuss what they need and why, and practitioners are able to observe the resources that are used the most and for what purpose. Through observations, practitioners will often notice that some areas of continuous provision are hardly used or only used by very few learners; this is often due to the adult making choices of what needs to be in this area rather than through consultation with the learners. It is often the case that 'less is more' in these areas with resources that are accessible and providing guidance on how things can be returned. Below are some examples of areas of continuous provision that have been planned and organised.

Monitoring and assessment

For the Foundation Phase to be successful, monitoring needs to take place on a number of levels. The whole school polices will be regularly monitored by senior leaders, and the Foundation Phase leader at the school will be responsible for ensuring that what is written in the policy for Foundation Phase practice is carried out in each year group. Through effective systems for long and medium term planning the Foundation Phase leader can track progression and ensure there is continuity in the pedagogical approaches; thus ensuring security and wellbeing for the learners as they progress through the phase. For day-to-day monitoring to be effective it is essential that all practitioners engage in daily discussions based on observations that have taken place. Observations are vital and practitioners need to have training and guidance on how to carry out observations effectively to ensure they inform next steps to learning. Within the Foundation Phase pedagogy, observations can be both spontaneous and planned. Spontaneous observations often take place where the practitioners observe learning experiences in the continuous or enhanced provision through a child initiated activity. Planned observations occur where the practitioner identifies specific skills that need to be observed and link directly to planning and assessment.

Children also need to monitor their own progress linking with assessment for learning to promote thinking skills and metacognition (WAG, 2008b). It is important that the children engage with the continuous provision through progressive strategies. By ensuring that stages of child development are accounted for, the children can access the provision on a range of levels that challenges their thinking and independence. Table 4.5 on page 196 provides an overview of how the use of provision is built up year on year.

Examples of progression in CP/EP

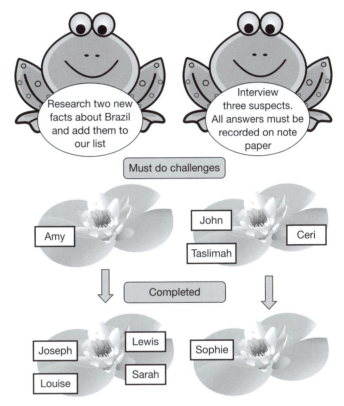

Challenges can be set for the children to practise and consolidate skills. To become independent learners children need to begin to take responsibility for their own work. As practitioners we have to devise ways to observe and monitor this work. This challenge board demonstrates how the learners are selected for the challenge by placing their names on the top lily pad. When they have completed their task they then move their name to the bottom pad. This allows practitioners to monitor who has completed the task and who still needs to complete the task when they are accessing the CP/EP.

Making the Foundation Phase a success
Perspectives on what makes the Foundation Phase work in practice

Challenge board – Gaer Infants Newport.

STUDENT REFLECTION

1. How can practitioners ensure they are meeting the statutory requirements of the numeracy and reading tests at the end of Year 2 whilst maintaining this pedagogical approach?
2. What do you consider the main changes need to be in classroom organisation to ensure the Foundation Phase is progressive through to Year 2?

Table 4.5 Overview of provision

Year group	Continuous Provision (CP) organisation (progressive)	Enhanced Provision (EP) organisation (progressive)	Assessment
Nursery	**All areas of CP set up.** Learners to access all areas freely and adults to observe & facilitate learning within the areas.	Linked to child initiated ideas Schematic learning Practising, consolidating and embedding newly taught skills planned by the practitioner, in selected areas of CP	Observation 'Knowledgeable other' Shared, sustained thinking
Reception	All areas of CP set up. **Learners to access all areas by selecting their names and placing them alongside the photographs of each area of CP. Each area will be limited to how many learners at one time can play in there.**	Linked to child initiated ideas Schematic learning **Challenge cards are provided in certain areas for the children to independently engage with.**	Observation 'Knowledgeable other' Shared, sustained thinking **Practitioners facilitate and support challenges set and monitor how independently children can work on a given task – feed into short term planning.**
Year 1	**Areas of CP set up that are essential on a daily basis.** **E.g. writing area; construction; workstation; discovery area; role play etc.** Children to access the provision as in Reception.	Linked to child initiated ideas Schematic learning **Challenge board set up in the classroom for learners to engage with and see which challenges they need to undertake throughout the week.**	Observation 'Knowledgeable other' Shared, sustained thinking Practitioners facilitate and support challenges set and monitor how independently children can work on a given task – feed into short term planning – **work completed should be of the same standard as work completed in a focus task; work is marked where applicable.**
Year 2	Areas of CP set up that are essential on a daily basis. E.g. writing area; construction; workstation; discovery area; role play etc. **Children to know how many are able to access each area at any one time and monitor on individual cards how many areas they have accessed each week and how many times.**	Linked to child initiated ideas Schematic learning Challenge board set up in the classroom for learners to engage with and see which challenges they need to undertake throughout the week.	Observation 'Knowledgeable other' Shared, sustained thinking Practitioners facilitate and support challenges set and monitor how independently children can work on a given task – feed into short term planning – work completed for a challenge should be of the same standard as work completed in a focus task; work is marked where applicable. **Children complete a weekly evaluation sheet to feedback on the CP/EP and how effectively they engaged with the learning experience.**

Note: Bold font indicates an extension of the provision.

CASE STUDY: NANT-Y-PARC PRIMARY SCHOOL: THE ROLE OF THE ADULT IN THE FOUNDATION PHASE

Nant-y-Parc Primary School is a community school for boys and girls from three to 11 years of age. Most of the 204 pupils come from the village of Senghenydd, near Caerphilly. Over the past three years, the number of pupils on roll has been on an upward trend. Pupils are taught in seven single-aged classes. It also accepts 'rising 3' children in both Spring and Summer terms.

Around 39 per cent of pupils are eligible for free school meals. This proportion is well above local and national averages. All of the pupils come from homes where English is the predominant language. Twenty-three per cent of pupils are identified as having special educational needs (SEN), one of whom has a statement of SEN.

The school holds the Basic Skills Quality Mark, stage 4 of the Healthy Schools Scheme and the Eco 2nd Green Flag Award.

The last school inspection was in October 2010. The Head teacher has been in post since June 2014. There have been significant staff changes since 2010 which has impacted positively on teaching and learning throughout the school.

Nant-y-Parc Primary School places great emphasis on the key role played by all adults supporting the Foundation Phase; this is viewed not only as key in the success and achievements of the standards but in the holistic development of each child. The recommended ratio is fully supported by the Head teacher, providing 1:8 ratios for nursery and reception and 1:15 in Years 1 and 2; however like many schools, staffing often needs to be flexible and therefore any additional adults who work with a level 3/4 position may be expected to provide cover supervision when needed.

Staff development and training

In order for staff to embrace the vision of the school and the Foundation Phase ethos, the school has a Foundation Phase Leader who ensures the practice and standards are carefully monitored. The Foundation Phase Leader (Kathryn Ford) plays an important role within the senior management team and ensures that all staff throughout the primary phase are fully aware of the work that is undertaken in the Foundation Phase so smooth transitions take place into K.S.2. Updated training is provided through the Education Achievement Service (EAS) as well as 'in house' training. Staff meetings that take place every Monday often ensure that feedback and updated information is provided to all staff regarding Foundation Phase practice. Within the Foundation Phase regular phase meetings are also timetabled to ensure key members of staff meet to review procedures and successes as well as areas for further development. In addition to the staff meetings, weekly planning meetings ensure staff have an opportunity to reflect on learning experiences, share ideas and inform future practice.

Monitoring and assessment

Planning feeds directly into the work that is carried out on a daily basis and is monitored by all teachers and support staff. For monitoring and assessment purposes marking is colour coded so there is a consistent approach throughout the school. All support staff mark work using green and the teachers mark in red which allows parents/carers and senior managers to know who has been supporting each individual, as well as the senior management ensuring marking is consistent with school policy guidelines and is of a high quality. Staff regularly carry out 'book looks' as part of monitoring and assessing; staff are given an opportunity to view others' work enabling targets to be monitored and moderation of books to take place.

In addition to daily discussions that take place between staff within each class, a half termly lesson observation is conducted. The staff members respond favourably to this and embrace constructive feedback to ensure the highest standards are achieved. Staff members are encouraged to view what is taking place in other classrooms within the school and share expertise. Clear school tracking systems have been set up and are updated frequently and ensure national priorities and assessments are adhered to.

The school operates an 'open door' policy and staff members ensure time is given each morning for brief daily discussions with parents and carers when required. Parental consultations are given great importance along with parental involvement and the school's involvement in community activities and historical context.

Areas of continuous provision

The areas for continuous provision are consistent throughout the Foundation Phase. Resources are well organised so that children can have easy access to the provision. Attention is paid to clear labelling (in English and Welsh) and resources are limited to avoid low level play experiences.

Within each area of learning, challenge cards are provided that meet with differentiated needs. The Foundation Phase leader reviewed this system in line with developing further literacy and numeracy skills and this was implemented from September 2014. Staff meetings and phase meetings ensure staff members are aware of how this provides consistency and progression in the continuous and enhanced provision throughout the phase. The outdoor provision was reviewed with new resources and systems to ensure play is of a high quality, and this was implemented from September 2014.

Current challenges and future directions

The following sections identify some of the major challenges facing the Welsh Foundation Phase, and how these might translate into policy for the future.

Review of Foundation Phase

Following the new appointment of the Minster for Education and Skills in Wales (2013), Huw Lewis commissioned an independent review of the Foundation Phase led by Professor Iram Siraj. The stocktake took place between September 2013 and March 2014 with a particular focus on how well the Foundation Phase is being implemented, linking to the current national priorities of literacy and numeracy and socio-economic deprivation.

Following the stocktake there are 23 recommendations that focus on all aspects of the implementation of the Foundation Phase, including training requirements and leadership opportunities that place emphasis on the importance of the Foundation Phase and the impact this can then have on transition into K.S.2 and the links between pre-school provision and maintained and non-maintained settings. There are ten short term priorities. The stocktake identifies good practice and notes that where there is successful Foundation Phase pedagogy and practice, Head teachers 'took a distributive or collaborative approach to leadership, they ensured that the Foundation Phase co-ordinator was in a strong position to lead and manage change' (Welsh Government, 2014a:33).

In addition to this stocktake the Welsh Government also commissioned an independent evaluation led by WISERD to focus on how productive the implementation is and its impact on learning. A particular finding from this research identified that the older the year group the less likely the practitioner was to promote Foundation Phase pedagogical approaches. Also child choice and outdoor learning were observed least often. This was often linked to staff attitudes and the adult–child ratios.

Literacy and Numeracy Framework (LNF)

Following the international PISA results, raising standards in literacy and numeracy has become a priority for schools across Wales. From September 2013 the implementation of the Foundation Phase became statutory with schools needing to ensure they plan for literacy and numeracy across the curriculum; the introduction of reading and numeracy tests that are stringently monitored and administered in Year 2. Following the release of this statutory framework it was quickly identified that the current LNF does not align with the Framework for Children's Learning document (WAG, 2008b) and the skills based curriculum in K.S.2 and as a result new documentation is currently under consultation to ensure that skills can be implemented using the indented curriculum.

The WISERD research commissioned by the Welsh Government (WISERD, 2014) identified that formal literacy and numeracy sessions are now being (re)introduced in some Year 2 classes to ensure that Year 2 perform well in reading and numeracy tests. This is a particular area that needs training and support to ensure that there is cohesion between the raising of standards in literacy and numeracy and the current skills framework for the Foundation Phase (recommendation 8 of the Foundation Phase stocktake).

Addressing child poverty

Arguably one of the greatest challenges facing the Welsh Foundation Phase is how best to mitigate the effects of poverty on children's lives. The issues surrounding child poverty and its effects are complex and multi-faceted, and cannot be addressed in any depth within this chapter. However, the impacts of such poverty on children's lives, wellbeing and learning are visible within many Foundation Phase settings, and many practitioners would argue that this situation has worsened under austerity measures as public resources to deal with the challenges posed by poverty have reduced significantly.

The Welsh Government has prioritised tackling poverty within its communities with a very strong emphasis on addressing the particular problems of child poverty. This has resulted in a more systematic, inter-departmental approach to the issue which attempts to:

1.   reduce the incidence of child poverty and
2.   mitigate the effects of child poverty where it arises.

However, many of the levers for addressing poverty currently sit outside Wales at Westminster, resulting in a call for an extension to current devolved powers to enable the Welsh Government to implement economic and social security related policies which meet the specific needs of Welsh communities, children and families.

Conclusions

The Welsh Foundation Phase represents a sound policy intent based on the principle that early years provision should offer a sound foundation for future learning through a developmentally appropriate curriculum. It offers a play-based pedagogy which helps 'create the conditions for combining intended learning outcomes with the possible outcomes that emerge from children's interests, engagement and participation' (Wood, 2008:28). A number of studies have highlighted overwhelming support from stakeholders for the Foundation Phase approach with its greater emphasis on active learning and play, and its real potential to enable children to play, learn, grow and meet their potential.

However, it is not sufficient simply to have the right policy intent; this needs to be coupled with robust implementation. Within this aspect there is too much variation across Wales, resulting in differences in quality and outcomes. Management theory suggests that effective policy implementation demands concerted effort in the following areas:

- resources
- planning and processes
- leadership
- foster a culture of commitment
- technology.

(Economist Intelligence Unit, 2010)

Largely, this echoes the findings of the recent stocktake on the Foundation Phase in Wales. In order for the Foundation Phase to deliver against its stated aims, a number of key priorities need to be addressed. First, whilst it is unlikely that there will be additional resources for the Foundation Phase in a time of financial austerity it is essential that existing funding be used effectively to maximise opportunities for children. There is much good practice in delivering the Foundation Phase, so this practice needs to be widely disseminated across the early years sector to improve quality and enable more consistency in practice and outcomes. Training, underpinned through robust theory and research, is also essential in order to ensure that staff at all levels have the knowledge, understanding and skills to deliver high quality early years experiences that enable children to meet their potential. Stronger links with Initial Teacher Training Providers and advisory services will further enhance this aspect. Strong leadership from Head teachers, fostering a culture of commitment to the Foundation Phase and to deliver high quality early years provision will be key to future development and success. Getting these key ingredients in place will enable the Foundation Phase to move forward into the future, delivering exciting, high quality early childhood experiences for children and providing them with strong foundations for learning and for life.

References

Allen, G. (2011) *Early Intervention: The Next Steps.* London: Department for Work and Pensions and Cabinet Office.

Andrews, M. (2012) *Exploring Play for Early Childhood Studies.* London: Sage Publications.

Baker, C. (1996) *Foundations of Bilingual Education and Bilingualism.* 2nd Edition. Clevedon: Multilingual Matters Ltd.

Bertram, T. and Pascal, C. (2002) What Counts in Early Learning? In Saracho, O.N. and Spodek, B. (eds) *Contemporary Perspectives in Early Childhood Curriculum,* pp. 241–256. Greenwich, CT: Information Age.

Craft, A. (2005) *Creativity in Schools: Tensions and Dilemmas.* London: Routledge.

Dahlgren, G. and Whitehead, M. (1991) *Policies and Strategies to Promote Social Equity in Health.* Stockholm: Institute for Future Studies.

Eco-Schools (2006) *Eco-Schools Handbook for Wales.* Online: www.npted.org/schools/primary/stthereses/Ecp%20Schools/Eco%20schools%20handbook.pdf. Accessed 12 May 2015.

Economist Intelligence Unit (2010) *In Search of Insight and Foresight. Getting More Out of Big Data.* Online: www.oracle.com/us/solutions/ent-performance-bi/business-intelligence/eiu-oracle-insights-1930398.pdf. Accessed 12 May 2015.

Estyn (2009) *Best Practice in the Reading and Writing of Pupils Aged 5–7 years.* Cardiff: Estyn.

Estyn (2010) *A Report on Ysgol Bryn Gwalia CP Clayton Road Mold CH7 1SU.* Cardiff: Estyn.

Estyn (2011) *Outdoor Learning: An Evaluation of Learning in the Outdoors for Children Under Five in the Foundation Phase.* Cardiff: Estyn.

Estyn (2013a) *A Report on Abertillery Primary School.* Cardiff: Estyn.

Estyn (2013b) *Supplementary Guidance: Education for Sustainable Development and Global Citizenship.* Cardiff: Estyn.

Estyn (2013c) *Best Practice Ysgol Feithrin Pont-y-Pŵl.* Cardiff: Estyn. Online: www.estyn.gov.uk/download/publication/301637.7/developing-welsh-skills-through-an-imaginative-learning-environment/&rct=j&frm=1&q=&esrc=s&sa=U&ei=9ANRVYqXLoe07QbmqoG4Ag&ved=0CBoQFjAB&usg=AFQjCNEfUgqsj-zreNxdH3-vADn-DpwNZQ. Accessed 12 May 2015.

Fisher, R. (2005) *Teaching Children to Think.* Cheltenham: Nelson Thornes.

Howard, J. (2014) The Importance of Play. In Mukherj, P. and Dryden, L. (eds) *Foundations of Early Childhood,* pp. 122–140. London: Sage Publications.

Isaacs, S. (1951) *Social Development in Young Children.* London: Routledge.

James, A., Jenks, C. and Prout, A. (1998) *Theorizing Childhood.* Bristol: Policy Press.

Katz, L.G. (1993) *Dispositions: Definitions and Implications for Early Childhood Practices.* Catalogue No. 211 Perspectives from ERIC/EECE: Monograph series no. 4. Online: http://ceep.crc.uiuc.edu/eecearchive/books/disposit.html. Accessed 2 May 2014.

Kuhl, P.K. (2008) Linking Infant Speech Perception to Language Acquisition: Phonetic Learning Predicts Language Growth. In McCardle, P., Colombo, J. and Freund, L. (eds) *Infant Pathways to Language: Methods, Models, and Research Directions,* pp. 213–243. New York: Erlbaum.

Laevers, F. (1993) Deep Level Learning: An Exemplary Application on the Area of Physical Knowledge. *European Early Childhood Education Research Journal, 1*(1), pp. 53–68.

Liebschner, J. (1992) *A Child's Work: Freedom and Guidance in Froebel's Educational Theory and Practice.* Cambridge: Lutterworth Press.

Macblain, S. (2014) *How Children Learn.* London: Sage Publications.

McDowall Clark, R. (2013) *Childhood in Society for the Early Years.* London: Sage Publications.

Malaguzzi, L. (1993) For an Education Based on Relationships. *Young Children, 11*(93), p. 10.

Montessori, M. (2012) *The 1946 London Lectures* (Volume 17). Amsterdam: Montessori-Person.

Mosley, J. (2014) Turn your School Around. Online: www.circle-time.co.uk/. Accessed August 2014.

Moyles, J. (1994) *The Excellence of Play.* Buckingham: Open University Press.

National Foundation for Educational Research (NFER) and King's College London (2004) *A Review of Research on Outdoor Learning.* Shrewsbury: Field Studies Council.

Nutbrown, C. (2011) *Threads of Thinking.* London: Sage Publications.

OFSTED (2003) *Taking the First Step Forward ... Towards an Education for Sustainable Development.* Online: www.eauc.org.uk/sorted/files/taking_the_first_step_forward_towards_an_education_for_sustainable_development.pdf. Accessed June 2014.

OFSTED (2008) *Schools & Sustainability: A Climate Change.* Online: http://staffcentral.brighton.ac.uk/clt/ESD/documents/ofstedschoolsandsustain.pdf. Accessed June 2014.

OFSTED (2009) *Education for Sustainable Development: Improving Schools – Improving Lives.* Online: http://dera.ioe.ac.uk/1089/1/Education%20for%20sustainable%20development.pdf. Accessed June 2014.

Oldfield, L. (2012) *Free to Learn: Steiner Waldorf early Childhood Care and Education.* Stroud: Hawthorn Press.

ONS (Office for National Statistics) (2012) *Regional Labour Market Statistics.* Online: www.ons.gov.uk/ons/rel/subnational-labour/regional-labour-market-statistics/august-2012/stb-regional-labour-market-august-2012.html. Accessed 14 November 2014.

ONS (Office for National Statistics) (2013) *Regional Gross Value Added Statistics.* Online: www.ons.gov.uk/ons/rel/regional-accounts/regional-gross-value-added—income-approach-/december-2013/stb-regional-gva-2012.html. Accessed 14 November 2014.

Prensky, M. (2001) Digital Natives, Digital Immigrants Part 1. *On the Horizon, 9*(5), pp. 1–6.

Prowle, M.J. (2012a) Examination Reform and the Limits of Welsh Devolution, *Click on Wales – Institute of Welsh Affairs Blog.* Online: www.clickonwales.org/2012/10/examinations-reform-and-the-limits-of-welsh-devolution/. Accessed 14 November 2014.

Prowle, M.J. (2012b) Monopolistic Self-Interest Rules Welsh Education, *Click on Wales – Institute of Welsh Affairs Blog.* Online: www.clickonwales.org/2013/04/monopolistic-self-interest-rules-welsh-education/. Accessed 14 November 2014.

Prowle, M.J. and Potter, C. (2012) Unpublished briefing paper for BBC Wales on the current state of health and health services in Wales.

Rickinson, M., Dillon, J., Teamey, K., Morris, M., Choi, M.Y., Sanders, D. and Benefield, P. (2004) *A Review of Research in Outdoor Learning.* Shrewsbury: Field Studies Council.

Robson, S. (2012) Children's Experiences of Creative Thinking. In Fumoto, H., Robson, S., Greenfield, S. and Hargreaves, D.J. (eds) *Young Children's Creative Thinking*, pp. 93–106. London: Sage Publications.

Save the Children (2014) Statistics. Online: www.savethechildren.org.uk/where-we-work/united-kingdom/wales. Accessed 11 September 2014.

Siencyn, S.W. (2011) *Early Childhood Bilingualism.* Conference presentation to Children in Wales Annual Conference, Cardiff. Online: www.childreninwales.org.uk/wp-content/uploads/2014/02/Sian-Wyn-Siencyn.pdf. Accessed 12 May 2015.

Siencyn, S.W. (2015) Approaches to the Early Years Curriculum: A Critical View from Wales. In Reed, M. and Walker, R. (eds) *A Critical Companion to Early Childhood*, pp. 205–216. London: Sage Publications.

Siraj, I. (2014) *An Independent Stocktake of the Foundation Phase in Wales Report.* Cardiff: WAG.

Sylva, K., Melhuish, E., Siraj-Blatchford, I. and Taggart, B. (2004) *The Effective Provision of Pre-School Education (EPPE) Project.* Final Report. London: DfES.

Tabors, P. (1997) *One Child, Two Languages.* Baltimore, MD: Paul Brooks Publishing.

WAG (Welsh Assembly Government) (2001) *The Learning Country: A Paving Document.* Cardiff: WAG.

WAG (Welsh Assembly Government) (2003a) *The Learning Country: Foundation Phase 3–7 Consultation Document.* Cardiff: WAG.

WAG (Welsh Assembly Government) (2003b) *Iaith Pawb – A National Action Plan for a Bilingual Wales.* Cardiff: WAG.

WAG (Welsh Assembly Government) (2004) *Children and Young People: Rights to Action.* Cardiff: WAG.

WAG (Welsh Assembly Government) (2007) *Out of Classroom Learning.* Department for Children, Education, Lifelong Learning and Skills (DCELLS). Cardiff: WAG.

WAG (Welsh Assembly Government) (2008a) *Education for Sustainable Development and Global Citizenship – A Strategy for Action Updates (January 2008).* Department for Children, Education, Lifelong Learning and Skills (DCELLS). Cardiff: WAG.

WAG (Welsh Assembly Government) (2008b) *The Foundation Phase: Framework for Children's Learning for 3–7 Year Olds in Wales.* Department for Children, Education, Lifelong Learning and Skills (DCELLS). Cardiff: WAG.

WAG (Welsh Assembly Government) (2008c) *Learning and Teaching Pedagogy.* Department for Children, Education, Lifelong Learning and Skills (DCELLS). Cardiff: WAG.

WAG (Welsh Assembly Government) (2008d) *Play/Active Learning Overview for 3 to 7-Year Olds.* Cardiff: WAG.

WAG (Welsh Assembly Government) (2008e) *Skills Framework for 3 to 19-Year-Olds in Wales.* Cardiff: WAG.

WAG (Welsh Assembly Government) (2008f) *Child Development Profile Guidance.* Cardiff: WAG.

WAG (Welsh Assembly Government) (2009) *Outdoor Learning Handbook: Foundation Phase.* Online: http://learning.gov.wales/docs/learningwales/publications/140828-foundation-phase-outdoor-learning-handbook-en.pdf. Accessed June 2014.

WAG (Welsh Assembly Government) (2010a) *Educational Guide: A Safety Guide for Learning Outside the Classroom.* Cardiff: WAG.

WAG (Welsh Assembly Government) (2010b) *Iaith Fyw: Iaith Byw – A Strategy for the Welsh Language.* Cardiff: WAG.

WAG (Welsh Assembly Government) (2010c) *The Welsh Medium Education Strategy.* Cardiff: WAG.

WAG (Welsh Assembly Government) (2011) *End of Foundation Phase Assessment. Exemplification of Outcomes.* Cardiff: WAG.

Welsh Government (2013) *Average Gross Weekly Earnings by UK Country/English Region and Year.* Online: https://statswales.wales.gov.uk/Catalogue/Business-Economy-and-Labour-Market/People-and-Work/Earnings/AverageWeeklyEarnings-by-UKCountryEnglishRegion-Year. Accessed 21 October 2014.

Welsh Government (2014a) *An Independent Stocktake of the Foundation Phase in Wales.* Cardiff: Welsh Government.

Welsh Government (2014b) *Out-of-Work Benefit Claimants by GB country/English Region, Measure and Client Group.* Online: https://statswales.wales.gov.uk/Catalogue/Business-Economy-and-Labour-Market/People-and-Work/Key-Benefit-Claimants/BenefitClaimants-by-GBCountry-EnglishRegion-Measure-ClientGroup. Accessed 21 October 2014.

Welsh Government (2014c) *Wales National Health Survey 2013.* Cardiff: Welsh Government.

White, J. (2008) *Playing and Learning Outdoor. Making Provision for High Quality Experiences in the Outdoor Environment.* London: Routledge.

White, R. (2014) Physical Development and the Role of the Physical Environment. In Mukherj, P. and Dryden, L. (eds) *Foundations of Early Childhood*, pp. 339–357. London: Sage Publications.

Whitehead, M. (2010) *Language and Literacy in the Early Years 0–7*. London: Sage Publications.

Williams-Siegfredsen, J. (2012) *Understanding the Danish Forest School Approach: Early Years in Practice*. London: David Fulton.

WISERD (2014) *Evaluating the Foundation Phase: Key Findings on Reported Impacts*. Commissioned by the Welsh Government. Online: http://dera.ioe.ac.uk/20535/1/140506-evaluating-foundation-phase-reported-impacts-en.pdf. Accessed 26 June 2015.

Wood, E. (2008) Developing a Pedagogy of Play. In Anning, A., Cullen, J. and Fleer, M. (eds.) *Early Childhood Education: Society and Culture*. 2nd Edition, pp. 27–38. London: Sage Publications.

Woodhead, M. (2005) Early Childhood Development: A Question of Rights, *International Journal of Early Childhood*, *37*(3), pp. 79–98.

5   A conversation between the home nations

Diane Boyd, Nicky Hirst, Glenda Walsh, Claire Warden, Lynn McNair, Alison Prowle and Linda Davidge-Smith

Question 1: What is the rationale for the development of a National identity within your curriculum?

A response from England

Research has been conducted on the development of National identity in childhood and from a developmental psychology perspective, it has been suggested that children 'are able to talk about their own national identity' and this 'increases significantly between 5 and 11 years of age' (Barrett, 2000: abstract). The findings of this study suggested that 'at 5 years of age, children often feel very positively about the people who belong to their own national group, and far less positively about foreigners' (Barrett, 2000: abstract). This idea of the 'other' is important and the subjective sense of National identity has been considered in the context of the Early Years Foundation Stage (EYFS) (DfE, 2012) and is embedded within the statutory requirements under the guise of diversity, inclusion and equal opportunities, thus, this was revised and the subheading of 'equal opportunities' (DfE, 2012:26:3.66) was replaced with reference to 'Special Educational Needs' (DfE, 2014:29:3.67). The Early Learning Goal for Understanding the World: People and Communities states that children 'know about similarities and differences between themselves and others, and among families, communities and traditions' (Early Education, 2012: 38). However, the idea of an *English* National identity is absent from any documentation and this may be due in part to a centralised government perspective where the English EYFS has been developed with representation from the four home nations and the idea that a British identity encompasses more than an 'Englishness that is often crabby and xenophobic' (Harris, 2014). Geographically, Britain is an inclusive, outward looking place but writing in *The Guardian* in 2014, Harris suggests that a solitary England would represent something much more problematic and too often displays of English national identity, such as the English flag, have been hijacked by far right political ideologies such as the BNP. The idea of multiculturalism is reiterated in the desire to support young children to identify their place in a community context. John Siraj–Blatchford cites research conducted by the University of Kent for the documentary series *A Child of Our Time*, and this research was influenced by the fact that 'racial intergroup bias and stereotypes emerge at an early age' (Siraj–Blatchford, 2008: 68) and the analysis that 'children who had more contact with the other groups showed less racial bias' is significant as it is translated into early years practice and the author noted back in 2008 that the original EYFS 'provided a platform for good practice in this area' (2008:69).

A response from Northern Ireland

Northern Ireland (NI) is a country slowly emerging from a troubled past. For over three decades NI has been fraught with much political and sectarian conflict (Walsh, 2007;Walsh and McMillan, 2010). Peace was finally restored as a result of the paramilitary ceasefires in 1994 and the subsequent Belfast Agreement in 1998 (Palaiologou et al., 2013). However, the impact of such violence has had detrimental effects on some young children's social and emotional development, where according to Connolly et al. (2002), by the age of six, one in six children in NI are making sectarian and racial remarks. More recently there has also been an increase of people from minority ethnic groups moving to NI to such an extent that it is now considered to be a 'multi-racial and multi-cultured society' (Fearon and Mearns, 2012:140). However, Fearon and Mearns recognise that despite such a change bringing many opportunities to experience other cultures and traditions, attitudes to those who are different can still vary greatly in NI, both within and between communities, particularly between the two main traditions, i.e. Protestants and Catholics (Fearon and Mearns, 2012).

Against this backdrop of renewed peace and reconciliation, juxtaposed with an evidence-base of deep-rooted hostilities and unease, much work is being undertaken in NI to promote notions of inclusivity and a shared future. It is on this premise that the content of the Foundation Stage (FS) curriculum is placed, encouraging children to learn from a young age the need to respect and value the opinions and beliefs of others. It is clearly stipulated within the general content of the primary curriculum that learning opportunities should be provided which enable children and young people to develop as contributors to society where they:

- develop an awareness and respect for:
  - the different lifestyles of others; and
  - similarities and differences in families and people in the wider community;
- understand some of their own and others' cultural traditions; and
- are aware of how we rely on each other.

(CCEA, 2007:4)

More specific information about how such skills can be fostered in the FS of schooling are referred to within the Area of Learning entitled Personal Development and Mutual Understanding in the FS curriculum. In an effort to encourage children to respect themselves and learn to respect others, it is emphasised that teachers:

> should help children to become aware of the world beyond their immediate environment and to learn about others from a basis of tolerance, respect and open-mindedness. They should encourage them to understand similarities and respect differences in people in the local and wider community.

(CCEA, 2007:40)

Further educational initiatives in the form of the Media Initiative for Children (www. early-years.org/mifc/) and Sesame Tree, the NI version of Sesame Street (www.early-years. org/sesame-tree/), have been supported by the local government and funded by a range of organisations (including the American Ireland Fund, The International Fund for Ireland, the NI fund for Reconciliation and the US Peace Initiative Institute) in an effort to support early years professionals and FS teachers to address issues such as mutual respect, empathy, diversity and reconciliation within the early years setting/classroom. Research has shown that both initiatives have had a positive impact on children's attitudes to difference and inclusion (see Larkin et al., 2009; Connolly et al., 2010).

It is also worthy of note that the NI Primary Curriculum is available both in English and Irish and the NI Curriculum website for the FS has a particular section written in Irish for the Irish-medium sector in NI (www.nicurriculum.org.uk/irish_medium/). Currently there is a total of 86 schools providing Irish-medium education to over 5,000 children from all faiths and backgrounds at pre-school, primary and post primary level throughout NI (www.comhairle.org/english/) where the emphasis is placed on promoting the Irish language and Irish culture.

Likewise a recent initiative known as the Ulster-Scots Flagship Programme (Ulster Scots Agency, 2012) has been designed to support primary schools in the development of high quality educational and curricular opportunities for children and young people to learn more about the Ulster-Scots tradition and culture. Currently there are over 20 schools working towards their Flagship status throughout 2014.

So it would seem that with the tides shifting towards greater inclusivity and shared education programmes within the context of NI, there is an innate drive on the part of the two main traditions to ensure that their particular identity and culture will remain recognised and appreciated within the field of education.

A response from Scotland

At the point of writing this chapter on 18 September 2014, Scotland had a key referendum asking the residents if they wanted independence from the United Kingdom. The outcome of the vote was narrowly in favour of remaining in the union. We already sit with a devolved parliament for Scotland in terms of many of our budgets and spending, especially in terms of education and health. The National identity is very strong and often when travelling internationally people are keen to link themselves to Scotland.

It has a rich diversity of languages. Scots is spoken by 1.6 million people in Scotland today and therefore has a key role in the culture, identity and language of our country.

Scottish Gaelic is our native language. The 2011 census of Scotland showed that a total of 57,375 people (1.1 per cent of the Scottish population aged over three years old) in Scotland could speak Gaelic at that time, with the largest intensity being in the Outer Hebrides.

The Curriculum for Excellence (CfE) seeks to build the National identity of Scotland through its celebration of who, what and where we are. The singing of Scots nursery rhymes, through to the structured teaching of Ceilidh dancing and chanter (bagpipe) in primary school into a strong tradition of Kilt wearing and understanding of the Plaids does give a strong image of Scotland. Yet we have a culture of thinking and ways of approaching life that run far deeper than the external image. The CfE is structured to ensure that we celebrate the past but also allow the development of the National identity for a modern world.

In the Building the Curriculum 1, the Language section (Scottish Executive, 2006: 13–17) explores Scots and the Gaelic. It states:

I develop and extend my literacy skills when I have opportunities to:

- engage with and create a wide range of texts *(1)*
- develop my understanding of what is special, vibrant and valuable about my own and other cultures and languages
- explore the richness and diversity of language *(2)* and how it can affect me

(1) Texts ... may also include writing in Scots and the Gaelic.

(2) The languages of Scotland will include the languages which children and young people bring to the learning environment.

Education in Scotland has not always been conducive to fostering a sense of National identity. In 1872, Parliament passed the Education (Scotland) Act which resulted in changing the Scottish education system to mimic the English one. It removed any Gaelic instruction and children speaking the language were given corporal punishment. As a result of this, there are no monolingual Gaelic speakers in Scotland. The Gaelic Language (Scotland) Bill was passed in 2005 by the Scottish Parliament and ensured that Gaelic would be an official language of Scotland; Gaelic was placed in the curriculum and it was put into a national plan for the slowing down of its decline.

In the social studies aspects of the curriculum experiences and outcomes there is a new focus on Scottish studies. The initial outline in 2011 recommended that:

- learning about Scotland should be embedded across the curriculum from early years to senior phase;
- the Scottish Qualification Association (SQA) should investigate how an award in 'Scottish studies' might be initiated;
- guidance, resources and support should promote and enable learning about Scotland using a variety of contexts and making the most of Scotland's rich landscape;
- professional development to build confidence on Scottish themes should be rolled out; and
- opportunities to learn Scotland's languages should be promoted.

In 2014, all of the above elements are well underway if not achieved.

Within any broad based curriculum there are choices and decisions about the delivery style of the curriculum in terms of the contexts and fascinations that arise from children. In Building the Curriculum 3 (2008) it states very clearly that the emphasis is on our Scottish national identity: 'Throughout this broad curriculum it is expected that there will be an emphasis on Scottish contexts, Scottish cultures and Scotland's history and place in the world. This planning should demonstrate the principles for curriculum design' (Scottish Executive, 2008:5).

The tenacity and commitment of practitioners in Scotland have been shown to us over a number of years. Their commitment to stand up for what they believe has been demonstrated through the lobbying for educational reform, the refusal to accept SAT testing, the tenacity to stimulate a Risk debate in Parliament and the writing of reforms to bring back our National identity. The rights-based education we have empowers children to have a voice within the consultative planning frameworks, with awards such as Investing in Children[1] (European Commission, 2014), pupil councils in primary school, the Children's Parliament at the government level and most recently The Children and Young People (Scotland) Act (2014) that are encouraged by the cross party commissioner for children and young people. The Act makes it very clear that there is a duty to consult children, youth and families about their care and education so that the voice of the child is paramount but more importantly can be used to evoke change.

A response from Wales

The Foundation Phase contributes to the Curriculum Cymreig by developing children's understanding of the cultural identity unique to Wales across all Areas of Learning through an integrated approach. Children should appreciate the different languages, images, objects, sounds and tastes that are integral to Wales today, and gain a sense of belonging to Wales, and understand the Welsh heritage, literature and arts as well as the language (WAG, 2008a).

The last few decades have seen a growing emphasis on National identity and Welsh culture both within government policy and within society as a whole. The creation of the Welsh Assembly and increasing levels of devolution have contributed to this process. Whilst it is important not to stereotype Welsh culture, some aspects generally associated with Welsh culture (e.g. St David's Day, welsh folklore and Welsh music and dance) do have a role to play within the curriculum. Indeed many schools enter enthusiastically into the local and national Eisteddfodau (Festival of Welsh Culture) and children gain rich experiences as a result. However, any conversation about Welsh identity and culture would be incomplete without reflecting some of the diversity of cultures represented within the country and its communities. The Foundation Phase recognises this: 'Over time children will learn about different backgrounds and lifestyles, to respect them equally and appreciate the varied contributions that different cultures make to communities in Wales' (WAG, 2008b:10).

Hence, it is incumbent upon practitioners to provide opportunities for children to interact and learn together, thus realising that there are more than one perspective and opening their minds to other possibilities and cultural ideas and norms.

The Welsh language is perhaps the most distinctive feature of the education system in Wales and the emphasis on bilingualism is embedded from the Foundation Phase onwards. (Chapter 4 considers this aspect in detail.) Whilst the Foundation Phase makes a bold attempt to enable all children to acquire Welsh language skills as an entitlement, there is some debate about how effective this is in practice and whether this approach is capable of delivering functional bilingualism. What is clear is that the Welsh Government has put much store on international evidence to support the efficacy of introducing a second language in early years. Although the recent census showed a slight decline in Welsh speaking, particularly in the Welsh speaking heartlands, there has been a phenomenal growth in South East Wales, in particular in Welsh-medium education, which perhaps hints at a growing regard for the language amongst parents, both in relation to the educational benefits of a second language but also for the value of Welsh in itself as a symbol of culture and National identity.

Question 2: How do you think the child is constructed within your framework?

A response from England

The English early years framework reiterates the need for practitioners to promote 'teaching and learning to ensure school readiness' (DfE, 2014:5) and that children need to 'complete' the EYFS 'ready to benefit fully from the opportunities ahead of them' (DfE, 2014:7). The idea of *completion* is reminiscent of the Piagetian 'ages and stages' approach that was dominant in the English education system from the 1960s; however, the suggestion of a linear approach is at odds with the notion of an inclusive framework where each child is perceived as an individual with 'unique' characteristics. The English EYFS is a goal orientated framework where children are expected to achieve specific goals by a predetermined date in an academic calendar and Pugh and Duffy suggest that the 'unintended consequences may be that some children are viewed as failing before they even start statutory schooling' (2013:120). There is a sense in the English EYFS of a construction of the child as *incomplete*, and McDowall Clark (2013:108) suggests that this adult/child distinction can be really useful when considering children's rights and their participation and the non-statutory guidance (Early Education, 2012) explicitly states:

> Children have a right, spelled out in the United Nations Convention on the rights of the child, to provision which enables them to develop their personalities, talents and abilities irrespective of ethnicity, culture or religion, home language, family, background, learning difficulties or gender.

The key person role, defined within 3.26 of the Statutory Framework, presents a lean statement, capturing the idea that relationships are important; however, the notion of the child's involvement is glaringly absent and McDowall Clark reminds us how children's rights are recognised in legal frameworks such as the Children Acts 1989 and 2004 and internationally in the UNCRC (United Nations, 1989); however, 'this is not a straightforward story of continual improvement and progress; children's voices do not carry as much weight as those of adults and their rights to participation within society are still frequently overruled in the name of protection' (Handley, 2009, cited in McDowall Clark, 2013:107).

It could be argued that the English framework places a great deal of emphasis on the future contribution that children will make and this discourse reflects what Lee (2001, cited in McDowall Clark, 2013:109) describes as 'human becomings'. This perspective is also captured by Peter Moss who notes the exaggeration of children as a commodity and as a person in a state of 'becoming', exemplified through the repetitive suggestion that children need to be 'ready' for school.

There are many contradictions in the English EYFS and whilst the framework draws on many familiar theoretical ideas, the uniqueness of each child is at odds with the language embedded in the early years outcomes document where the language is firmly embedded in developmental psychology with the suggestion of 'typical and atypical behavior' (DfE, 2013a). This, it could be argued, is in contrast with the guidance embedded in Development Matters which concentrated on a more holistic approach with explicit reference to an ecological understanding of the child. The *image* of the child is reflected in Malaguzzi's world renowned Reggio philosophy as a 'rich' child who is inherently inquisitive and strong; however, the adult needs to 'see' the competencies of the child rather than the deficit view postulated by the overuse of negative language such as 'issues', 'concerns' and a lack of 'reaching or achieving developmental levels' in the EYFS guidance.

A response from Northern Ireland

The NI FS curriculum (CCEA, 2007) paints a picture of the young child as a competent learner, recognising that he/she has already had a variety of differing experiences in their young lives, whether it be at home or at pre-school, which should be built and developed upon in the foundation phase of their educational journey. In this way, it would seem that the NI FS curriculum recognises that 'children bring more to school than their backpack' (Margetts, 2003:5) and it is these interests and curiosities that should be embraced by the FS teacher and used to promote effective learning in the classroom. Young children are perceived, therefore, in the FS curriculum to be active agents who are involved to some extent in the planning, reviewing and reflecting on what they have done and have some degree of choice, autonomy and independence in their learning programme (CCEA, 2007). It could be argued, therefore (see, e.g., Hunter and Walsh, 2014), that the FS curriculum in NI aligns itself with a combination of child and teacher initiated activities which positions active learning as an appropriate pedagogical approach, 'valorising play and adult responsiveness to children' (Stephen, 2010:318). As CCEA (2007:9) states:

> In the Foundation Stage children should experience much of their learning through well planned and challenging play. Self-initiated play helps children to understand and learn about themselves and their surroundings. Motivation can be increased when children have opportunities to make choices and decisions about their learning, particularly when their own ideas and interests are used, either as starting points for learning activities or for pursuing a topic in more depth.

However, as detailed within the content of the NI chapter, the rhetoric does not always meet with the reality. There is much evidence to suggest that teachers in the early years of primary schooling struggle with this new image of the child as active learner in the classroom (Walsh et al., 2010; McInness et al., 2011; Wood, 2013). Hunter and Walsh (2014: 14) contend that:

> Teachers in NI need to shift beyond the confines of a prescriptive pedagogy, to pedagogy based on responsiveness, skilful interactions and playful experiences, in order to ensure a high-quality holistic learning experience for the youngest children in primary schools. Entering into the play scenario and engaging in a model of co-construction, where children and adults unite to extend and progress the learning experience did not seem to come naturally to many of the Year 2 teachers observed.

This backdrop of evidence would suggest that despite the good intentions of the NI FS curriculum in recognising the need for young children to be actively involved in the learning process, policy statements alone will not ensure that such practice becomes a reality in our early years classrooms throughout NI (Hunter and Walsh, 2014).

A response from Scotland

The CfE construct of the child is that the child is an active, knowledgeable and socially participative being, and that '[e]ach child has an enormous capacity for learning and the potential to achieve in different ways' (Scottish Executive, 2004a:9).

'Global, social, political and economic changes' (Scottish Executive, 2004a:10) have ensued shifting representations resulting in current local constructions of the child as an *individual* and not, significantly, a homogenised child. Thus, currently, there is a heightened awareness of the diversity of children and this mindfulness takes into account inequalities of children's experiences (Mundane and Giugni, 2006; Gonzalez-Mena, 2008; Killen and Rutland, 2011). This is due to the vast disparities in the social and economic conditions of children's lives, as already noted, and of consequence, this does not impede the implicit CfE construct that all children are rich, capable and able learners (James and James, 2012). Instead the impetus is on the educational practitioner to sensitively plan experiences for the capable and able child.

The child is also viewed as both a *human being* and a *human becoming* (Corsaro, 2005; Qvortrup, 2005; Brownlie and Sheach-Leith, 2011) with the child occupying multiple locations. As practitioners from the various educational sectors demonstrate oppositional dichotomies resulting in different constructions of the child, e.g. in early years settings, a child-centred focus is taken where the CfE experiences and outcomes are planned and built around what the child is interested in, whereas, enigmatically, as the child progresses through the sectors there is a pedagogical shift on the child of the future, and what the adult decides what the child/young person will *need* to become as a valuable contributing member of society, e.g. a member of the workforce. This embodies a specific view that the child/young person is 'not quite an adult', but is an adult in the making for the adult world (Hillman, 2006; Gill and Howard, 2009).

Declarations from the global children's rights movement (The Convention) is imbued in the CfE (Munro, 2012). The child/young person as a person with rights (Alderson, 2001) is both implicitly and explicitly written throughout the document. Our Scottish journey is definitely changing with practitioners, at different steps on their journey, adopting a social justice (Fennimore, 2008; Konstantoni, 2010) and rights-based approach. This construct of the child evokes a certain amount of zealotry and inspires participatory approaches (Wood, 1998; Burman, 2009) that include the child in decision-making processes as subjects with rights, who has his/her voice heard and, significantly, acted upon (Clark et al., 2005; Tisdall et al., 2009). As mentioned earlier, not everyone is there … people are complex, ambiguous and at times uncertain. Our CfE allows for that uncertainty; the journey to excellence is not a destination it is a journey with many paths. Children are creative, imaginative beings (Davis et al., 2012) … there are many paths they can take on the journey to excellence.

A response from Wales

The Foundation Phase construct of the child is very positive, painting a picture of the child as strong and capable and able to drive their own learning. The child is seen as more than a social actor, but rather as a social agent who can influence the world around them, and there is recognition that even very young children can make choices and exert agency. This emphasis on the child's voice is evident throughout the Welsh Government Children and Young People's agenda. The Welsh Government has adopted the United Nations Convention on the Rights of the Child as a principle which underpins all planning. The Rights of Children and Young Persons (Wales) Measure 2011 received unanimous cross party support when it was passed at the National Assembly for Wales in January 2011. This measure further strengthened the rights-based approach of the Welsh Government to making policy for children and young people in Wales. The anti-smacking campaign 'Children are Unbeatable' has received much political support in Wales, with a strong all party lobby advocating a change of law to prevent the physical chastisement of children. At present, this remains a non-devolved area of legislation, but given that in the plenary debate the vast majority of members voted for a change to the current law, then it is likely that with further devolution this would be a priority for the Welsh Government.

Other examples of an on-going commitment to children's rights and participation include becoming, in 2001, the first country to appoint a Children's Commissioner and the establishment of Funky Dragon, The Children and Young People's Assembly for Wales. Interestingly, however, this proud history is currently under threat of severe funding shortages with the likelihood that Funky Dragon will cease to exist unless funding can be found to sustain it. The rhetoric for children's rights and participation is certainly sound within Wales, but without an infrastructure to support and develop this on the ground then one must wonder how likely policy is to empower children and give them a voice.

One important issue in relation to delivering a child-centred approach with an emphasis on the child's voice within the Foundation Phase is the extent to which practitioners 'buy in' to the vision and are equipped to translate it into effective practice. The evidence from the recent stocktake suggests that this is inconsistent across settings, and that there is a real need for on-going high quality training and development opportunities for staff, designed to equip them to effectively deliver the Welsh Government's ambitious agenda for children.

Question 3: What are the practitioner ratio/qualifications needed to work within early years and are there any debates around this contentious issue?

A response from England

Within the Statutory Framework (DfE, 2014:20) it states that the 'daily experiences of children' are dependent on practitioners having 'appropriate qualifications, training, skills and knowledge as well as a 'clear understanding of their roles and responsibilities'. This topic has been a contentious issue within the English early years sector for a number of years. In June 2012, Professor Cathy Nutbrown published an independent review of early education and childhood qualifications in England. She made 19 recommendations which were warmly welcomed across the sector; however, in the government response, 'More Great Childcare' (DfE, 2013b:42) there was only acknowledgement and acceptance of five of the recommendations 'in full' and seven 'in principle'. The remaining recommendations were either 'still under consideration' and 'subject to consultation' (x3), 'kept under review' (x1), 'not accepted' (x2) and 'no action for government' (x1) (DfE, 2013b:42–43). Nutbrown responded immediately with 'Shaking the Foundations of Quality?' (2013), questioning the apparent disregard to her recommendations. The various titles attributed to those working with young children in England has historically been associated with a mixed bag of level 3 qualifications and it was this confusion that prompted a review which culminated in the updated criteria for 'full and relevant' qualifications. An interesting omission is the need for childminders to achieve any recognised 'level' as long as they 'complete training which helps them to understand and implement the EYFS' (DfE, 2014:21), and Nutbrown incredulously suggests that childminders have lost a 'battle' as they do not have parity with other practitioners who work within the EYFS.

According to Nutbrown, many of her recommendations have been misinterpreted and she strongly asserts that one of these recommendations was the establishment of a specialist early years route to Qualified Teacher Status (QTS) to demonstrate 'pedagogical expertise' (2013:3). These experts would lead an effective team of early years practitioners at level 3 who hold a new full and relevant level 3 early years qualification (Teaching agency qualifications 2014). The government rejected this route and opted to replace the Early Years Professional Status (EYPS) with 'Early Years Teacher Status' (EYTS) as they noted that the change would simply give 'one title of teacher across the early years and schools sectors' which would, they claim, 'increase status and public recognition' (Nutbrown, 2013:43). However, this has been strongly contested, not least by Cathy Nutbrown who states that the notion of 'changing the label on the tin' will mislead parents as well as practitioners who would not be rewarded with the same remuneration in terms of salary, associated benefits, career opportunities and she asks 'why is the title "teacher" being used to mean something quite different from the commonly understood and accepted meaning?' (Nutbrown, 2013:7).

The Statutory Framework (DfE, 2014) notes that staffing arrangements must meet the needs of all children and ensure their safety and it could be argued that the discourse around safety is at odds with the recommendation to ensure that all babies and young children are given the care, love and support of familiar adults. Read the revised Statutory Framework paying particular attention to 'Staff:Child ratios' (DfE, 2014:21).

A response from Northern Ireland

As the FS in NI currently concentrates only on Years 1 and 2 of primary school, those responsible for educating 4–6-year-old children in this phase are all practising teachers. DENI Circular 2007/22 details the qualifications required to be eligible to teach in grant-aided schools in NI (DENI, 2007). In summary, they all have qualified teacher status having acquired either a Bachelor of Education or a degree in a subject area such as English or a particular discipline such as psychology or early childhood studies followed by a Post-graduate Certificate in Education, or another degree course with an approved Teacher Education element.

It is stipulated by DENI that the number of pupils in any Foundation Stage class should not exceed 30 children (DENI, 2011). However it would appear that ratios are dependent on individual school budgets. A FS factor has been added to the Common Funding Scheme as part of the local management of schools (see DENI, 2013), to provide primary schools with additional funds to support the use of classroom assistants and classroom resources in an effort to ensure that the FS of primary schools is delivered effectively. As a result all Year 1 classes and a number of Year 2 classes have the support of a classroom assistant but the number of hours they spend in these classes on a daily basis appears to be at the discretion of individual schools' governance.

A response from Scotland

Adult:child ratios

In non-domestic premises, e.g. early years settings, the practitioner ratios are:

Age of child	Ratio
Under 2 years of age	1:3
2 years to under 3 years	1:5
★3 years and over	1:8
8 years and over	1:10

Source: The Scottish Government (2005:31)

Note: ★Where children aged three years and over attend facilities providing day care for a session which is less than a continuous period of four hours in any day, the adult:child ratio may be 1:10 providing individual children do not attend more than one session per day.

There is an expectation that there will be two practitioners with the children at any one time.

In domestic premises the ratios are:

Age of child	Ratio
★Children under 12	1:6

Source: The Scottish Government (2005:31)

Note: ★Of whom no more than three are not yet attending primary school and of whom no more than one is under one year.

Qualifications

Table 5.1 is a guide to qualifications for a career in working in early education, childcare and playwork.

Table 5.1 Table of main qualifications

Qualification	Description
Introductory qualifications	
Scottish Group Award in Care (Intermediate 2)	School/college based award. Introductory level. Relevant to anyone thinking of working with young children.
National Qualification – Higher Early Years Care and Education	School/college based National Course designed to introduce candidates to child development, behaviour and health.
Professional Development Award (PDA) Certificate for Classroom Assistants	College based introductory level qualification, with some aspects assessed in the workplace, specifically aimed at people wanting to be classroom assistants.
Professional Development Award (PDA) Certificate for Support for Learning Assistants	College based introductory level qualification, with some aspects assessed in the workplace, specifically aimed at people wanting to be support for learning assistants.
SVQ 2 Early Years Care and Education (formerly Childcare and Education)	Work based intermediate qualification. Relevant for most occupations that include working with children aged between 0 and 8 years.
SVQ 2 Playwork	Work based introductory qualification. Relevant for most occupations that include working with children aged between 5 and 15 years, especially play situations (e.g. out of school care, adventure playgroups, mobile play projects and holiday schemes).
Scottish Group Award Early Years Care and Education (Higher)	One year full-time college based award. Contains 3 National Courses at Higher level and core skills. This SGA was available from 2002.

(continued)

Table 5.1 (Continued)

Qualification	Description
More advanced qualifications	
Higher National Certificate (HNC) Childcare and Education	One year full-time (2 years part-time) college based intermediate qualification. Relevant for most occupations that include working with children. Most providers recognise people holding this qualification as being 'fully qualified'.
Higher National Certificate (HNC) Supporting Special Learning Needs	One year full-time (2 years part-time) college based intermediate qualification aimed at those who wish to work with children and adults with special learning needs.
SVQ 3 Early Years Care and Education (formerly Childcare and Education)	Work based intermediate qualification. Relevant for most occupations that include working with children aged between 0 and 8 years. Most providers recognise people holding this qualification as being 'fully qualified'.
SVQ 3 Playwork	Work based qualification. Relevant for most occupations that include working with children aged between 5 and 15 years in a supervisory capacity, especially play situations (e.g. out of school care, adventure playgroups, mobile play projects and holiday schemes).
Higher National Diploma (HND) Supporting Special Learning Needs	Two year full-time (4 years part-time) college based intermediate qualification aimed at those who wish to work with children and adults with special learning needs. The HNC in Supporting Special Learning Needs forms Year 1 of this HND.
Professional Development Award (PDA) Childcare and Education	College based advanced award providing progression for experienced staff from the HNC in Childcare and Education. Suitable for those in promoted posts or seeking promotion.
SVQ 4 Early Years Care and Education	Work based qualification. Aimed at managers and senior practitioners. The management aspects will also be applicable to managers in the Playwork sector.

Source: The Scottish Government (2002)

Debates/contentions

The *Making the Difference* report (2012) researched the impact of staff qualifications on children's learning in the early years; the researchers found:

> In the most effective practice, high quality experiences for children resulted from the combined strengths and talents of the range of professional staff involved. Staff demonstrated an understanding of early years methodology and were committed to putting this into practice to support children's learning. High quality learning experiences were provided in an enjoyable and supportive environment for all children. Settings showed strong leadership which allowed staff to develop their skills. Through improvements in self-evaluation staff were able to reflect on practice and make changes which were leading to improvements for children. This effective practice

was due in some cases to the ability to access a pre-school teacher with a background in early years methodology and in others due to the increasing impact of higher qualifications for staff who achieved additional qualifications such as, the BA in Childhood Practice.

(Education Scotland, 2012:1)

The *Making the Difference* report (2012) researchers expressed that they were observing quite significant professional changes in the sector:

In local authorities where teachers continue to be employed in nursery schools and classes, they tend to lead curriculum implementation and related development. This is to ensure that children receive a high quality of experience and appropriate outcomes for learning. Evidence shows that, in some instances, as teachers in nursery schools and classes leave, authorities are replacing them with other staff, for example a senior early years worker. There is as yet no substantial evidence to say that this affects the quality of the experiences provided.

(Education Scotland, 2012:6)

This evidence may suggest that practitioners who have a General Teaching Council Qualification and practitioners who hold a BA in Childhood Practice illustrate similar skills in the workplace; skills that lead to high quality provision. This has caused some tension in the workplace as BA Childhood Practice qualified practitioners begin to occupy positions that General Teaching Council practitioners previously held.

A further report, *Taking the First Steps: Is Childhood Practice Working?* (Davis et al., 2014) reported positively on the impact of the qualification, as Davis (2014) expressed:

The "Taking the First Steps – is Childhood Practice Working?" report demonstrates significant increase in techniques of developed leadership and service users participation. It illustrates the abilities of all staff, children and parents whatever their background to lead the direction that provision takes. The Childhood Practice degree has had an impact on managers and settings in relation to delivering a creative curriculum, enabling participatory leadership, listening to parents, promoting the views of children and putting knowledge of children's rights into practice. It has enabled professionals to be more thoughtful, gain greater status in their local areas, gain employment opportunities and build much stronger relationships with parents and children.

(Davis, 2014:5)

What Davis et al. (2014) highlighted is that practitioners in Scotland are experiencing positive change filled with promising, inspirational leadership. What the Scottish Social Services Council are aiming for in the early years sector is a highly skilled and qualified professional workforce. In Scotland, currently, practitioners have more opportunities than ever to grow organically in the workforce. Change in the workplace is inevitable and is viewed positively.

A response from Wales

The current recommended ratios for working with children in the Foundation Phase is 1:8 for those in Nursery and Reception and then 1:15 for Years 1 and 2. Schools that have a Nursery allocation tend to have a qualified teacher to lead the team of practitioners; however, often in non-maintained settings there is no qualified teacher and staff are qualified as teaching assistants with level 1, 2 or 3 in CACHE or NVQ qualifications. The funded non-maintained settings benefit from a link teacher who works closely with the setting to support the implementation, observation and assessment of the children. Training for funded non-maintained settings has ensured that all practitioners have accessed the modules for the implementation of the Foundation Phase. Nutbrown (2012) reinforces the importance of highly qualified practitioners working with younger children and this has been highlighted in the independent stocktake of the Foundation Phase commissioned by the Welsh Government in 2013. It has been noted that with the recommended ratios, on occasion cheaper and less qualified staff have been appointed to accommodate the ratio rather than supporting the implementation of an effective pedagogy. For some maintained settings there has also been an impact for teachers who have little or no experience of managing extra staff, thus leading to inappropriate deployment of staff, i.e. staff being used to support behaviour issues or withdrawal of small groups to target specific learning needs. Recommendation 17 of the stocktake requests that all teaching assistants 'benefit from continued professional development (CPD) processes and support within maintained schools and that literacy and numeracy training is available for those that need it'.

Question 4: How is observation and formative assessment embedded into practice to ensure that assessment is not perceived from a linear viewpoint?

A response from England

Observation and assessment is a key feature of the English EYFS and there is a great deal of guidance for practitioners who *must* 'consider the individual needs, interests, and stage of development of each child in their care, and must use this information to plan a challenging and enjoyable experience for each child in all areas of learning and development' (DfE, 2014:8).

Practitioners are targeted as adults who 'must' assess children's progress and 'respond' and 'consider' are frequently used terms; however, the term 'observation' is considered within the section on assessment and is subsumed in the narrative around observing to recognise children's 'level of achievement, interests and learning styles' to 'shape learning experiences'. There are two elements of assessment within the EYFS with the progress check at two (for children aged between two and three) and the profile which is in the final term of the year in which the child turns five (DfE, 2014:14). The progress check is completed as an early intervention strategy and is targeted at all children who attend an early years setting. Regular assessment is a requirement in the EYFS and a cycle of observation, planning and assessment is articulated as a way of getting to know children; however, there are tensions in the English framework where the purpose of observation is perceived to be targeted at assessment and the focus on outcomes may take precedence over the personal, social and emotional needs of very young children. Practitioners must record a summary of the child's development in the three prime areas and they must identify the child's strengths and any areas where the progress 'is less than expected' and this is to be shared with parents and carers. This focus on observation as assessment is disconcerting for many observers who note the possible anxiety that parents may feel and this in turn raises the validity of Nutbrown's recommendation (2012) where she hoped for an incremental increase in the qualifications of the early years workforce. In short, practitioners need to understand the purpose of formative observation to scaffold children's interests beyond summative assessment. It could be argued that mapping through observations onto plans using the prime areas and characteristics of effective learning reduces the idea of holistic development and questions the idea of practitioners thinking in 'areas'. A linear development sequence that represents 'typical' development suggests a certain path to follow; however, Ang (2014:15) opines this is as long as the child 'fits in' with the age and stage requirements of the EYFS (DfE, 2014). The 'assessment and reporting arrangements' are highlighted in the profile guidance from the DfE (2014:16) and highlight how practitioners need to provide a written summary against all the Early Learning Goals within each area of learning, make comments on general progress and summarise whether children are 'meeting', 'exceeding' or 'emerging' in each area. Additionally, practitioners must make comments on general progress including the characteristics of effective learning and this must be shared with parents. In contrast to the 'Early Years Outcomes' document (DfE, 2013a), 'Development Matters' (Early Education, 2012) reflects a more holistic picture with emphasis on the cycle of observation, assessment and planning with a visual reminder of the interconnectedness of the prime, specific areas and the characteristics of effective learning.

A response from Northern Ireland

Like other contexts within the United Kingdom, the NI Guidance on Assessment in the FS (CCEA, 2012) also attributes much value to the process of observations in the early years classroom. 'Observations are perceived as the natural and essential part of effective assessment practice' (CCEA, 2012:10) where it is recognised that the FS teacher must find time for both planned and spontaneous observations to allow children's individual needs to be effectively taken into account and to inform future planning. Advice on what to observe within the document embraces content, skills and learning dispositions allowing a full picture of individual children's development to be collated and acted upon.

Unlike the rest of the primary school in NI, the Assessment Guidance for the FS is non-statutory. In this way, although FS teachers are required to assess pupils' progress on each of the cross-curricular skills and on each of the Areas of Learning within the curriculum, they are not required to report formally on these regarding levels of progression and numerical outcomes. They are required only to meet with parents to discuss their child's progress and provide an annual report to parents at the end of the school year.

However, as the FS Assessment Guidance contains reference to developmental stages in learning for each of the three cross-curricular skills, namely Communication, Using Mathematics and Using ICT, and the FS curriculum refers to statutory requirements for each of the Areas of Learning, there is a degree of concern that early years pedagogy and practice will become subordinated to a set of educational goals and targets (Hunter and Walsh, 2014). In turn the power of formative assessment or Assessment for Learning could, it is feared, become subservient to Assessment of Learning in the early years classroom.

It is also worthy of comment that in NI we still have a very selective system in place where the majority of parents opt for their children to undertake an examination/s in the early stages of Year 7 in primary school, which allows them to be considered for entry into the grammar schools system in Year 8. These tests focus solely on Literacy and Numeracy and although primary schools are not supposed to prepare children for these tests, it depends on where you live and the pressure from parents as to whether this happens or not in reality. Likewise the fact that these examinations are still taking place and still hold such significance on the part of children and parents may impose a narrowing of the curriculum throughout the primary school context, where Literacy and Numeracy are prioritised from the outset.

A response from Scotland

In Building the Curriculum 5: A Framework for Assessment (Scottish Executive, 2011) there is an emphasis on what, when and how we assess. Woven through this document we read about the need to support learners, to consider their engagement, to explore a variety of approaches and range of evidence so that assessment is fit for purpose. The need to share information with colleagues is part of the collegiate working that is an expectation of the reporting on progress and achievement (Scottish Executive, 2004b).

There is a linear viewpoint in terms of the development of children through time, but each stage of that learning journey is supported through observation and formative assessment in play and active learning (Scottish Executive, 2007). There are summative points on that pathway that are indicators of achievement. The requirement by the government for a transition record on entry to Primary one and the end of year reporting systems can create pedagogies that focus on the attainment of experiences and outcomes rather than the process of learning.

To balance this there is, however, a strong movement to support the voice of the child through social and educational policy. The presence of the Children's Commissioner at Government level has given children and youth a real place of empowerment. The culture of this forum has seen children and youth make changes in policy and their voices are sought in national consultation such as 'A Right Wee Blether'[2] (Education Scotland, 2014: unlisted).

The Inspectorate for Education and the Care Commission have supported approaches to planning that raise the child voice from the play room floor to being pivotal in deciding their next steps for learning. These voices are documented in a variety of models such as Talking and Thinking Floorbooks and Talking Tubs (Warden, 1994), Learning Stories (Carr and Lee, 2012), family books, learning journals, individual profile books, online blogs, etc.

Within these approaches to formative assessment and consultative and participatory planning there are details laid out within the CfE and 'Pre-Birth to Three: Positive Outcomes for Scotland's Children and Families' (The Scottish Government, 2010) about 'Getting it Right for Every Child' (The Scottish Government, 2012). This clearly supports the emphasis of an 'I can' approach to assessment rather than a deficit model of 'I can't'.

The need for data still sits as a challenge to these formative models. A tension exists between the paperwork required by practitioners who run two systems of formative and summative assessments in order to appease everyone. The question that sits at the heart of the assessment process is: Who is the assessment for? How will it impact on the lives of children and their families, dialogue should surely evoke change?

The rights of the child are valued in Scotland and as such settings are being respectful about the amount they photograph, to the point where they ask the child if it is okay if an adult records the moment. Most do, but the important point in our work is that the child has been asked and if they say no, then we as practitioners need to respect that (Dahlberg et al., 1999).

Given that Scotland is made up of 32 local authorities it will follow that there are some variations in the level of empowerment children have within their own self-assessment and the way that observation and formative assessments are documented.

For example, in an attempt to raise standards certain Scottish local authorities have introduced 'Pre-Five Planning and Assessment Trackers' in the subject areas of Literacy and Mathematics (Hall, 1996). These literacy and mathematic 'tools' are designed to facilitate, enhance and maximise the child's 'normal' development (based on developmental psychology ideology). The trackers are regulated, governed and sanctioned by early years practitioners during the period of time the child attends the early years setting. The child's 'progress' (the hard data) in the specific areas is normalised and classified by 'ticking and dating boxes' method. Further, there is a local authority expectation that the (plethora of) boxes are 'ticked' prior to the child starting primary school.

Since Literacy and Mathematics are the only subjects externally required there is, of course, a danger that practitioners in early years settings will focus their observations on these subjects to the exclusion of others. Other subjects such as health and wellbeing may be denuded in order to make way for literacy and mathematic observation and practitioners may be lulled into a culture of teaching for literacy and mathematics assessment. In some local authorities the trackers replace the child's transition record.[3] The transition record contains holistic information on the child, e.g. it emphasises the child's social and emotional wellbeing as well as his/her academic achievement. However, it could be argued that the literacy and mathematics trackers are working against a holistic ideology. Further concern has been raised by practitioners who argue that the child may not have all the boxes 'ticked' resulting in the child being labelled as 'failing'. MacNaughton (2005) warns: 'Knowledge that is sanctioned institutionally can produce such an authoritative consensus about how to "be" that it is difficult to imagine how to think, act and feel in any other way' (MacNaughton, 2005: 32). In other words, there is a concern that assessment trackers may carry such institutional authority that limits another way of seeing the child and all they are achieving (Freire, 1996; Goldstein, 1997).

A response from Wales

Observations are a key focus for the role of the adult from three to seven years. The stages of child development are used in conjunction with the *Framework for Children's Learning* (WAG, 2008a) to ensure that the continuous and enhanced provision support the holistic development of each individual. Where practice is good, practitioners focus on specific observations to track learner progress as well as allowing the practitioners time to observe child initiated learning. It is often through the child initiated learning that observations demonstrate the level of understanding of a particular task and how the child sets their own challenges to further develop thinking skills and problem-solving abilities. Observations must be used to inform the next steps of learning and short-term planning provides specific and measureable learning objectives that can accurately be assessed. Tracking of progress for each individual supports this cyclical process and ensures that learners engage in activities that are differentiated to meet their individual needs.

Following the recent research summary (WISERD, 2014a) case study observations noted that where practitioners had accessed the Foundation Phase modules they felt they 'had a better understanding and more positive views of the Foundation Phase'; however, there is a general feeling that practitioners would like to have more 'structured and tailored guidance'. Researchers also noted in the paper that there was a link between child choice and 'physically active, explorative, first-hand pedagogies' with high involvement and wellbeing. The work of Ferre Leavers focuses particularly on the importance of high involvement resulting in deep level learning.

Observations in the Foundation Phase can only be carried out effectively where the deployment of the adults is appropriate. Where adults are used to support a range of focus tasks rather than observing, independent learning opportunities are often missed and assessment does indeed become a linear process as its main focus is based on the areas of learning and intended learning objective rather than the holistic development of the child. For the pedagogy to be effective, the model provided by the Welsh Government states that only one-third of the time allocation goes to focus task activities with two-thirds allocated to continuous and enhanced provision. The research carried out indicated that some practitioners and key stakeholders were 'of the opinion that children were becoming overly dependent on high adult:child ratios and high numbers of additional practitioners in the classroom' (WISERD, 2014b).

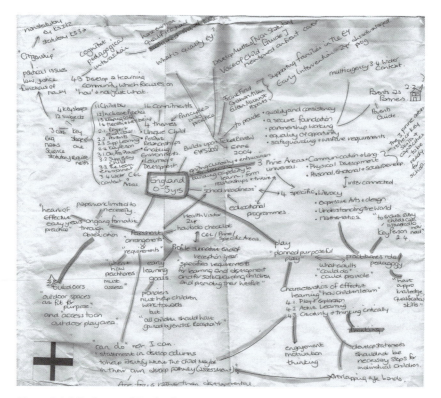

Figure 5.1 Mind map of England.

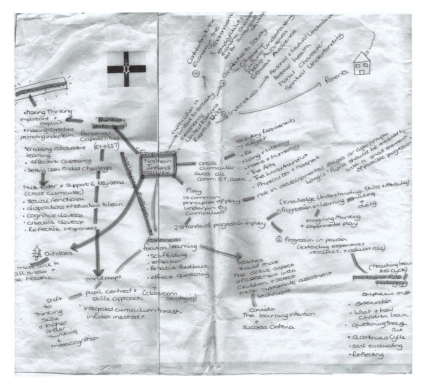

Figure 5.2 Mind map of Northern Ireland.

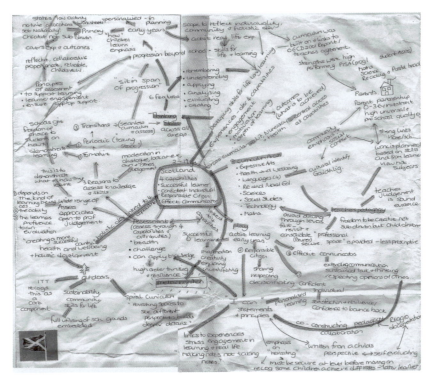

Figure 5.3 Mind map of Scotland.

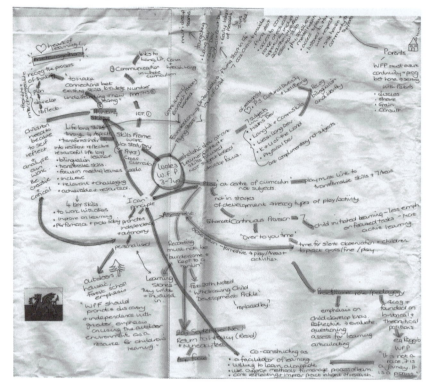

Figure 5.4 Mind map of Wales.

Notes

1 Investing in Children is an organisation that promotes the human rights of children and young children.
2 A report of the 2011 initiative which aimed to raise awareness of Scotland's Commissioner for Children and Young People (SCCYP) and to provide children with an opportunity to express opinions on things that matter to them.
3 The transition record is the record of the child's holistic achievements. It travels with the child to primary school. It generally includes both children and parents' comments on the child's early years experience.

English references and further reading

Ang, L. (2014) *The Early Years Curriculum: The UK Context and Beyond.* London: Routledge.
Barrett, M. (2000) *The Development of National Identity in Childhood and Adolescence.* Inaugural Lecture presented at University of Surrey, 22 March 2000 [online]. Available at: http://epubs.surrey.ac.uk/1642/1/00_Inaugural_lecture.pdf [accessed December 2014].
DfE (Department for Education) (2012) *Statutory Framework for the Early Years Foundation Stage: Setting the Standards for Learning, Development and Care for Children From Birth to Five.* Runcorn: DfE Publications.
DfE (Department for Education) (2013a) *Early Years Outcomes: A Non-Statutory Guide for Practitioners and Inspectors to Help Inform Understanding of Child Development Through the Early Years.* London: DfE Publications.

DfE (Department for Education) (2013b) *More Great Childcare: Raising Quality and Giving Parents More Choice*. London: DfE [online]. Available at: https://www.gov.uk/government/uploads/system/uploads/attachment_data/file/219660/More_20Great_20Childcare_20v2.pdf [accessed December 2014].

DfE (Department for Education) (2014) *Statutory Framework for the Early Years Foundation Stage: Setting the Standards for Learning, Development and Care for Children From Birth to Five*. Runcorn: DfE.

Early Education (2012) *Development Matters in the Early Years Foundation Stage (EYFS)* [online]. Available at: www.early-education.org.uk/development-matters-early-years-foundation-stage-eyfs [accessed April 2015].

Harris, J. (2014) England's Identity Crisis: What Does it Mean to be English? *The Guardian*, 20 May [online]. Available at: www.theguardian.com/uk-news/2014/may/20/england-identity-crisis-english-euro-scottish-elections-ukip-patriotism [accessed January 2015].

McDowall Clark, R. (2013) *Childhood in Society for the Early Years* (2nd Edition). London: Sage.

Nutbrown, C. (2012) *Foundations for Quality: The Independent Review of Early Education and Childcare Qualifications*. Final Report (Nutbrown Review). London: DfE.

Nutbrown, C. (2013) *Shaking the Foundations of Quality? Why 'Childcare' Policy Must Not Lead to Poor-Quality Early Education and Care* [online]. Available at: www.shef.ac.uk/polopoly_fs/1.263201!/file/Shakingthefoundationsofquality.pdf [accessed August 2014].

Pugh, G. and Duffy, B. (2013) *Contemporary Issues in the Early Years* (2nd Edition). London: Sage.

Siraj-Blatchford, J. (2008) The Implications of Early Understandings of Inequality, Science and Technology for the Development of Sustainable Societies. In Samuelsson, P. and Kaga, Y. (eds), *The Contribution of Early Childhood Education to a Sustainable Society*. Paris: UNESCO, pp. 67–71.

United Nations (1989) United Nations Convention on the Rights of the Child (UNCRC). Geneva: United Nations.

Northern Irish references and further reading

CCEA (Council for the Curriculum Examinations and Assessment) (2007) *The Northern Ireland Curriculum: Primary*. Belfast: CCEA.

CCEA (Council for the Curriculum Examinations and Assessment) (2012) *Foundation Stage: Non-Statutory Assessment Guidance*. Belfast: CCEA.

Connolly, P., Miller, S. and Eakin, A. (2010) *A Cluster Randomised Trial Evaluation of the Media Initiative for Children: Respecting Difference Programme*. Belfast: The Centre for Effective Education [online]. Available at: http://pure.qub.ac.uk/portal/en/publications/a-cluster-randomised-trial-evaluation-of-the-media-initiative-for-children-respecting-difference-programme(f511556f-3dd9-45e5-9c30-ac13c882ee8a).html [accessed 15 November 2014].

Connolly, P., Smith, A. and Kelly, B. (2002). *Too Young to Notice? The Cultural and Political Awareness of 3–6 Year Olds in Northern Ireland*. Belfast: Community Relations Council.

DENI (Department of Education in Northern Ireland) (2007) Qualifications of Teachers in Nursery, Primary, Secondary and Special Schools, DENI Circular 2007/22 [online]. Available at: www.deni.gov.uk/dc2007-22.pdf [accessed March 2015].

DENI (Department of Education in Northern Ireland) (2011) Class Sizes for Pupils in Years 1–4 (Foundation Stage and Key Stage 1), DENI Circular 2011/01 [online]. Available at: www.deni.gov.uk/circular_class_sizes_foundation_and_key_eng_ver.pdf [accessed March 2015].

DENI (Department of Education in Northern Ireland) (2013) Common Funding Scheme [online]. Available at: www.deni.gov.uk/final_version_2013-2014_cfs.pdf [accessed March 2015].

Fearon, K. and Mearns, E. (2012) The Media Initiative for Children: Using Early Years Programmes to Tackle Sectarianism and Racism, *The International Journal of Diversity*, 11(5): 139–147.

Hunter, T. and Walsh, G. (2014) From Policy to Practice? The Reality of Play in Primary School Classes in Northern Ireland, *International Journal of Early Years Education*, 22(1): 19–36.

Larkin, E., Connolly, P. and Kehoe, S. (2009) *A Cluster Randomized Controlled Trial Evaluation of the Effects of the Sesame Tree Outreach Pack on Young Children's Attitudes and Awareness (Report 3)*. Belfast:

The Centre for Effective Education [online]. Available at: http://pure.qub.ac.uk/portal/en/publications/a-cluster-randomized-controlled-trial-evaluation-of-the-effects-of-the-sesame-tree-outreach-pack-on-young-childrens-attitudes-and-awareness-report-3(0fba05e6-3459-4315-b8bd-7db65e7535ce).html [accessed 15 November 2014].

McInness, K., Howard, J., Miles, G. and Crowley, K. (2011) Differences in Practitioners' Understanding of Play and How this Influences Pedagogy and Children's Perceptions of Play, *Early Years*, 13(2): 121–133.

Margetts, K. (2003) Children Bring More to School than Their Backpacks: Starting School Down Under, *European Early Childhood Education Research Journal*, Monograph Series no. 1: 5–14.

Palaiologou, I., Walsh, G., MacQuarrie, S., Waters, J. and Dunphy, E. (2013) The National Picture. In Palaiologou, I. (ed.) *The Early Years Foundation Stage* (2nd Edition). London: Sage, pp. 37–53.

Stephen, C. (2010) The Early Years Research-Policy-Practice Nexus: Challenges and Opportunities. In Yelland, N. (ed.), *Contemporary Perspectives on Early Education*. Buckingham: Open University Press, pp. 248–264.

Ulster Scots Agency (2012) Ulster-Scots Flagship Programme [online]. Available at: www.ulster scotsagency.com/fs/doc/flagship-schools-programme/USA_Flagship_Programme_(Final_Version). pdf [accessed February 2015].

Walsh, G. (2007) Northern Ireland. In Clark, M. and Waller, T. (eds), *Early Childhood Education and Care*. London: Sage, pp. 51–82.

Walsh, G. and McMillan, D. (2010) War and Peace in Northern Ireland: Childhood in Transition. In Clark, M. and Tucker, S. (eds) *Early Childhoods in a Changing World*. Stoke-on-Trent: Trentham.

Walsh, G., McGuinness, C., Sproule, L. and Trew, K. (2010) Implementing a Play-Based and Developmentally Appropriate Curriculum in Northern Ireland Primary Schools: What Lessons Have we Learned?, *Early Year*, 30(1): 53–66.

Wood, E. (2013) *Play, Learning and the Early Childhood Curriculum* (3rd Edition). London: Sage.

Scottish references and further reading

Adichie, C.M. (2009) *The Danger of a Single Story* [Streaming Video] [online]. Available at: www.ted. com/talks/ [accessed November 2014].

Alderson, P. (2001) *Young Children's Rights: Exploring Beliefs, Principles and Practice*. London: Jessica Kingsley Publications.

Brownlie, J. and Sheach-Leith, V.M. (2011) Social Bundles: Thinking Through the Infant Body, *Childhood*, 18(2): 196–210.

Burman, L. (2009) *Are You Listening? Fostering Conversations that Help Young Children Learn*. St Paul, MN: Redleaf Press.

Carr, M. and Lee, W. (2012) *Learning Stories: Constructing Learner Identities in Early Education*. London: Sage.

Clark, A., Kjorholt, A.T. and Moss, P. (Eds) (2005) *Beyond Listening: Children's Perspectives on Early Childhood Services*. Bristol: Polity Press.

Corsaro, W. (2005) *The Sociology of Childhood* (2nd Edition). London: Sage.

Dahlberg, G., Moss, P. and Pence, A. (1999) *Beyond Quality in Early Education Childhood Education and Care: Postmodern Perspectives*. London: Falmer Press.

Davis, J.M. (2014) *Childcare is Already a Game Changer* [online]. Available at: http://newsnetscotland. com/index.php/scottish-opinion/9571-childcare-is-already-a-game-changer#comments [accessed 24 August 2014].

Davis, J., Aruldoss, V. and McNair, L. (2012) Enabling Creativity in Learning Environments: Lessons from the CREANOVA Project.

Davis, J.M., Bell, A. and Pearce, M. (2014) *Taking the First Steps: Is Childhood Practice Working?* [online]. Available at: file:///C:/Users/Kurt%20Mischa/Downloads/Taking%20the%20first%20steps%20 -%20is%20Childhood%20Practice%20working%202014.pdf [accessed 24 August 2014].

Education Scotland/Foghlam Alba (2012) *Making the Difference* [online]. Available at: www.educationscotland.gov.uk/Images/Making%20the%20Difference_tcm4-735922.pdf [accessed 24 August 2014].

Education Scotland/Foghlam Alba (2014) *Transforming Lives Through Learning* [online]. Available at: www.educationscotland.gov.uk/earlyyearsmatters/a/genericcontent_tcm4674091.asp [accessed 20 October 2014].

European Commission (2014) *Investing in Children: Breaking the Cycle of Disadvantage* [online]. Available at: http://ec.europa.eu/justice/fundamental-rights/files/c_2013_778_en.pdf [accessed November 2014].

Fennimore, B.S. (2008) Talk About Children: Developing a Living Curriculum of Advocacy and Social Justice. In Geniski, C. (ed.), *Diversities in Early Childhood Education: Rethinking and Doing*. New York: Routledge, pp. 185–200.

Franklin, B. (1995) *Handbook on Children's Rights: Comparative Policy and Practice*. London: Routledge.

Freire, P. (1996) *Pedagogy of the Oppressed*. London: Penguin.

Gill, D. and Howard, S. (2009) *Knowing Our Place: Children Talking About Power, Identity and Citizenship*. Camberwell, VIC: Australian Council for Educational Research Press.

Goldstein, L. (1997) *Teaching with Love: A Feminist Approach to Early Childhood Education*. New York: Peter Lang Publishing.

Gonzalez-Mena, J. (2008) *Diversity in Early Child Care and Education: Honouring Differences* (5th Edition). Washington DC: National Association for the Education of the Young.

Hall, N. (1996) Why is Mathematics So Important, *Every Child*, 2(4).

Hillman, M. (2006) Children's Rights and Adults' Wrongs, *Children's Geographies*, 4(1): 61–67.

James, A. and Prout, A. (1997) *Contemporary Issues in the Sociological Study of Children: Constructing and Reconstructing Childhood*. London: Falmer Press.

James, A. and James, A. (2012) *Key Concepts in Childhood Studies*. London: Sage.

Kearns, K. (2010) *Birth to Big School* (2nd Edition). Frenchs Forest, NSW: Pearson Australia.

Killen, M. and Rutland, A. (2011) *Children and Social Exclusion: Morality, Prejudice and Group Identity*: Maiden, MA: Wiley-Blackwell.

Konstantoni, K. (2010) Young Children's Perceptions and Constructions of Social Identities and Social Implications: Promoting Social Justice in Early Childhood. PhD in Education: The University of Edinburgh.

McLeod, W. (Ed.) (2006) *Revitalising Gaelic in Scotland: Policy, Planning and Public Discourse*. Edinburgh: Dunedin Academic Press.

MacNaughton, G. (2005) *Doing Foucault in Early Childhood Studies. Applying Poststructural Ideas*. London: New York.

Mundane, K. and Giugni, M. (2006) *Diversity and Difference: Lighting the Spirit of Identity*. Watson ACT: Early Childhood Australia.

Munro, J. (2012) Education Systems That Support Inclusion. In Ashman, A. and Elkins, J. (eds), *Education for Inclusion and Diversity* (4th Edition). Frenchs Forest, NSW: Pearson Australia.

Qvortrup, J. (ed.) (2005) *Studies in Modern Childhood: Society, Agency and Culture*. Basingstoke: Palgrave Macmillan.

Qvortrup, J., Corsaro, W. and Honig, S.M. (2009) *The Palgrave Handbook of Children's Studies*. Basingstoke: Palgrave.

Robertson, J. (2006) Focussing the Lens: Gazing at 'Gaze'. In Fleet, A., Patterson, C. and Robertson, J. (eds), *Insights: Behind Early Childhood Pedagogical Documentation*. Castle Hill, NSW: Pademelon, pp. 147–162.

Robinson, K.H. and Jones-Diaz, C. (2006) *Diversity and Difference in Early Childhood Education: Issues for Theory Policy and Practice*. Maidenead: Open University Press.

Scotland's Census (2011) *National Records of Scotland. Table QS211SC – Gaelic language skills* [online]. Available at: www.scotlandscensus.gov.uk/documents/censusresults/release2a/healthboard/QS211SC_HB.pdf [accessed 20 October 2014].

Scottish Executive (2004a) *The Curriculum for Excellence: The Curriculum Review Group* [online]. Available at: www.educationengland.org.uk/documents/pdfs/2004-scottish-curriculum-review.pdf [accessed November 2014].

Scottish Executive (2004b) *A Smart, Successful Scotland: Strategic Direction to the Enterprise Networks and an Enterprise Strategy for Scotland* [online]. Available at: www.gov.scot/Resource/Doc/26800/0027981.pdf [accessed May 2015].

Scottish Executive (2006) *A Curriculum for Excellence: Building the Curriculum 1. The Contribution of Curriculum Areas* [online]. Available at: www.educationscotland.gov.uk/Images/building_curriculum1_tcm4-383389.pdf [accessed 20 October 2014].

Scottish Executive (2007) *Building the Curriculum 2: Active Learning in the Early Years* [online]. Available at: www.educationscotland.gov.uk/images/Building_the_Curriculum_2_tcm4-408069.pdf [accessed 20 October 2014].

Scottish Executive (2008) *A Curriculum for Excellence: Building the Curriculum 3: A Framework for Learning and Teaching* [online]. Available at: www.educationscotland.gov.uk/Images/building_the_curriculum_3_jms3_tcm4-489454.pdf [accessed 20 October 2014].

Scottish Executive (2010) *Curriculum for Excellence through Outdoor Learning* [online]. Available at: www.educationscotland.gov.uk/images/cfeoutdoorlearningfinal_tcm4-596061.pdf [accessed 20 October 2014].

Scottish Executive (2011) *Building the Curriculum 5: A Framework for Assessment* [online]. Available at: www.educationscotland.gov.uk/Images/BtC5Framework_tcm4-653230.pdf [accessed 20 October 2014].

The Scottish Government (2002) *A Guide to Qualifications and Career in Early Education, Childcare and Playwork* [online]. Available at: www.scotland.gov.uk/publications/2002/04/14534/2764 [accessed 20 October 2014].

The Scottish Government (2005) *The National Care Standards: Taking Care of You* [online]. Available at: www.nationalcarestandards.org/files/early-education.pdf [accessed 20 October 2014].

The Scottish Government (2010) *Pre-Birth to Three: Positive Outcomes for Scotland's Children and Families* [online]. Available at: www.educationscotland.gov.uk/Images/PreBirthToThreeBooklet_tcm4-633448.pdf [accessed 20 October 2014].

The Scottish Government (2012) *A Guide to Getting it Right for Every Child* [online]. Available at: www.scotland.gov.uk/Resource/0039/00394308.pdf [accessed 20 October 2014].

Thinkersinresidence (2012) The Competent Child [Video file] [online]. Available at: www.youtube.com/watch?v=meuYauSzt7U [accessed 20 October 2014].

Tisdall, E.K.M., Davis, J.M. and Gallagher, M. (2009) *Researching with Children and Young People, Research Design, Methods and Analysis*. London: Sage.

Warden, C. (1994) *Talking and Thinking Floorbooks*. Crieff: Mindstretchers.

Wood, L. (1998) Participation and Learning in Early Childhood. In Holden, C. (ed.), *Children as Citizens: Education for Participation*. London: Jessica Kinglsey Publishers, pp. 31–45.

Welsh references and further reading

Department for Education and Skills (2014) *An Independent Stock Take of the Foundation Phase in Wales: Final Report September 2012–March 2014*. Cardiff: Welsh Government.

Nutbrown, C. (2012) *Foundations for Quality: The Independent Review of Early Education and Childcare Qualifications. Final Report (Nutbrown Review)*. London: DfE.

Taylor, C., Maynard, T., Davies, R., Waldron, S., Rhys, M., Power, S., Moore, L., Blackaby, D. and Plewis, I. (2013) *Evaluating the Foundation Phase: Annual Report 2011/12*. Cardiff: Welsh Government Social Research.

WAG (Welsh Assembly Government) (2008a) *The Foundation Phase: Framework for Children's Learning for 3 to 7 Year Olds in Wales*. Cardiff: WAG.

WAG (Welsh Assembly Government) (2008b) *Personal and Social Development, Well-Being and Cultural Diversity.* Cardiff: WAG.

WISERD (2014a) *The Outcomes of Foundation Phase Pupils (Report 1).* Report commissioned by the Welsh Government. Cardiff: Welsh Government.

WISERD (2014b) *Evaluating the Foundation Phase: Key Findings on Reported Impacts.* Commissioned by the Welsh Government [online]. Available at: http://dera.ioe.ac.uk/20535/1/140506-evaluating-foundation-phase-reported-impacts-en.pdf [accessed 26 June 2015].

Index